SEE PAGE 89. *

Praise for *Homesteading the Plains:*

"*Homesteading the Plains* unsettles longstanding homesteading myths and histories alike. Provocative and illuminating, it brings new data, technologies, and questions to open new historical terrain."—ELIZABETH JAMESON, professor of history at the University of Calgary and past president of the Western Historical Association

"Solidly researched, clearly written, logically organized, and cogently argued. The publication of *Homesteading the Plains* will not only be a contribution to knowledge but also field-altering in terms of the way scholars must hereafter write and teach about the Homestead Act."—R. DOUGLAS HURT, professor of history at Purdue University

"This careful empirical analysis provides a long overdue corrective to frequently cited but flawed 'facts' about homesteading in the nineteenth-century West. The authors persuasively demonstrate the impressive achievements of the Homestead Act and incisively evaluate the degree of fraud and Indian land dispossession on the homesteading frontier."—BRIAN Q. CANNON, professor of history at Brigham Young University

"*Homesteading the Plains* fundamentally alters the dominant frame for understanding the costs and consequences of settling the Great Plains. . . . This book upends many tired and baseless myths about the settlement of the continent. The authors tell a nuanced, fascinating national story that is regionally rooted and beautifully illustrated with tables, charts, and maps."—KAREN V. HANSEN, professor of Sociology and Women's, Gender, and Sexuality Studies at Brandeis University

"A provocative plea for a new history of the homestead laws. . . . Anyone interested in understanding the place of these almost mythic laws in the American past must read *Homesteading the Plains.*"—MICHAEL GROSSBERG, Sally M. Reahard Professor of History and Professor of Law at Indiana University

Homesteading the Plains

for Neil and Pinckie,
with much love,
Rick

Homesteading the Plains

Toward a New History

Richard Edwards,
Jacob K. Friefeld,
and Rebecca S. Wingo

University of Nebraska Press
LINCOLN & LONDON

Contents

Illustrations

Tables

Acknowledgments

This project originated with Mark Engler, superintendent of the Homestead National Monument of America in Beatrice, Nebraska. Engler had a big dream: make all the records of the several million homesteaders widely available to the public. Those records are written and printed on old and fragile paper; most are locked away in boxes at the National Archives and Records Administration (NARA) in Washington DC, though some are lodged in other government sites around the country. NARA's collection alone may include files of 2 million homesteaders, each containing on average fifteen pieces of paper, or some 30 million in all. Using them in research is inconvenient and expensive. Engler's idea was to somehow make them easily and cheaply accessible to any member of the public wishing to use them.

Fifteen or so years later, after much effort and some false starts, the homestead records are gradually being digitized and made accessible by a consortium including the NARA, the National Park Service, Ancestry.com, FamilySearch, and the University of Nebraska. All the records of homesteaders in several states are now available; the Nebraska records, a huge cache, were digitized first. This book would not have been possible without those digital records, and Engler was the one who got the project started. We acknowledge our great debt to him and thank him.

Many people worked with us on this project, and we are grateful to all of them. Katie Nieland prepared all the illustrations, and she, Robert Shepard, and Michael Cooper were all crucial in creating the maps. Brandon Locke and Rhea Wick provided excellent research assistance, and we thank Adam Hodge for his contribution.

David Wishart and Clark Archer generously shared the data on which chapter 5 is based; see appendix 2 for a fuller description of their assistance.

The Center for Great Plains Studies at the University of Nebraska and its entire staff provided essential support and encouragement. The Center for Digital Research in the Humanities, at the University of Nebraska–Lincoln and directed by Katherine Walter, provided valuable help.

Elizabeth Jameson read our entire manuscript—twice! She first read it when it was a rough early draft, and her willingness to see its merits even in that form encouraged us to complete it. She and other participants at a special workshop, the "Homesteading Conclave," gave us outstanding comments and criticism, for which we are highly grateful. Other participants included Karen V. Hansen, Sara Gregg, Valerie Grim, Mikal Eckstrom, David Chang, and Mark Engler.

Our special thanks go to Tammy Hendrickson in Broken Bow and the volunteers at the Dawes County Historical Society in Chadron. Their kindness and knowledge of the region is unrivaled and appreciated.

In short, we have benefited from the help and kindness of many colleagues and friends, and we sincerely thank them. Of course, we remain solely responsible for any errors in our analysis or conclusions.

Homesteading the Plains

I

Competing Visions of Our Homesteading Past

Homesteading—free land!—in the government's vast western expanse has become a cherished part of our national story. Ordinary people, including many who had few worldly goods, moved to remote areas and staked their claims in a gamble to fashion better futures for themselves. The public reveres homesteaders as hardy and deserving recipients of federal largesse, common folks who used their opportunity to make farms for themselves, turn the United States into a food-producing colossus, and help create the vast American middle class. Popular culture celebrates homesteading as a big deal, a wise and highly democratic opening of valuable public lands to "actual settlers." Today probably 46 million adult Americans (20 percent of all American adults), and possibly as many as 93 million (40 percent), are estimated to be descended from homesteaders.[1] Many families, often living in cities far removed from where their forebears staked their claims, retain a treasured story, a photograph, or a memory of their homesteading ancestors.

The 1862 Homestead Act, signed into law by President Abraham Lincoln, was formally "an act to secure homesteads to actual settlers on the public domain." Under it, the federal government offered settlers free public land. There was a small processing fee to pay, you had to live on your claim for five years (later reduced to three), and then you "proved up" your claim. Homesteading was open to male citizens over twenty-one, war veterans of any age, widows and single women, married women who were heads of households, and even new immigrants if they simply affirmed their intention to become citizens. After 1866, when a civil rights act established that blacks were indeed citizens, African Americans could homestead, too, as could citizens of Asian descent after an 1898 Supreme Court decision.[2] The act permitted homesteading anywhere on "unappropriated" public lands (lands not set aside for other purposes) where such land was otherwise available for sale. The law, and later related legislation, thus opened lands in thirty states, though principally homesteading occurred in the states north of Texas and west of the Missouri River.

Daniel Freeman was the first homesteader. A physician, Civil War scout, and sometime sheriff, Freeman filed his claim to a farm site in Beatrice, Nebraska, a few minutes after the Homestead Act took effect at midnight on January 1, 1863. He likely had a little extra help from the Brownville, Nebraska, land office, which opened up in the middle of the night so he could be first. Five years later he obtained his patent. A half-century later, Isabel Proctor, a young, single teacher then living in Minnesota, received a letter from her brother in Montana: "Come out and homestead," he wrote. "The government is giving land away." Isabel moved to Rapelje, Montana, a remote community in the Stillwater County flatlands and staked her claim. Every weekday during the school year she rode her horse fifteen miles to and from town to teach her class, often riding through heavy snow and bitter cold. By residing on her land for three years with no lengthy absences, she fulfilled the residency requirement of the Homestead Act, allowing her to prove up her claim. She owned the 160 acres the rest of her long life. Freeman, Proctor, and approximately 1.6 million others successfully claimed free land under the act.[3]

Homesteaders claiming free land and building successful lives became deeply rooted in American culture, literature, and memory—in such books as Willa Cather's *O Pioneers!* and O. E. Rølvaag's *Giants in the Earth*, in histories like Mari Sandoz's *Old Jules* and personal journals like Elizabeth Corey's *Bachelor Bess*, in Elinore Pruitt Stewart's letters to the *Atlantic Monthly* (later published as *Letters of a Woman Homesteader* and the basis for the 1979

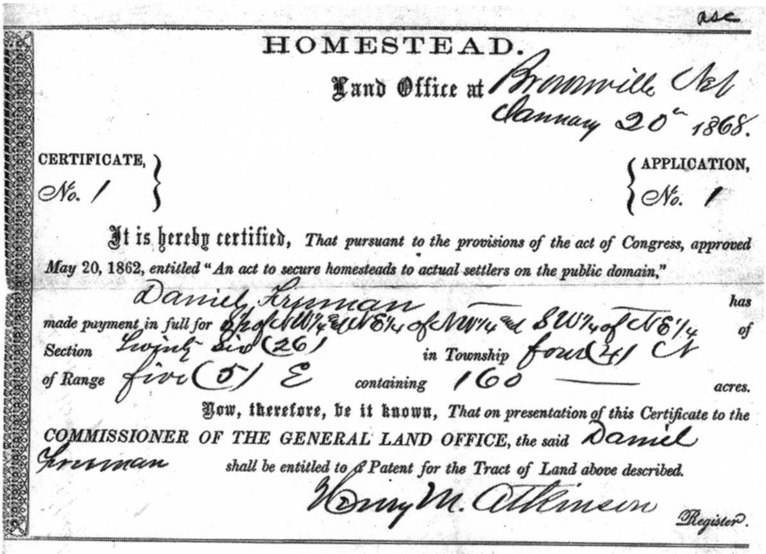

HOMESTEAD.

Land Office at *Brownville, Neb*
January 20ᵗʰ 1868.

CERTIFICATE, } No. 1

{ APPLICATION, No. 1

It is hereby certified, That pursuant to the provisions of the act of Congress, approved May 20, 1862, entitled "An act to secure homesteads to actual settlers on the public domain," *Daniel Freeman* has made payment in full for *the W¼ of NW¼ & SW¼ of NE¼* of Section *twenty six (26)* in Township *four (4) N* of Range *five (5) E* containing *160* acres.

Now, therefore, be it known, That on presentation of this Certificate to the COMMISSIONER OF THE GENERAL LAND OFFICE, the said *Daniel Freeman* shall be entitled to a Patent for the Tract of Land above described.

Henry M. Atkinson Register.

FIG. 1.1. Portion of Daniel Freeman's homestead filing, marked as "Certificate, No. 1" and "Application, No. 1." Courtesy Homestead National Monument of America.

movie *Heartland* starring Rip Torn and Conchita Farrell), and in Laura Ingalls Wilder's *Little House on the Prairie* and the hit television series based on it. Presidents on both the left and the right praised it: John F. Kennedy declared the Homestead Act to be "probably the single greatest stimulus to national development ever enacted." George W. Bush proclaimed, "In America's ideal of freedom, citizens find the dignity and security of economic independence. . . . This is the broader definition of liberty that motivated the Homestead Act." Barack Obama noted, "There are certain things we can only do together. . . . Only a union could harness the courage of our pioneers to settle the American West, which is why [Lincoln] passed a Homestead Act giving a tract of land to anyone seeking a stake in our growing economy." The author Mari Sandoz in 1963 declared simply, "The Homestead Act was the hope of the poor man." Conservative columnist George Will in 2005 enthused, "Rarely has a social program worked so well." In 2012 the left-leaning Center for American Progress named the

FIG. I.2. Daniel Freeman dressed up for his studio portrait.
Courtesy Homestead National Monument of America.

Homestead Act one of its "Top 10 Middle-Class Acts of Congress." Agreeing on little else, both sides concur that the Homestead Act was a huge American success.[4]

Conservatives and liberals praise the act because each finds in it something of value—the right celebrates the fact that it created many small property holders, and the left praises it because it was so democratic, not restricting its benefits to white men of property but rather opening opportunity to nearly everyone. Although the vast majority of homesteaders were white, some were African American, famously including the "Exodusters" fleeing postbellum oppression in the South. Moreover, the act was not a theoretical curiosum: millions of settlers staked their claims and, some years later, received their patents, legal proof that they now owned the land.

Colliding with the public's positive vision of homesteading, however, is another, much darker and even dismissive view constructed and accepted by most scholars. They see the whole homesteading venture as marginal and somehow unseemly, illicit, tainted—and clearly a failure. As historian Katherine Harris wrote, among New Western History scholars there have been many differing judgments on the success or failure of various western enterprises, and scholars have even debated what the very terms "success" and "failure" might mean. But, she observed, there is one striking exception: "One western enterprise, however, stands outside the debate, thanks to an uncharacteristic unanimity of opinion. Lacking glamour and now quaintly anachronistic, homesteading, all contenders agree, was a failure."[5]

Indeed, recent scholars have largely abandoned the study of homesteading per se and moved on. They focus instead on the broader process of how white settlement of the West intersected with Native American cultures, gender, the environment, and other topics of contemporary interest. In this broader settlement story, homesteading's role is usually conflated with settlement generally. There has been some outstanding research on a few homesteading topics, especially women's participation and ethnic settlement, but very little on homesteading in general.[6] Scholars' lack of interest in homesteading and its near disappearance in their telling of the American narrative would have been a surprising denouement for earlier generations of public lands scholars. Even homesteading's harshest critics in earlier generations understood the lure of free land to be the central and in many ways determining element in attracting settlers to the Great Plains and parts of the interior West. America's greatest public lands scholar, Paul Gates, declared the Homestead Act "one of the most important laws which have been enacted in the history of this country."[7] Now it is barely mentioned, virtually banished from the college textbooks. How did we arrive at the curious situation where one of the country's "most important laws," remembered with deep affection by the public, holds so little favor or even interest among today's scholars?

The sharp disconnect between the public's highly positive image of homesteading and scholars' negative and disapproving assessment is stunning. The schizophrenia of our historical memory is exquisitely but painfully illustrated in the beautiful and historically sensitive film *Land of Dreams: Homesteading America*, which introduces visitors to the impressive exhibits and grounds of the Homestead National Monument of America. The monument is the National Park Service's homage to homesteaders, built on the location of first homesteader Daniel Freeman's Nebraska farm. *Land of Dreams* includes vignettes of fourth- and fifth-generation descendants of white and black homesteaders who proudly describe the courage and persistence of their ancestors who staked their claims and made successful new lives for themselves despite the hostile and isolating prairie environment. These positive images are interspersed with interviews with Native Americans who describe, with palpable pain and sadness, how the land previously belonged to them but was stolen away, leaving them dispossessed. The viewer is left with strong feelings of admiration for homesteaders and an equally strong discomfort or even guilt for the historical injustice of the dispossession for which homesteading seemed to be the cause.

Homesteading was one way in which the federal government transferred parts of America's enormous public domain to private ownership. The U.S. government acquired nearly 1.5 billion acres in the lower forty-eight states between 1781 and 1853, through the Revolutionary War treaty, the Louisiana Purchase, the Mexican War cessions, the settlement of boundary disputes with the British over Canada, and a few other minor acquisitions. From the outset many individuals, whether landless or the mightiest land barons, mining companies, and speculators, eagerly looked on public land as a source of potential riches for themselves. But the government was also interested in moving public land into private hands for a variety of motives that shifted over time. Initially it sought to use land sales to fund the federal budget, but later it distributed land to stimulate canal and railroad growth, to occupy remote regions and thereby forestall threats from foreign powers, to populate the West in order to foster private economic development, and to create a land-owning, small-farmer middle class that would sustain a democratic society.

We can trace in broad terms the disposition of this 1.442 billion-acre public domain. The national government today continues possession of about 26 percent (380 million acres). It transferred approximately 22 percent (328 million acres) to individual states, most of which was sold, and homesteaders claimed about 19 percent (270 million, or possibly as much as 285 million, acres). The balance, roughly 32 percent (between 449 and 464 million acres) was transferred to private owners through sales, grants to railroad corporations, veterans' bonuses, agricultural college grants, and other distributions, or it was stolen, misappropriated, reserved, or otherwise caused to disappear from the public land rolls.[8] Homesteading accounted for between a quarter and a third of the public land transferred by the federal government to private owners.

Even if the federal government had not wanted to distribute its land, it would have found it nearly impossible to avoid it—indeed, in those instances where it tried to restrict settlement, it almost uniformly failed. The first pressure it faced was the constant rush of squatters onto public land. Throughout the nineteenth and early twentieth centuries, many people eagerly sought land in the unsettled regions of the public domain to make farms for themselves. Like the flow of illegal immigration today, squatting was pervasive, insistent, unstoppable, and enjoyed considerable public sympathy. Attempts to hold off unauthorized settlement proved futile, whether in the Military Tracts, the Black Hills, or Indian lands elsewhere. The modern eye might see nineteenth-century government land programs as similar to today's real estate projects, say, a new housing development where interested buyers show up to consider purchasing property that has been clearly defined and laid out. But squatting meant that the process occurred in reverse order: settlers moved into an unorganized region and claimed land, and the laws and surveys and titles raced to catch up.

The long history of preemption mapped this phenomenon. "Preemption" was simply a euphemism for legalizing squatters. Starting in 1830, Congress periodically passed preemption acts which, recognizing the reality on the ground, forgave intrusions by squatters and allowed them to legalize their claims. These bills in effect said that squatting was wrong, but as with medieval papal indulgences, the sin could be forgiven by payment, in this case usually $1.25 per acre. Preemptors had the first right to purchase land once it was surveyed, and since squatters typically arrived first to stake the best land, the preemption price was often a bargain. In the 1841 Preemption Act, Congress abandoned the idea that squatting was trespass and wrong and authorized (future) preemptions, but attempted to restrict them to already surveyed lands. By 1853 Congress had abandoned this restriction, too, in recognition of the fact that squatters just moved in wherever they wanted, whether or not the land had been surveyed. Many factors contributed to the momentum to legalize preemptions, but the most basic was simply the impossibility of stopping the flow of people onto the land.[9]

A second pressure forcing the government to divest itself of its land were speculators, or less pejoratively, land investors, who were a continual presence. Squatters took action right on the land, but speculators operated everywhere, not only on the ground but in nearby cities like Omaha and Denver, in fashionable New York and Boston offices, and in the halls of Congress. The Nebraska

City *News* in September 1867, for example, noted that "seven thousand acres of land lying west of Lincoln were entered by a gentleman from Pennsylvania" and the *Kansas Farmer* groused that the worst land monopolists used agricultural college scrip to gobble up vast tracts.[10] Although it was (and is) easy to focus on the few immensely successful and therefore notorious speculators, the truth was that nearly every landowner tried to profit from rising land prices. Indeed, many players both large and small invested in land, a long-established activity that was hardly dishonorable. Aside from Henry George and the Single-Taxers, no serious effort was made to prevent people from profiting from the rising value of their land, for the simple fact that it was widely assumed to be the landowner's right, and besides, so many hoped to benefit.

Stories of speculators profiting from insider dealing, fraud, and outright theft provoked great outrage because most people distinguished between those landowners, labeled "speculators," who were only interested in profiting from the rising value of their holdings, and the quicker the better, and other landowners, "actual settlers" in the words of the Homestead Act's title, who wanted land as a long-term holding on which to build a farm and create a lifetime livelihood. The St. Paul *Weekly Pioneer*, observing that two whole counties had nearly been gobbled up by speculators using agricultural college scrip and military bounty warrants, thundered, "These two counties had far better have been visited by the locusts of Egypt or the grasshoppers of the Red River than by these speculators." The fact that some actual settlers did not succeed, and others changed their plans after the hard experience of trying to make a farm in hostile conditions, did not change matters. Moreover, as Gilbert Fite has noted, "Despite the fact that millions of acres fell into the hands of corporations and speculators who held them for profitable prices, there was no real lack of good land on the Minnesota, Dakota, Nebraska, and Kansas frontier in the late 1860s and early 1870s." Nineteenth-century farmers were said to be perpetually overinvested in land, betting that land prices would rise, and as historian Roy Robbins explained, "Many settlers had invested in lands on credit hoping to pay out of the increase in the value of their holdings. . . . Some were able to do so but many were not."[11] Investors who grabbed title to public land simply to profit from its rising price were widely disliked, although they had much influence in the halls of Congress and other power centers.

So when President Lincoln signed the Homestead Act of 1862, he was bringing to a close a long struggle by free-land advocates like *New York Tribune* editor Horace Greeley, Speaker of the House Galusha Grow, the Free Soil Party, and others to provide free government land to actual settlers. If preemption legalized squatting, it still required squatters to purchase their land when they wanted to secure title. The Homestead Act was designed to be different, permitting the would-be settler or "entryman" to claim as much as 160 acres of public land (later legislation allowed larger claims), or 80 acres if the land was on a government-retained section within a railroad grant. The settler just needed to register his or her claim and pay the $14 filing and recording fee, live on the land for five (later three) years, make some minor improvements on it including building a small house and plowing ten acres for crops, and then prove up. Soon the General Land Office (GLO) in Washington would send out the patent (title), and the homesteader owned the land.

In some regions homesteading played a very large role in land distribution. In Nebraska, for example, 45 percent of the entire state was patented by homesteaders, a figure perhaps reached in North Dakota as well; in South Dakota, about 41 percent; in Montana and Oklahoma, 34 percent; in Colorado, 33 percent. Such a calculation does not measure the economic value of homesteaded land compared to other dispersals, nor does it measure the enormous indirect effects of homesteading, such as attracting settlers who wanted free land but wound up purchasing land or who purchased land in addition to claiming a homestead, nor does it fully convey the cultural significance of homesteading. In the homesteading regions, free land was the central force attracting settlers and driving settlement—whether or not it was the means by which they ultimately acquired title.[12]

The idea of free land created a frenzy, and settlers poured into states where land was available. Yet in practice the land was hardly

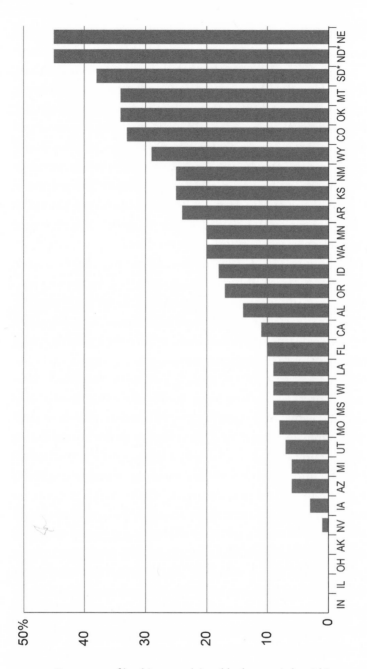

FIG. 1.3. Percentage of land in state claimed by homesteaders (thirty homesteading states). For sources and calculation, see chapter 1, note 12; land homesteaded in Dakota Territory allocated to North and South Dakota.

free. Successfully creating a farm required years of the entryman's labor, plus investments in a house and fields, livestock, a barn, and fencing. And settlers paid in other ways, too, enduring long freezing winters and hot searing summers, often losing crops to drought or wind or disease or grasshoppers, and suffering deep social isolation. As a common old saw put it, "The government bets you a quarter-section that you can't survive on the land for five years," and many who took the bet failed. Despite the obstacles, roughly 1.6 million homesteaders successfully earned title to their piece of the public domain. Before 1900, the average claim was about 134 acres; later claims, including some made under the Enlarged Homestead Act, averaged about 185.[13]

Throughout this book we use "homesteading" to refer narrowly to any claims for free public land made under the Homestead Act of 1862 and its amending and related successors, including the Kinkaid Act (1904) and the Enlarged Homestead Act (1909).[14] In that sense, we distinguish homesteading from the broader process of "settlement" more generally, wherein hide hunters, miners, soldiers, railroaders, squatters, gamblers, Indian agents, land companies, adventurers, and others entered new territory, town builders plated new towns, and (some) farmers obtained land through preemption, purchase, or renting ground. We divide the homesteading process, as Paul Gates did, into its "first phase" from the late 1860s through the mid-1890s, and its "second phase" from the late 1890s through the 1920s. (After 1930 homesteading claims declined to a trickle, and the last homesteader obtained his patent in Alaska on May 5, 1988.) The two phases differed by geography as well as timing—the first phase was concentrated in the central plains (Nebraska and Kansas) and the far west (Oregon and California), whereas the second phase filled in the Dakotas, Oklahoma, Montana, Wyoming, and Colorado. Later we explore some additional distinguishing characteristics between the two phases.

Scholars have described homesteading as deeply flawed or unimportant or both; what's the basis for their being so critical and dismissive? Their negative view is based on several shared understandings about homesteading—some scholars would call these characterizations "received wisdom," lawyers would call them "stipulations," and social scientists would term them "stylized facts." They are what everyone "knows" to be true or agrees to treat as true, a simplified presentation of a perhaps more complicated train of empirical findings that adequately serves most purposes. Stylized facts operate as the preamble or premise, not the targets, of analysis. As we document in detail in succeeding chapters, scholars have adopted four findings about homesteading as stylized facts:

- Homesteading was a minor factor in farm formation; most farmers purchased their land.
- Most homesteaders failed to prove up their claims.
- The homesteading process was rife with corruption and fraud.
- Homesteading caused Indian land dispossession.

If these four assertions are true, it is easy to see why scholars would have a censorious view of homesteading and treat it as a minor factor in settlement.[15]

The first stylized fact is that while homesteading has received a lot of popular attention, it was unimportant in creating actual farms; the historical reality, it is said, is less dramatic or romantic, and it is that most farmers simply bought their land. For example, mid-twentieth-century historian Fred Shannon declared that "less than a sixth of the new homes [i.e., farms] and a little over a sixth of the acreage [was] on land that came as a gift from the government. Eighty-four out of each hundred new farms had to be achieved either by subdivision of older holdings or by purchase." In 2000 historians Robert V. Hine and John Mack Faragher asserted, "Most western settlers, it turns out, were not homesteaders."[16] The last generation or two of scholars have used the presumed unimportance of homesteading as reason enough to ignore it, increasingly treating it as a kind of ephemera of the period, like the Grange or utopian communities—once considered important but now receding in more sober retrospection. Why spend time and attention on a minor land program?

Scholars have moved on to other western topics and issues, and we can see their abandonment of homesteading in their college textbooks. Every scholarly discipline tends to express its "consensus" views in its textbooks—authors want instructors to adopt their books, and they know that to gain acceptance, their books must in general reflect the profession's prevailing views (hence the often-lamented "lack of originality" in textbooks). Indeed, the common style is to omit source citations (except credits for reprinting copyrighted material) because, it is assumed, all the discipline's practitioners "know" this information. When we examine college textbooks of American history, we find that homesteading has largely been written out of them, and in at least one case, it has been completely forgotten.[17] Another way to see current historians' marginal interest in homesteading is the absence of research articles on homesteading; we searched article titles in the leading American history journal, aptly called the *Journal of American History*, from 1965 through 2015, using JSTOR; *JAH* published no articles on homesteading during that fifty-year span.[18] Homesteading, with its stylized facts, is no longer open to debate nor is it an appealing subject of research. One result of this abandonment is that virtually no one has worked to reconfirm or challenge the assertions and findings of the great mid-twentieth-century public land scholars like Benjamin Hibbard, Fred Shannon, Paul Gates, and Gilbert Fite, so when today's scholars cite homesteading-related statistics in support of the first stylized fact, they almost always have to rely on decades-old compilations or calculations.

The second stylized fact, that most settlers who tried homesteading failed at it, is also deeply entrenched in the scholarly literature. Fred Shannon, the most forceful proponent of this point, defined "failure" as an entryman who failed to prove up and receive his or her patent—that is, someone who abandoned his or her claim. He then provided a statistical analysis as proof, and a long line of scholars adopted his work as authoritative. His writings remain the most frequently cited authority on this topic. Echoing (though not citing) Shannon, historian Alan Brinkley in 2012 declared, "The Homestead Act rested on a number of misperceptions. . . .

Although [many] homesteaders stayed on Homestead Act claims long enough to gain title to their land, a much larger number abandoned the region before the end of the necessary five years."[19]

The third stylized fact, that homesteading was shot through with corruption and fraud, is the oldest point of consensus to be entrenched in the homesteading literature. In the 1880s public lands reformer Thomas Donaldson and GLO Commissioner William Sparks campaigned vigorously—so vigorously that Sparks was fired by President Cleveland—against land frauds.[20] Historians then picked up the theme, and a long line of twentieth-century scholars complained about fraud, including Hibbard, Shannon, Roy Robbins, and Gates. Present-day scholars tend to situate homesteading in the rowdy, expansionist, proudly self-aggrandizing, and corrupt post–Civil War era, where financiers manipulated markets, trusts and industrial combines monopolized markets, congressmen offered themselves for sale, and the government granted to railroad companies immense tracts of public land with virtually no oversight. They found their notion of fraud-infested homesteading fit seamlessly into the same narrative, and they expected to find the same evils perverting it as had led to the theft of other public lands and assets. So historian Louis Warren, perhaps thinking he was expressing nothing controversial, simply noted, "After 1862, the federal government deeded 285 million acres to homesteaders. Half their claims were fraudulent, backed by false identities, fake improvements, or worse."[21]

The scholars' final stylized fact is that homesteading contributed to an illegal and historically unjust dispossession of Indians from their lands. Although such expressions were not unknown in the nineteenth century, this issue is of more recent concern due to the greater prominence and sympathetic attention given Native American issues by today's scholars. This more comprehensive American history includes the disreputable progression of unequal treaties forced upon Indians by the federal government under compulsion of hunger or military might, followed by the appointment of corrupt, misguided, and sometimes megalomaniacal Indian agents, followed by U.S. failure to live up to even the minimal obligations of unjust treaties, followed by the replacement of the earlier treaties by even more unequal treaties or executive orders (and all that followed by the outrageous misman-agement and misappropriation of Indian "trust" lands and funds).

This litany of broken promises and mistreatment certainly runs through the history of white settlement of the West, but to what extent were the Homestead Act and homesteaders responsible for it? Scholars have not been reluctant to link the two. Historical sociologist Karen Hansen, in her outstanding treatment of home-steading at Spirit Lake (North Dakota) Reservation, noted that Norwegian "homesteaders gained their foothold as landowners and citizens through the Dakotas' dispossession." Cultural scholar Francis Kaye wrote that the homestead acts "dispossessed the peo-ple who were using the land sustainably [i.e., Native Americans]."[22]

But the scholarly consensus linking homesteading and dispos-session has emerged without much examination of the evidence of the role that homesteading *actually* played in dispossession; like the Bush administration's invasion of Iraq after the 9/11 attack perpetrated mainly by Saudis, the consensus may have focused on the wrong target. By submerging homesteading in the larger settlement story and deploring the larger story, scholars have pre-sumed homesteading was complicit.[23]

On the basis of these four widely accepted truths about homesteading—accepted so automatically that scholars have found little need to reexamine or justify them—most of today's scholars judge homesteading to have been a sham, a failure, and of minor importance.

Perhaps we are at a point where serious study of homesteading is again on the agenda. If so, then this question emerges: will the new studies merely replicate scholarship that adopts the stylized facts as their premise, adducing additional anecdotes and reana-lyzing deeply flawed statistics from long ago, or will something new be tried?

This volume offers a new look at all four of the stylized facts. We critically examine them to determine how adequately they

FIG. 1.4. A house twelve-by-fourteen. Albert D. Richardson, *Beyond the Mississippi: From the Great River to the Great Ocean*. Hartford CT: American, 1867.

accord with the relevant data and evidence available today. We also explore two further topics, the participation of women in home-steading and the formation of community in the homesteading process. We employ new methods and analyze both old and new data to examine these questions.

Our studies are motivated by the desire to bring data to bear in challenging accepted theories and deciding questions for which previous scholars have relied mainly on anecdotes and stories for their evidence. For example, one widely circulated story is of homesteaders taking advantage of an alleged government loophole.

It was claimed that the GLO, when setting out its rules for proving up, required homesteaders to testify that among the improvements they had made was a dwelling at least twelve-by-fourteen, but the GLO forgot to specify that the house was to be measured in *feet*. So, it is claimed, some homesteaders built their twelve-by-fourteen houses in *inches*. The Richardson drawing (fig. 1.4) has been reproduced in textbooks and the story often retold. The National Archives and Records Administration (NARA) includes it on its official website for K–12 teachers called "Teaching with Documents: The Homestead Act of 1862":

> Some land speculators took advantage of a legislative loophole caused when those drafting the law's language failed to specify whether the 12-by-14 dwelling was to be built in feet or inches. . . . The General Land Office was underfunded and unable to hire a sufficient number of investigators for its widely scattered local offices. As a result, overworked and underpaid investigators were often susceptible to bribery.

The problem is that there has never been a documented case where a homesteader received his patent using such a miniature house. The drawing in figure 1.4 was published to illustrate an alleged abuse of the *preemption* law, but the story is usually told about homesteading.[24] The fact that we have no documented case of a speculator actually benefiting from this alleged loophole, or that the usual homestead rule, in contrast to preemption, was a *ten*-by-fourteen house—none of this matters, and the story persists, too amusing and helpful to be dislodged by mere facts. (Nor, we might add, is there much evidence, as best that can be determined, for the assertion that land agents were "often susceptible to bribery." They may have been, but at present it's an assertion with little factual basis.) The history of homesteading has long been constructed on such "evidence."

By contrast, for our study of fraud we develop a study area database consisting of all the homestead entries in ten Nebraska town-ships—a full census of all 621 successful homesteaders in these townships—using digitized homestead case files not previously available, and supplemented by additional data from county land-entry records, claimants' land transfer, military, and census records, county historical society records, and original survey maps for each township, which we overlaid with modern geospatial data. The resulting dataset was utilized in both quantitative analysis and mapping studies.

Similarly, for our study of dispossession, we use data initially extracted by David Wishart from the Indian Claims Commission's proceedings combined with GIS mapping data constructed by J. Clark Archer (all sources are fully described in the relevant chapters and endnotes). Our purpose is to reanalyze old data and mobilize new data to reexamine these enduring homesteading questions.

We do not discount anecdotes—or personal stories, to use a less disparaging term—because we believe they bring depth and quality to any analysis. Indeed, we include exactly such descrip-tive or qualitative information in our chapters to provide dimen-sion to our more quantitative approach. It's just that when analysis is *solely dependent* upon personal stories, as for so long the schol-arship of homesteading has been, we have little way of knowing how representative or unrepresentative such stories are. Thus data and narrative must be woven together, and in combination they provide a much stronger fabric for understanding homesteading than either does separately.

As we will see, none of the categories we use—farm forma-tion, fraud, homesteading success, even dispossession—have sharp boundaries demarcating one outcome versus its opposite. Take farm formation: The seemingly simple question of how many homesteads resulted in real operating farms proves more elusive on close inspection. For how long, or at what point in time, must a homesteaded farm remain in operation for us to count it as hav-ing successfully resulted in a real operating farm? With proved-up homesteads, we know homesteading produced an operating farm for the five years of required residency, because the entryman usually had to plow at least ten acres and seed them to a crop to gain his or her patent. Is that sufficient? If afterward the homesteader continued to reside on the property and farm, as most did, then we may be satisfied that the claim did create a farm. But for how long must this continue? From the beginning of the homesteading era, if not before, the minimum efficient size of farms increased because of widening markets, mechanization, and other factors quite independent of homesteading. This process triggered a wave of farm consolidation and a corollary decline in the number of farms. Farms started on homestead claims were as much subject to this process as other farms. This means that the longer the span we require between the initial homestead claim and when we will count it as having generated a real farm—if we insist a homestead survives for twenty-five years instead of five, for example—the fewer homesteads will get counted as having generated real farms. But the observed decline would be mostly a numerical artifact of mechanization and farm consolidation, not a measure of homesteads failing to become real farms.

The same is true with fraud. Some fraud was clear and easy to define. Other cases, however, were less clear. The GLO issued numerous circulars to local land offices to explain its policies and provide guidance to local agents on how to interpret its rules in special cases. (Appendix 1 reviews these circulars.) The GLO worried about situations where the entryman had substantially complied with the law but through inadvertence or ignorance he or she violated or lacked some technical requirement. Usually headquarters wanted the case decided on the basis of the intent of the law, not the technicality. Was it fraud when settlers discovered that in the semiarid region beyond the 100th meridian, the 160-acre farm was simply too small to support a family, and so they often used a homestead claim, a preemption, and perhaps a timber culture claim to accumulate enough land to make a workable farm? If the Homestead Act's intent was to create viable farms, should such land agglomeration be seen as abuse or as an effective and desirable implementation of the law's underlying intent? Or even more extreme, it was alleged that sometimes an entryman with

FIG. 1.5. Isabel Proctor, with Ginger and Preacher, on her homestead claim near Rapelje, Montana, ca. 1912. Courtesy Richard Edwards.

no capital at all would file a claim, sell it as a relinquishment or make a deal for commuting it (both illegal), then take his proceeds and repeat the process in a different state (also illegal). After two or three filings, he would have amassed enough money to make a go of homesteading. Was this fraud or benign abuse?

The basic categories of farm formation and fraud inevitably have fuzzy boundaries, making it more difficult to sort into binary outcomes. So too the definitions of homesteading "success" and "failure" are nuanced. Consider Isabel Proctor, the single woman without financial assets who homesteaded her land, proved up, then moved back to town and led an extraordinarily productive and successful life in her community; she leased out her land for decades afterwards to successful farmers, so her land became part of real operating farms. Should her homesteading be judged as a success or failure? Certainly in her mind it was a big success.[25]

Thus it is possible that in the minds and estimations of homesteaders, success looked quite different from how the GLO or public lands scholars like Hibbard and Shannon saw it. For example, the critics tended to see the 160-acre farm, which was perfectly adequate for supporting a family in Pennsylvania or Ohio or even Iowa, as the proper allotment of public land to homesteaders, and they viewed farmers' efforts to build larger farms as abusing the spirit of the law, whether the additional public land was gained legally or fraudulently. But as settlement moved west, homesteaders learned they had to expand their holdings to survive and prosper, and so the intent of the Homestead Act increasingly came into conflict with its legal provisions. Even the same critics who complained about farmers misusing the laws to expand their holdings criticized the law for not recognizing the inadequacy of the 160-acre limit. Eventually even Congress acknowledged the disparity when it passed the Kinkaid Act (1904), permitting claims of 640 acres in the Sandhills region of Nebraska, and the Enlarged Homestead Act (1909), which allowed claims of 320 acres in other regions. Similarly, homesteaders and their neighbors might see other individual circumstances that justified the granting of a patent when a strict reading of the GLO's regulations might define the claim as fraudulent. Indeed, the GLO sometimes cautioned its local agents to try to implement the spirit rather than rigid technical compliance with the law.

But as tricky as such "boundary" cases and nuanced circumstances may be to interpret, we can nonetheless see the general patterns. Indeed, the assurance with which historians assert the stylized facts assumes that they have discerned general patterns despite the chaos and confusion of specific cases. In our reexamination of the stylized facts, *we adopt the most conservative analytical stance*: for example, we compare homestead patents issued with number of farms created, not attempting to "correct" for the effects of general farm consolidation; we treat as successful homestead claims only those for which the entryman obtained a patent, not seeking to bolster the total by including or excluding arguable boundary cases; and for fraud, we stick to legal or "technical" definitions, not dismissing those instances where circumstances (and contemporary interpretation) might suggest applying a looser criterion to categorize them differently. Our strategy is straightforward: if the stylized facts are found wanting on the basis of even such strict standards, then *a fortiori* they would seem to fail with more nuanced interpretations.

The public's highly positive understanding of the American homesteading experience stands in sharp contrast to scholars' negative and dismissive interpretation. As we will see in later chapters, our research tends to support the more favorable public understanding over the critical assessment of earlier scholars and the neglect and misstatements of many contemporary historians.[26] Of course neither the public's nor scholars' view is entirely supported by our analysis, which should hardly be surprising given that homesteading occurred over so many decades in such different places and circumstances. Nor do we believe our work is the last word on these matters—indeed, we know it is not and hope that it will stimulate or provoke a new burst of homesteading-focused research. Scholars should use the new data sources, digitized records, and powerful new analytic tools that are increasingly becoming available to fashion new understandings that better illuminate our homesteading past.

2

Recalculating Homesteading's Reach and Success

In this chapter we examine the first two stylized facts of the homesteading literature:

- Homesteading was a minor factor in farm making; most farmers purchased their land.
- Most homesteaders failed to prove up their claims.

While these assertions may be found earlier, they found their firmest foundation and most powerful expression in Fred Shannon's writings. Through his various articles and especially his 1945 book, *The Farmer's Last Frontier: Agriculture, 1860–1897*, Shannon became one of the most prominent historians of homesteading. A mark of his continuing influence is that scholars today regularly cite and quote him and rely on his well-known quantitative picture of homesteading. Examples of Shannon's influence are not hard to find. In 1982 Yale's Alan Trachtenberg wrote, "As historian Fred Shannon has shown, perhaps only a tenth of the new farms settled between 1860 and 1900 were acquired under the Homestead Act." In 2000 University of California–Riverside professor Robert V. Hine and Yale's John Mack Faragher wrote, "After a detailed study, historian Fred Shannon estimated that between 1862 and 1900 half of all homestead entries were fraudulent." In 2014 Columbia University's Eric Foner advised about *The Farmer's Last Frontier*, "Remains an excellent introduction to the experience of farmers in the last four decades of the nineteenth century."[1]

Even when he's not explicitly named, it doesn't take much digging to find Shannon's influence. In 1979 University of Minnesota historian Willard W. Cochrane published a well-respected volume, *The Development of American Agriculture: A Historical Analysis*. Cochrane provides a thinly veiled and mostly unattributed paraphrasing of Shannon, even calling his relevant chapter "The Last Frontier: 1860–1897," in which he restates or repeats many of Shannon's statistics and arguments. In a 2014 book called *Sod Busting*, published by the prestigious Johns Hopkins University Press, University of North Dakota's David Danbom, citing Hine and Cochrane, asserts, "Most of the land on the Great Plains—perhaps as much as 80 percent—was purchased rather than acquired under the Homestead Act."[2] Many other examples of Shannon's influence, particularly his serving as a source for statistics, can be found in the homesteading literature.

Published nearly three-quarters of a century ago, Shannon's book would normally deserve little attention today, but because it continues to be so influential, it is important that we reexamine his arguments. Most scholars have naively accepted his overarching conclusions and especially his statistical claims about homesteading during the last four decades of the nineteenth century, and indeed they rely on his calculations as a principal authority when asserting the claims in the first two stylized facts. Unfortunately, Shannon's quantitative results are wrong or seriously misleading, as are more recent scholars' paraphrases and restatements of his work.

Shannon's Misguided Calculations

Shannon reported numerous statistics and findings, but he never showed exactly how he arrived at his results; in some cases his calculations are obvious, whereas in others we must do some detective work. Although his published work has many merits, accuracy and care when reporting and analyzing statistics are unfortunately not among them. Some of his most frequently cited statistics are based on simple mistakes, while others are stated in a deceptive way. To compound the problem, a number of later scholars make similar wrong calculations or specious claims. Here we examine

Shannon's most-cited quantitative assertions and assess how valid they are, and we also reexamine some other scholars' restatements, using different supporting data, that arrive at similar conclusions; then we turn to correcting the historical record.

Shannon and others had a paucity of data with which to work and did a poor job of analyzing the data they did have. Thomas Donaldson compiled the first compendium of public land statistics, a great service, but his numbers ended in 1880 (or 1883, in a few cases) with publication.[3] Later scholars depended on data from the General Land Office, which was often overwhelmed by the volume of its work and unable to provide reliable numbers. It is unclear whether these authors (excepting Paul Gates) understood how poor their data were. In any event, whether due to concerns about data reliability or simply lacking the data needed, they relied heavily on anecdotes and individual stories to support their argument. Such dependence makes it difficult to know how representative the anecdotes are and how reliable the scholars' conclusions are.

As one of us has argued elsewhere, homesteading data are of poor quality, and the calculations below require manipulating numbers from different sources.[4] Some sources (e.g., *Historical Statistics of the United States*), while authoritative, have severely rounded their numbers; others (e.g., the BLM's "Homesteads" brochure) report numbers with many significant digits, giving the impression of much greater precision than seems warranted. The results reported below should therefore always be read as indicating approximate magnitudes rather than precise numbers; nonetheless, they are highly instructive.

Examining Stylized Fact 1

- Homesteading was a minor factor in farm making; most farmers purchased their land.

This point is sometimes argued on the basis of the *number of farms* created via homesteading versus other mechanisms, and at other times it is argued on the basis of the *number of acres* transferred from the public domain to nonfederal owners via homesteading as compared to other programs. Those two metrics produce somewhat different results.

Shannon claimed that homesteading was so unimportant in the larger context of land transactions during the period 1860 to 1900 that "even if all the homesteaders had kept and lived on their holdings, less than a sixth of the new homes ... would have been on land that came as a gift from the government. Eighty-four out of each hundred new farms had to be achieved either by subdivision of older holdings or by purchase." This is the specific claim that Alan Trachtenberg found compelling for his 1982 book.[5] If true, farm formation via homesteading ("gift from the government") apparently was a minor sideshow.

Shannon focused on the number of farms and obtained his estimate as follows: Using data from the decennial censuses, he reports that there were 2,000,000 farms in the United States in 1860 and 5,737,000 farms in 1900, so 3,737,000 new farms had been formed during the forty-year period.[6] The GLO reported that it had issued 599,402 patents on proved-up homestead claims during the period, so we divide 599,402 by 3,737,000 to obtain 16.0 percent; on this calculation free farms accounted for 16.0 percent or "less than a sixth" (less than 16.6 percent) of new farm formation.[7] The arithmetic here is correct, but Shannon's presentation is very misleading. In the context of his discussion, he clearly suggests he is analyzing the twenty-nine homesteading states or perhaps just the West, but his data cover the entire United States, including both homesteading and nonhomesteading states. It is hardly surprising that homesteading played a negligible role in farm formation in those eastern and southern states where homesteading was not allowed!

There are several ways to obtain a more straightforward presentation. First, we can look at just the twenty-nine homesteading states between 1860 and 1900, excluding the nineteen nonhomesteading states. We also exclude Alaska, which was not part of Shannon's analysis (Alaska and Hawaii are not included in the 1860 or 1900 censuses). In the homesteading states, there were 1,017,000 farms in 1860 and 3,328,000 in 1900, an increase of 2,311,000 farms. With 599,402 homesteading patents issued during this period, homesteading would account for 25.9 percent of new farm growth in the homesteading states. That is, restricting our analysis (as it should be) just to states where homesteading was actually permitted increases its role to more than a quarter, not "less than a sixth" as Shannon claimed.

However, Shannon also failed to account for successful homesteads initially filed between 1896 and 1900, an obvious mistake. These farms were homesteads in the making, clearly part of the homesteading process. (Note that we include only those homesteads filed during 1896 and 1900 that were successfully proved up, and when we speak of homesteads "in-process," it includes *only* homesteaders who ultimately gained their patents, not all initial claimants.) He should either have added them to his numerator, thereby making it "proved-up plus soon-to-be successful" homesteads," or excluded them from his denominator.[8] He did neither, thereby artificially lowering his numerator without adjusting his denominator and biasing his calculation toward underreporting homesteading's role in farm formation. We can easily correct his mistake: according to the GLO, there were 154,272 homesteads that received their patents between 1901 and 1905, that is, successful homesteads whose initial claims were made before 1900. If we add this figure to 599,402, we obtain 753,674 homesteads that had either been proved up or were in the process of successfully proving up between 1863 and 1900. This means that homesteads initially filed between 1863 and 1900 would account for 32.6 percent—nearly a third—of new farm growth in the twenty-nine homesteading states, roughly double Shannon's figure.

A second and better recalculation would also exclude three other states—Ohio, Indiana, and Illinois—where homesteading was legal, but there was virtually no homesteadable land available. Those states had already been largely settled when homesteading began. Ohio had only 110 final homestead entries between 1863 and 1905, Indiana 26, and Illinois 73. These were homesteading states in law but not in practice. If we exclude them to get a more realistic appraisal of homesteading's role in the areas where it actually operated, then in the twenty-six remaining states there were 562,000 farms in 1860 and 2,565,000 in 1900, or an increase of 2,003,000 farms. With 753,465 (599,402 + 154,272 − 209) homesteading patents issued or homesteads-in-process during the period in the included states, homesteading would account for 37.6 percent of new farm growth.

But this is still highly misleading, because nearly all discussion of homesteading takes place in the context of the settlement of the West. We see this in the textbooks, whether those volumes are specifically "History of the American West" or more general "History of the United States." For example, James A. Henretta and coauthors in their *America's History* (7th ed.) discuss homesteading in a section called "Incorporating the West." Eric Foner, in his *Give Me Liberty!* textbook, notes, "Congress . . . had already offered free land to settlers in the West in the Homestead Act of 1862."[9] So instead of calculating homesteading's reach by including homesteads and farm formation in Florida, Alabama, and Michigan, let's look directly at "the West"—the sixteen states west of the Missouri River plus Minnesota.[10] How important was homesteading in farm formation in the West? This would produce a more relevant recalculation.

Looking just at the West shows how misleading Shannon's presentation was. In these seventeen states, the number of farms in 1860 was 66,000 and in 1900 was 898,000, meaning settlers established 832,000 new farms during the forty-year period. The General Land Office issued 401,392 patents in these states between 1868 and 1900; an additional 130,490 homesteads were patented between 1901 and 1905 for a total of 531,882. *So in the West, homesteading may have accounted for as much as 63.9 percent (531,882/832,000) of new farm formation.* In the West, most new farms came from homesteading.

Other scholars have adopted Shannon's conclusion but based their argument on *acres transferred* rather than number of farms. They compare the number of public-domain acres transferred to private owners via homesteading versus other federal land grants and programs. Hine asserted, "More than 700 million acres were

FIG. 2.1. The seventeen states of "the West." Map created by Katie Nieland.

bought rather than granted from the public domain during [the homesteading period]—three or four times as many as were given free. Most farmers who went west did not homestead."[11] Willard Cochrane argued, "The total land in farms increased from some 407 million acres in 1860 to some 839 million acres in 1900. But of this increase of 432 million acres, only some 80 million acres were added through [homesteading]. . . . The Homestead Act played a role in the disposal of the public domain in the nineteenth century, but only a small role."[12] Danbom asserts, "Most of the land on the Great Plains—perhaps as much as 80 percent—was purchased rather than acquired under the Homestead Act. About 300 million acres was transferred to the states and the railroads. . . . Over 100 million more acres were held by the federal government and not opened to homesteading [but sold]."[13] Danbom cites Hine and Cochrane as authorities for his statement.

Unfortunately both of Danbom's sources prove to be as unreliable as Shannon. Hine's assertion that "three or four times as many [acres were sold] as were given free. Most farmers who went west did not homestead" is wrong: as shown above, in the West between 1863 and 1900, homesteading accounted for a majority of new farms, leaving those who purchased land in a minority.[14]

Hine is probably correct that more farmland was purchased than obtained through homesteading, though our estimates below suggest the ratio was about two to one, not the "three or four times" that Hine suggests. Both statements—that homesteaders constituted a majority of new farmers and that more farmland was purchased than homesteaded—can be true. Hine makes a logical error in drawing a conclusion about the number of farmers from his calculation about acres; it would be possible for there to be more acres sold than homesteaded, yet homesteaders outnumbered other farmers, if homesteaders on average had smaller holdings than those farmers who purchased their land. Indeed, this seems highly probable, since homesteaders were limited to 160 acres, somewhat more if they also used preemption or timber culture claims, whereas purchasers could buy as much land as they wanted—"a million acres at $1.25 per acre, if you have the money," in Thomas Donaldson's exasperated complaint. But we do not need to follow such a treacherous logical path; as we saw, much more direct estimates from the decennial censuses suggest that homesteading was responsible for a majority of farmers in the West, and a calculation below shows that homesteading accounted for almost a third of farmland in the West. Hine's conclusion is simply a non sequitur.[15]

Cochrane's evidence is doubly irrelevant. His first stumble is that his figure of 432 million acres of total farmland added between 1860 and 1900 refers to the total increase *in the United States*. Again, it is not surprising that the Homestead Act played little role in increasing farmland in nonhomesteading states like Georgia or Pennsylvania. His second mistake, identifying increases in total farmland with "disposal of the public domain," is simply specious. Farmland increased in many ways other than the sale of land in the public domain—for example, by conversion of a privately owned Georgia forest to cropland—but Cochrane used aggregate data that cannot distinguish among them, so he mistakenly attributed all increases in farmland to withdrawals from the public domain.

Some scholars adopted the false conclusion without revealing what they based it on. Eric Foner simply declared, "Hundreds of thousands of families acquired farms under the Homestead Act, and even more purchased land from speculators and from railroad companies." Pauline Maier and coauthors in *Inventing America: A History of the United States*, write, "Between 1862 and 1890, nearly 2 million people claimed free land under provisions of the Homestead Act. The typical westward migrant, however, *bought* land."[16] Neither gives a citation.

We can make a more direct and useful calculation using acres as follows.[17] In 1860 farmland in the seventeen-state West was 17,839,000 acres and in 1900 was 249,222,000 acres; therefore, the growth in farmland was 231,383,000 acres; with 76,480,436 acres homesteaded (counting proved-up and in-process), the percent of farmland gained via the Homestead Act was 33.1 percent, hardly the "small role" Cochrane asserted.

In sum, correcting Shannon's analysis shows that his estimate of "less than a sixth" of the new farms originating from homesteads is badly misleading. In the twenty-nine homesteading states, we found that 32.6 percent of new farms probably developed from homesteads. But more relevantly, in the seventeen-state West, we calculated that 63.9 percent of new farms created originated in homestead claims, contrary to Shannon's assertions and those of the many historians who repeated them. And we found that 33.1 percent of new farmland in the West derived from homestead claims, making the ratio of purchased to homesteaded land about two to one, not the "three or four times" Hine asserted. The bottom line is that between 1863 and 1900 homesteading accounted for approximately two out of three new farms created and one-third of the new farmland in the West.

Examining Stylized Fact 2

• Most homesteaders failed to prove up their claims.

Scholars' second stylized fact is the assertion that most settlers who filed homestead claims didn't last the five years (later three years) to prove up. Shannon claimed that "two-thirds of all homestead claimants before 1890 failed at the venture."[18] This contention or some variant (e.g., "most homesteaders failed") has frequently been repeated and has become a kind of bedrock quantitative assertion supporting scholars' generally negative consensus on the Homestead Act. Indeed, if most homesteaders failed, that would seem to bolster the (false) claim that homesteading was a minor factor in farm creation, the first stylized fact.[19] It is therefore worth examining the failure rate in detail. It turns out Shannon's claim is simply false, either a mistaken or intentional misuse of the underlying statistics, and those who repeated his assertion and relied on him as their authority are also wrong.

For support of this claim, which was made in *Farmer's Last Frontier*, Shannon cites his own 1936 paper, "The Homestead Act and the Labor Surplus." That paper cites page 355 of Thomas Donaldson's *The Public Domain: Its History with Statistics*. Note first that Donaldson provides data only until 1880, not 1890, so on the basis of Donaldson's data Shannon can make no statement about the failure rate "before 1890." Let us assume Shannon made a mistake and meant to refer to "before 1880" for which Donaldson provides the relevant data: year-by-year and summary statistics for "Homesteads—Entries" and "Final Homesteads—Entries" for 1863 through June 30, 1880. We can follow the calculation Shannon probably made: Using the summary statistics of 469,782 initial entries and 162,237 final entries (or patents), we subtract the latter from the former to obtain 307,545 cases of initial filings unaccompanied by patents (i.e., "failures"); dividing 307,545 by 469,782 yields 65.5 percent, very close to Shannon's more approximate statement of "two-thirds . . . failed at the venture."

What's wrong with this calculation? The cumulative total (469,782) contains initial entries made in the years immediately prior to 1880, which of course *were not yet eligible for proving up*; even if highly successful, they would show up in Shannon's analysis as "failures," once again biasing his results. If we correct for this elementary mistake, we can obtain a better estimate. First we must note that homesteaders had up to seven years to prove up their claims and often had an incentive (such as avoiding land tax) to delay final entry as long as possible; since we cannot distinguish in the data between "five-year prove-ups" and "seven-year prove-ups" or any in-between, we need to calculate upper and lower bounds for the failure rate.

We can calculate the upper-bound or highest estimate of the failure rate by adding to the total of final entries (that is, 162,237) the additional in-process homesteads, amounting to 95,158, which were patented during the years 1881–85; entrymen on these in-process homesteads made their initial claims in 1880 or earlier and successfully proved up by 1885. The new total of (completed + in-process) final entries is 257,395. Unsuccessful initial claimants would then be 469,782 less 257,395, or 212,387, and the failure rate is 212,387 divided by 469,782, or 45.2 percent, or said differently, at least 54.8 percent of initial claimants between 1863 and 1880 were successful homesteaders. On this calculation, the failure rate was not Shannon's two-thirds but rather at most 45.2 percent. "Most" entrymen (at least 54.8 percent) succeeded in obtaining their patents.

In a similar manner, we can also calculate a lower-bound or lowest estimate of the failure rate as follows: we add all final entries that could have been started with initial entries made in 1880 or earlier, that is, final entries filed from 1881 to 1887 (this likely includes some entries filed in 1881 and 1882). The total of these final entries is 134,380. The new total of final entries that began with initial claims between 1868 and 1880 is 162,237 + 134,380, or 296,617. With initial entries of 469,782, unsuccessful homesteaders would be 469,782 less 296,617, or 173,165, producing a failure rate of perhaps as little as 36.9 percent; the corresponding homesteader success rate would be 63.1 percent. By this calculation, nearly two-thirds (63.1 percent) of entrymen succeeded in obtaining their land.

Thus correct analysis of Donaldson's statistics yields a failure rate before 1880 somewhere between 37 percent and 45 percent—nowhere near the two-thirds that Shannon cites—or to put it differently, between 55 percent and 63 percent of homesteaders before 1880 *succeeded* in obtaining patents. Moreover, even this estimate accepts Shannon's highly dubious assumption that whenever an initial claimant did not prove up, it was a failure. For example, if the initial claimant died during the required residency period and had no inheritor to prove up his claim, this would be counted a failure. (It also accepts his implicit definition of nonfailure as any proved-up claim.) So, too, any commuted homesteads would be counted as failures. Thus even the 37–45 percent range of failure may be a misleading overestimate.

We can go beyond Donaldson's data to extend this analysis for the period 1881–1900, as follows: the *Historical Statistics of the United States* provides data for 1881–1900 on acres claimed in initial homestead filings and acres in final, proved-up claims.[20] These data show that there were 132,540,000 acres claimed in initial homestead filings between 1881 and 1900, and between 1886 and 1905—the years when claims filed in the earlier period would have been eligible to be proved up—there were patents issued for 73,022,000 acres. Using acres as a proxy for number of claims, we find that 55.1 percent of homesteaders who filed between 1881 and 1900 succeeded. Thus the *Historical Statistics* figure for 1881–1900 accords closely with the range of 55 percent to 63 percent successful homesteaders we calculated from Donaldson's data for the period 1863–80.[21]

Ironically Shannon's misrepresentation of the homestead data was largely irrelevant to the case he was trying to make. According to Shannon, "the first and one of the greatest defects" of the Homestead Act was that it failed to "provide means to get poor families to the farms, extend them long credit for all the rest of their needs for at least the first year, and give them guidance in farming." He was accurate in describing the act, because it did not include any provision for extending credit or advice to homesteaders, but he was quite wrong in suggesting that poor people did not benefit from free land. Many poor people somehow succeeded in homesteading despite being poor, as for example the "landless, poor, young, and single" Norwegian emigrants studied by Karen V. Hansen.[22]

Shannon's second complaint was that the act "failed to stop the public auctioning of [federal] lands and [sales of] railroad grants, or gifts to states" as well as sale of Indian lands reverting the government, soldiers' pension warrants, and preemption."[23] Elsewhere he added land disbursed via agricultural college scrip to the list. Few would dispute that the government's distribution of land under these programs was highly profligate and sometimes corrupt, or that it had the unhappy unintended consequence of creating a bonanza for speculators. Shannon's is a curious criticism of homesteading, however: the act is faulted because it did not cure the sins of *other* government land giveaways and because those programs did not include the exacting strictures (such as the 160-acre limit, the residency requirement, and so on) required of homesteaders. It would have been better, Shannon seems to be saying, if *all* government land had been given away under the rules of the Homestead Act. This seems a reasonable complaint to make of *other* programs but hardly a persuasive criticism of homesteading. On this basis, the cure for polio would be criticized because it didn't also cure malaria and the Ebola virus. In making these and other criticisms, Shannon mistakenly felt compelled to charge the Homestead Act itself as a failure and either misunderstood or misrepresented the homesteading statistics.

A more troubling question is why Shannon's numerically wrong calculations and misleading statistical presentation have lingered for so long and found such ready acceptance among today's scholars. The reasons scholars uncritically accepted his results are fundamentally unknowable, but the pattern is consistent with the hypothesis that having accepted that homesteading was somehow a sham, these scholars quickly welcomed any supporting evidence without checking it. It is long past time when such "evidence" should shape our understanding of homesteading.

Correcting the Historical Record

We can collect the findings from above to present a more accurate picture of homesteading in the period 1863–1900 in the West. First, we find that homesteading's role in creating farms varied substantially among the seventeen states, as shown in figure 2.2. States where homesteading was very important in farm formation are Colorado (86.6 percent), Idaho (84.6 percent), South Dakota (80.3 percent), and Washington (96.7 percent). In some states, those with the highest density of homesteads, the number of homesteads patented actually exceeded the number of new farms created and still surviving by 1900—for example, Montana (109.6 percent), North Dakota (113.3 percent), Oregon (114.5 percent), and Wyoming (109.6 percent).

Although initially puzzling, this pattern (exceeding 100 percent) is quite understandable in areas where farms were undergoing the long-term process of farm consolidation. Imagine a section of land, one square mile, where there were no farms in 1860; in the next decade, four homesteaders each file 160-acre claims and prove up. In 1870 there would be four farms, all derived from homesteads, so we would say 100 percent of the farms in this section started as homesteads. Then, over the next thirty years, three of the four homesteaders sold out to the fourth. By 1900, our square mile would have four times (400 percent) the number of homesteads filed as functioning farms. As the example shows, how many homesteads resulted in functioning farms is highly time-dependent in a context of consolidation: the longer the period, the higher the ratio of original homesteads to functioning farms. For the West as a whole, that is, the sixteen states west of the Missouri River plus Minnesota, homesteading likely contributed up to 63.9 percent of the new farms created.

These findings are broadly consistent with Gilbert Fite's conclusion: the charge that not many settlers actually obtained free land "is definitely not true if applied to the Minnesota-Dakota-Nebraska-Kansas frontier in the late 1860s and 1870s. . . . [Between 1863 and 1880] 86,169 farmers in Minnesota, Dakota, Nebraska, and Kansas obtained patents [and another] 50,673 who had filed entries before June 30, 1880, gained their title [later]. Thus between 1863 and 1880, 136,842 of the 242,000 new farms were settled as homesteads. . . . This was about 56.5 percent of the total farms created. . . . About two-thirds of the farms in Minnesota were originally established by homesteaders."[24]

Homesteading was also important but less so in the proportion of land newly converted to farming in the West. As shown in figure 2.3, the states with the highest proportions are Idaho

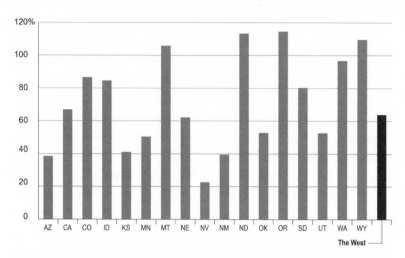

FIG. 2.2. Homesteads as a percentage of new farms, 1860–1900, seventeen western states, and "the West."

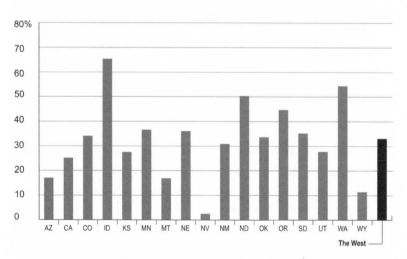

FIG. 2.3. Homesteaded acres as a percentage of new farmland, 1860–1900, seventeen western states and "the West."

(65.4 percent), Washington (54.4 percent), North Dakota (50.3 percent), and Oregon (44.7 percent). Overall in the seventeen-state West, homesteading accounted for 33.1 percent of farmland added. Since homesteads accounted for a much larger percentage of farms than homesteaded acres did of new farm acres, the obvious implication is that homesteaded farms were on average smaller than farms obtained through purchase or other methods. This result would be expected, given that homesteads were capped at 160 acres (except under the Kinkaid and Enlarged Homestead Acts), whereas farms created via purchase, military warrants, agricultural college scrip, or other methods were not. This result again demonstrates why one cannot draw conclusions about the *number* of homesteaders vs. other farmers based on *acreage* unless one also knows the average size of each group's farms.

What picture of homesteading, then, emerges from the more soundly grounded statistics reviewed above? Considering the West during the period 1863–1900, and remembering our earlier caution about the approximate nature of the data, both of the stylized facts we began the chapter with have been shown to be incorrect. The first assertion, that homesteading was a minor factor in farm making and most farmers purchased their land, might be replaced, based on the data in figure 2.2, with this finding:

◇ Homesteading was a major factor in farm making in the West; before 1900 it was responsible for nearly two out of every three new farms and almost a third of the new land brought into farming.

The second stylized fact, that most homesteaders failed to prove up their claims, is refuted by a corrected reanalysis of Donaldson's data for the period 1863–80 and by the *Historical Statistics* evidence for 1881–1900; instead, it might be replaced with:

◇ Most homesteaders—between 55 percent to 63 percent before 1900—succeeded in obtaining title to their land during the first phase of homesteading.

This is a nearly complete reversal of what scholars for more than a half century have accepted as the received wisdom on homesteading and have been teaching their students.

3

Evolving Views on
Homesteading Fraud

In this chapter and the next one, we examine the third stylized fact of the homesteading literature:

- The homesteading process was rife with corruption and fraud.

Fraud stained the bright dream of those who agitated for a homestead act. Galusha Grow, Speaker of the U.S. House of Representatives in 1862, had long advocated using America's vast public domain to make free grants of land to settlers. When Congress debated the Homestead Act, Speaker Grow articulated the lofty hopes held by many when he declared that "the best disposition that can be made of the public domain is to set it apart and consecrate it forever in homes for freemen."[1]

Nearly 150 years later, scholars have settled on a consensus narrative in which homesteading is seen as a program of minor importance marked by sham and fraud. The National Archives and Records Administration expressed this consensus on its official website as follows: "Unfortunately, the [Homestead] act was framed so ambiguously that it seemed to invite fraud, and early modifications by Congress only compounded the problem. Most of the land went to speculators, cattlemen, miners, lumbermen, and railroads. Of some 500 million acres dispersed by the General Land Office between 1862 and 1904, only 80 million acres went to homesteaders." We might note that the statement begins by describing the Homestead Act, then by sleight-of-hand switches to *all* land distributed by the General Land Office, arriving at the claim that "only 80 million of 500 million went to homesteaders." But land did not go to cattlemen, miners, railroads, etc., via the Homestead Act (except for trivial amounts) but rather through other public land policies. NARA conflates homesteaded land with all land granted by the GLO, wrongly attributing the scandal of most land going to "speculators, cattlemen, miners, lumbermen, and railroads" to the ambiguity of the Homestead Act. Thus what began as a critique of the Homestead Act morphs through factual inaccuracy, conflation with other land laws, and sloppy writing into a misstatement asserting enormous Homestead fraud. Nonetheless, for any but the most careful reader, the statement blames the Homestead Act for land fraud.[2]

How did we get from Speaker Grow's soaring dream of a consecrated land for freemen to modern historians' casual dismissal of it? This issue is a tricky one, because acts or behaviors that constituted fraud changed over time. The General Land Office (GLO) periodically issued circulars fine-tuning its definition of fraudulent acts. In this chapter we examine those regulations to map the GLO's evolving specification of fraud. Then we explore how historians and others saw the problem of fraud. Not surprisingly, some acts clearly constituted fraud, others were defined as fraud or not depending on the specific circumstances of the case or local sentiments, and still others depended on interpretation or the eye of the beholder.

Totaling just one and a half pages, the Homestead Act of 1862 was a concise piece of legislation with one big idea: free land to actual settlers. Due to its brevity, Congress tasked the commissioner of the GLO with producing the definitions, procedures, and policies needed to implement the law, stating that he was "hereby required to prepare and issue such rules and regulations, consistent with this act, as shall be necessary and proper to carry its provisions into effect." So it was left to the GLO to issue regulations giving practical and concrete meaning to what constituted fraud and how best to implement the law. The GLO quickly discovered that local land agents needed detailed instructions for how to interpret the various provisions of the act. Within five years the GLO began to clarify the homesteading law by annually issuing what it pithily called the *Circular from the General Land Office Showing the Manner of Proceeding to Obtain Title to Public Lands under the Pre-Emption, Homestead, Timber Culture, and Other Laws*, or more simply, the General Land Office circular. Each circular addressed the entire land distribution system, not just homesteading, up to the time of its annual publication. The circulars included instructions to the land offices, descriptions of the new laws that added to or amended the land system, regulatory changes made to each section, and copies of all the required forms.

For homesteading in particular, the circulars contained specific guidelines to the local land offices, filling in the necessary procedural detail where the original law had been silent. Special agents tasked with unearthing fraud sent reports to the GLO that included instances of fraud they had encountered.[3] GLO headquarters in Washington depended on these reports and other complaints from its local land agents to help it monitor unwanted or illegal homesteader behavior; it then issued preventative regulations against repeated offenses. We map changes in the circulars from 1867 to 1904, covering the "first phase" of homesteading. From these circulars we in effect generate a guide to how the GLO understood homesteaders' fraudulent or unauthorized actions and its regulatory changes in response to them. In this way we can see how the GLO understood, defined, and responded to fraud.[4]

The GLO intended each local land agent to interpret its regulations in response to local circumstances or specific factors in the claimant's case in order to achieve the Homestead Act's original intent: establishing "actual settlers" on the public domain. The commissioner, land agents, and entrymen alike treated the regulations in the circulars more as guidelines rather than rigid rules. In one case Commissioner Noah C. McFarland (1881–85) wrote to a land office clerk, "Such rules are made to aid in the just and equitable disposition of the public lands by the government to its citizens, and should not be held to hinder and delay such disposition." McFarland continued to scold the clerk for following his office's rules to the detriment of a bona fide settler seeking to own land. In fact, the circulars charged the commissioner, secretary of the interior, and attorney general to decide favorably in cases where "there has been substantial compliance with the law but lacking in some formality resulting from ignorance, accident, or mistake satisfactorily explained, to be decided on principles of equity and justice." In other words, the rules could be bent if it meant giving land to genuine settlers.[5]

This flexible administration of its rules continued a long GLO practice, predating passage of the Homestead Act, of prioritizing achieving the intent of the law above pettifogging insistence on exact rule compliance. In regard to preemptions and squatters, for example, the GLO granted considerable flexibility to local land agents in dealing with the many illiterate claimants or claimants who had little or no fluency in English, little experience in dealing with officials, or little familiarity with the subtleties of GLO regulations. While such flexibility potentially opened opportunities for corrupt agents and corrupting speculators, it was probably essential to achieve effective administration when agents implementing the law were so distant from headquarters.

Although the GLO worried about many kinds of fraud, three types dominated its thinking: speculation, marriage fraud, and stolen soldier identities. It also recognized problems with improper residency and exceeding the 160-acre limit, but for these concerns the GLO devised satisfactory regulations. Finally it grappled with the question of commutations, which was not precisely fraud (because they were fully allowed by the law) yet seemed inconsistent with the aims of the Homestead Act. In appendix 1 we provide an annotated listing of GLO circulars from 1867 through 1904 and the relevant entries from Henry N. Copp's *Public Land Laws Passed by Congress*. Copp assembled the most important official documents covering the years 1869 to 1890 with the intent of presenting "a repository of important decisions of the Land Department during that period."[6] These public land compendia chronicle revised statutes, land laws, decisions, opinions, and instructions, making Copp a complementary source to the circulars.

FIG. 3.1. Seal of the General Land Office, ca. 1865. U.S. Department of the Interior, Bureau of Land Management.

Speculation

The circulars classified speculation, which they defined as claiming land under the Homestead Act without the intent to settle, as undeniable fraud, and it was by far the category of fraud which most concerned the GLO. If the entryman did not intend to settle the land, or was making his or her claim for the benefit of some other person, then the claimant was committing fraud, since the law specifically stated that the free land was to go only to "actual" settlers. The Homestead Act stipulated that a claimant had to sign an affidavit upon making an initial claim, swearing that the entryman intended to live on the land and would use the land for his or her own exclusive benefit and that moreover this oath was "liable to the pains and penalties of perjury."[7] Congress intended the original affidavit to be the first line of defense against speculation, and it lasted thirty-three years before eventually requiring an overhaul. The revised affidavit required entrymen to swear explicitly that they in no way meant to use the land they claimed for speculation purposes and that no one else had a right to their land.[8] Requiring an oath on pain of perjury created a deterrent effect, though ultimately the affidavit was probably most effective when claimants believed the land office could prove speculation in other ways.

Relinquishment and commutation opened other possibilities for speculation. If the entryman chose not to stay for the five years (later reduced to three) of required residency, he or she faced two options. The first was simply to abandon the claim, called a relinquishment; a relinquished claim reverted to the government. Legally the entryman had no property to sell; however, entrymen still sometimes found ways to "sell" their relinquishments. For example, in return for a payment from a speculator, the claimant could agree to show up at the land office with the speculator, so that as soon as the seller had officially relinquished his claim, the speculator, standing next in line, could claim it. The second option, commutation, meant that an entryman could purchase his or her claim after six months (later extended to fourteen months) of living on the land. So it was possible for a speculator to "purchase" a relinquishment by advancing funds to the entryman to legally purchase (commute) his or her claim, with the understanding that the entryman would afterwards transfer the now legally purchased land to the buyer. In order to address this problem, the GLO added a series of amendments that dealt with relinquishments. The 1867 circular clarified that an entryman could not sell his or her homestead before receiving a patent. If the entryman sold his or her claim prematurely, the GLO assumed it proved that the claimant had no intent to be an "actual settler" on the land and only intended to profit from its sale. The circular three years later prohibited entrymen from relinquishing their homesteads to predetermined people.[9]

Unhelpfully, Congress passed two acts in 1880 that seemingly encouraged speculation. Most of the officials and clerks of the GLO (despite occasional bad apples) apparently attempted to administer the law fairly and prevent what they saw as fraud, and the GLO acted as the most consistent official force countering fraud. Congress and sometimes the president were another matter: they were much more open to political pressures and bribes from big-time speculators, railroads, and other land-seekers. One act passed by Congress retroactively legalized homestead transfers, essentially legalizing speculative transfers before 1885. Another act required land office clerks only to accept relinquishments when the claimant appeared in person in the land offices, theoretically restricting the ability of speculators to prepurchase relinquishments; however, it also streamlined the procedure by requiring no further action on the part of the GLO prior to putting a relinquished claim back on the market.[10] This new and improved process made it easier to relinquish land to a certain person, as the speculator just had to make sure he or she stood next in line behind the homesteader relinquishing the claim. Through these acts, Congress both restricted *and* assisted speculation.

Speculators could also gain control over land by filing fraudulent contestations. Speculators recognized this legal loophole after an 1878 circular gave legal preference, in any case where the contestation was successful, to the person who had contested the claim. In 1884 Commissioner McFarland explained, "Attorneys file contests, sell the right of contest, withdraw the original contest, and file another in the name of another party, thus controlling the disposition of the tract for speculative purposes." In anticipation of problems similar to this, federal legislators passed a law in 1878 requiring that anyone contesting a claim on the grounds of abandonment had to post notice in a local newspaper. Requiring contestants to announce their challenges to the claim allowed bona fide homesteaders to defend themselves more adequately.[11]

Marriage Fraud

Couples sometimes manipulated their marital status to obtain more than a quarter section of homestead land. If a man and a woman, unmarried, both filed claims, later wed, and then both proved up their claims, the family would obtain 320 acres, twice the amount allowed by the Homestead Act for one person or family. The original act did not address marriage as a method of defrauding the government. As such, land office agents and the commissioner himself often dealt with these cases in a way that contradicted the original intent of the law. In 1877 a potential homesteader asked Commissioner James A. Williamson (1876–81) if marriage would invalidate one or both of the unfinished claims of a man and woman wishing to marry. Williamson responded that as long as the pair both remained living on their claims, the claims would remain valid. However, if one moved to the other's residence, this would constitute abandonment. In one instance noted, a couple utilized this legal gray area when they entered adjoining land and built their residence on the dividing line. They were both allowed to receive patents, although this violated the spirit of the law. It did perhaps improve their chances for success and remaining on semiarid land.[12]

In response to the GLO's inconsistent handling of marriage fraud, the 1889 circular asserted that marriage did not preclude a woman from proving up her homestead; however, if she abandoned her homestead, she could not perfect her claim. But the GLO assumed that once married, a woman would move into her husband's residence. Indeed, in 1888 Acting Commissioner Strother M. Stockslager (1888–89) wrote that "a husband and wife, living as one family, can not maintain separate residences at the same time."[13] In other words, if a woman possessed an unpatented claim and married a man with the same, the GLO would assume they lived together and hence one of them would have to abandon his or her residence. Any attempt to finalize the abandoned claim would be considered fraudulent. The 1895 circular attempted to clarify the previous conflicting statements by declaring that if two applicants with yet unpatented homestead entries got married, they could prove up both homesteads only if they resided separately; implicitly assuming that married couples lived together, it went on to state that such couples could only prove up the claim on which they resided together.[14]

Stolen Soldier Identity

Stealing a soldier's right to homestead was an unequivocally fraudulent but potentially lucrative endeavor, since soldiers received special privileges within the homesteading system. Originally soldiers loyal to the Union who served more than fourteen days in any war could receive exemption from the law's requirement that the entryman be twenty-one years of age.[15] The law also allowed anyone who served in the military for at least ninety days to claim 160 acres of double minimum lands—land previously allocated for railroads or public works and priced at twice the cost of minimum lands—which was twice what civilians could legally homestead.[16] The most profitable benefits emerged in 1872 when Congress passed an act allowing any marines, officers, sailors, or soldiers who had served in the Civil War on the side of the Union for ninety days to homestead whether or not they met the law's requirements and on several extremely favorable terms.[17] For instance, they could file an entry through an agent and count either their time served in the military or their term of enlistment, if they received discharge due to injury, toward their residency requirements. If they died in the war, their widows or minor children—through a guardian if both parents had died—inherited their right to homestead under these special privileges, with the deduction of the deceased's term of enlistment from the residency requirement. Finally, if a soldier abandoned his homestead claim to serve in the military, the law permitted him (or his heirs, if deceased) to make a second entry.[18] An 1872 report of the commissioner additionally allowed soldiers who previously homesteaded less than 160 acres to make a second claim for a cumulative 160 acres.[19]

The special privileges created weak points that forced the GLO to take further action to ensure that soldier benefits went to the correct recipients. After the passage of the 1872 law, Commissioner Willis Drummond (1871–74) implemented a system that required all soldiers or their proxy claimants to submit appropriate documents or affidavits upon application to demonstrate their eligibility. Strengthening the procedures for proving a service record or eligibility minimized the risk of fraudulent application and

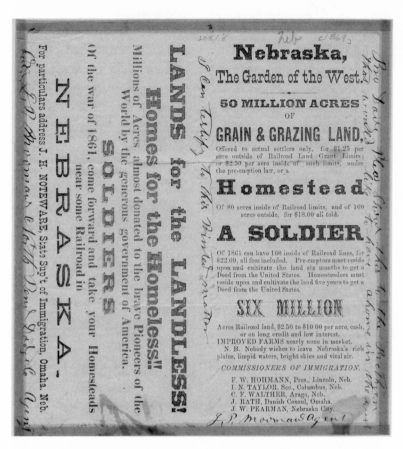

FIG. 3.2. Advertisement for homesteaders, especially soldiers, to claim land in Nebraska, "The Garden of the West," written in 1869 by J. H. Noteware, state superintendent of immigration. Courtesy Duke University.

restricted these rights to actual soldiers or their heirs. For example, George W. Benton was a contract surgeon, meaning he did not actually serve in the army; he attempted to claim the soldier's special right to double minimum lands, but the GLO denied his application because he did not officially serve as a solider or officer. Previously, in order to act as an agent for a soldier, a person had to submit proof that he had power of attorney for the soldier. The 1884 circular required that anyone attempting to make a declaratory statement on behalf of a soldier had to take an oath establishing that the claim was for the sole benefit of the claimant and that the agent had "no interest, either present or prospective, direct or indirect, in the claim." That same circular also emphasized that agents could only make a declaratory statement on the soldier's behalf; they could not make an actual entry. During homesteading's first phase, the GLO took no further action to protect soldiers' special right to homestead.[20]

In addition to these three major categories of fraud, the GLO also provided guidance and issued regulations governing other forms of abuse of the homestead laws. In the case of improper residency and exceeding 160 acres, the regulations mostly cleared up ambiguity in the requirements. In the case of commutations, the GLO tightened its rules regarding residency, although it continued to be concerned about the use of commutations.

Improper Residency

Residency requirements were a way to restrict the homestead privilege to bona fide settlers only. The original act required homesteaders to swear upon application their intent to settle and cultivate their claim and to reside on it for five years with no single absence exceeding six months. Indeed, "It was the intention [of] Congress to give homesteads to those persons who in good faith would settle upon and cultivate unappropriated public land."[21]

Questions about improper residency quickly arose, however, precipitating an early change in the 1867 circular explicitly stating that when homesteaders perfected their claims they had to prove continuous residence and cultivation. The need for this clarification indicates confusion among both land clerks and entrymen. For instance, in 1872 a land agent sent a letter to Assistant Attorney General W. H. Smith about a difficult case: "The only question is, whether residence on the land is essential." Smith, of course, asserted that it was, since residency was integral to the law from its very inception. While improper residency bears many similarities to speculation, it forms a different category for two reasons: speculators did not necessarily have to violate residency requirements, and noncomplying entrymen did not necessarily have to intend to sell the property for profit.[22]

Land agents and their supervisors soon realized that proving residency required eyes on the ground. Because the sheer volume of claims made it impossible to investigate every entry that came through their offices, the land agents relied on the integrity of each claimant's witnesses for proof of residency. Lacking community regulation potentially enabled claimants with untruthful witnesses to acquire land by fraud with few or no repercussions. To deter such frauds, Congress sought to enlist the vigilance of the community to assist agents in policing homestead filings. On March 3, 1879, it passed a law requiring every claimant intending to prove up to publish that fact in a local newspaper for five consecutive weeks.[23] The new process of finalization alerted neighbors and others living nearby, giving them the opportunity to formally object or bring other local influence to bear.

Additionally, the law gave contestants thirty days to exercise their right to the land following successful contestations. The absence of this provision in earlier circulars meant that the first claimant who otherwise satisfied eligibility requirements could get the land; this claimant sometimes was not the contestant whose effort and money had secured the cancellation of the contested entry.[24] Previously the process had occasionally penalized contestants, but now the law gave a preference right to the contestant; it created a clear incentive to report fraudulent homesteads and a tangible reward for succeeding. This change, by enlisting the wider community as enforcers of the law, decreased the need for the underfunded, understaffed land offices to root out fraudulent claims themselves. Unfortunately it also incentivized fraudulent contestations, making necessary the previously mentioned countermeasures against speculative contestations.

In addition to creating an incentive to report fraudulent claims, the GLO also tightened its rules about residency requirements while simultaneously providing flexibility for certain hardships. The 1884 circular explicitly stated that entrymen needed to establish residence within six months of application and that the period of continuous settlement and cultivation started after the establishment of residence. Twenty-seven years after the enactment of the

Homestead Act, the commissioner still felt the need to state the absolute necessity of proper residency, separate from speculation. The 1889 circular thus further defined residency, making it clear that entrymen could not simply visit their land every few months. Rather, homesteaders were required to reside on their plots without an interruption lasting more than six months. They also had to improve and cultivate their land.[25]

When the lofty ideals of the legislation met the harsh realities of homesteading, some compromise on this issue became necessary. For example, from 1874 to 1877 a grasshopper plague swept the Great Plains, destroying hundreds of thousands of acres of crops each year. With no livelihood left to sustain them, entrymen needed to leave their land to make money to feed themselves and their families. According to law, an absence of six months or more constituted abandonment and triggered the loss of the claim even for bona fide settlers. Congress responded by passing laws allowing extended leaves of absence for grasshopper damage, crop destruction, climatic hindrances, and wildfires. Going a step further, in 1894 Congress passed an act allowing second homestead entries for anyone who had lost his or her claim due to an absence that would have been covered by these forbearance laws.[26] Despite this leniency, claimants typically had to prove the extent of their crop loss using affidavits from disinterested witnesses.

Exceeding 160 Acres

The GLO also worried that, in addition to manipulating marital status, homesteaders might attempt in other ways to gain more than their allotted 160 acres. For example, some individuals tried to acquire second homesteads when their original homesteads failed; in response, the 1867 circular stated that anyone who relinquished or abandoned his or her initial claim could not file a second entry. That circular did not provide any exceptions, but the GLO soon realized that its proscription was too constricting to be practical. The circular three years later added a concession: "In the case of the illegality of [a claimant's] entry he may make a second claim." This was intended to address cases where confused claimants, through lack of understanding of the law's nuances, would inadvertently file claims later judged to be illegal, or where the clerk made a mistake, such as allowing a claimant to make entry before he or she reached twenty-one. The circular gave the land clerks leeway to allow second claims in the event of such minor illegalities or mistakes.[27]

This adjustment did not place limitations on the circumstances surrounding the illegality, thereby creating a sizeable loophole. The GLO then amended the exemption to state that if an entry-man's claim was "canceled as invalid for some reason other than abandonment, and not the willful act of the party"—if, for example, after filing, the land became unfit for cultivation because a dam built nearby had flooded it—the claimant could make a second entry. This stipulation addressed realities of homesteading not accounted for in the original law, such as catastrophic crop failure and other unforeseeable troubles. The latitude for climatic hindrances was not infinite, however; the 1884 circular clarified that if a homesteader lost his or her original claim due to negligence when choosing a plot, a second claim was prohibited.[28]

Later Congress amended the 160-acre limit because as settlement pushed further into the semiarid regions, it became increasingly apparent that 160 acres was an inadequate basis for a viable farm. Congress passed the Kinkaid Act in 1904, permitting 640-acre homesteads in western Nebraska, and the Enlarged Homestead Act in 1909, allowing 320-acre homesteads in other parts of the plains.

Commutation

Commutation allowed settlers to file a homestead claim and after six months (later extended to fourteen months) to purchase their land for the government price without completing homesteading's residency requirement. In the original Homestead Act, Congress only required a commuter to prove "settlement and cultivation as provided by existing laws granting preemption rights." Preemption requirements were not nearly as strict as those placed on homesteading, making commutations a source of great conflict for those overseeing the land system. In 1885 Commissioner William A. J. Sparks (1885–88) specified to his special agents that "commuted homestead entries, made without actual residence upon and improvement and cultivation of the land for the prescribed period, are fraudulent." Furthermore, his instructions asserted that "commuted homestead entries, made in the interest of speculation or monopoly, are an extensive and dangerous class of frauds, and need to be closely watched and rigorously investigated." Yet commutation remained. Why? Entrymen had a variety of completely legitimate reasons for commuting—most important, it gave homesteaders a title that could be used as collateral to obtain a mortgage or other credit. Given this ambiguity, the GLO could not condemn commutation as wholly wrong.[29]

In order to distinguish commutation as an avenue for speculation and fraud from its legitimate use by entrymen, the GLO sought to use residency requirements to restrict the practice to bona fide settlers. Originally the act only required claimants to comply with the standards of the preemption laws before commuting their claim. Preemption as well as homestead laws mandated proof of actual settlement and cultivation. They differed in that whereas homesteading required settlement of five years, preemption needed proof of residency within one year of settlement—a stipulation irrelevant to homesteaders. Preemption requirements proved unsatisfactory for homesteading, however. In 1870 the GLO more explicitly stated that in order to commute, homesteaders had to live on their land continuously for at least six months and present proof of their residency in the form of an affidavit and testimony from two credible witnesses. Even the GLO and the land agents disagreed about what this actually meant. For example, in 1881 John J. McKay did not settle on his claim within six months of making entry and as such the local land office denied his commutation application. However, Commissioner McFarland overturned this decision, stating that in commuting his homestead the entryman turned it into a preemption and that as such he only had to comply with preemption rules. In order to put this issue to rest, in 1891 Congress passed a law requiring residency for fourteen months before allowing commutation.[30]

In addition to mandating a certain length of residency, the GLO restricted commutations to bona fide settlers by requiring visible residency. The 1884 circular required entrymen to continuously reside on and cultivate their homestead in order to commute, under pain of prosecution. In 1889 the GLO in cases of commutation made full compliance with the law mandatory, with no exceptions for environmental disasters or similar hardships.[31]

The General Land Office circulars over time responded to what it heard from its agents about fraud, most commonly speculation, marriage fraud, and theft of a soldier's identity. It clarified the requirements concerning residency and multiple homestead filings. And it struggled with how to deal with commutation, wanting to diminish what it perceived as phony filings by people never intending to be "actual settlers" while recognizing that both the law allowed and circumstances often justified true homesteaders exercising their legal right to commute. It issued increasingly complex regulations to combat fraud. In effect, its changing regulations demonstrate how the bureaucracy defined and understood fraud and provides us with a working definition of homesteading fraud.

While the GLO was grappling with how to define fraud and educate its land agents on the changing definitions, others were quick to find problems. The first extensive evaluation of homesteading in practice was conducted by a congressionally chartered Public Land Commission in 1880. The five-member commission included John Wesley Powell, Thomas Donaldson, and other well-known advocates for reforming the public land laws. Commissioners traveled throughout the West and heard a good deal of testimony. When their five-volume report was published, Congress mostly ignored it, but the study received much wider notice when Donaldson separately republished and extended the report as *The Public Domain: Its History with Statistics*. He remained a true believer in homesteading itself: "The homestead act is now the approved and preferred method of acquiring title to the public lands. It has stood the test of eighteen years ... [and] stands as the concentrated wisdom of legislation for settlement of the public lands." Donaldson continued, "It protects the Government, it fills the States with homes, it builds up communities, and lessens the chances of social and civil disorder by giving ownership of the soil, in small tracts, to the occupants thereof. It was copied from no other nation's system. It was originally and distinctively American, and remains a monument to its originators."[32]

But Donaldson was outraged by what he saw as the rampant misuse and often criminal abuse of the laws on preemption, timber culture, railroad grants, commutation, and public land sales, and he believed the frenzy to abuse these laws inevitably corrupted the homestead law, too. He had heard testimony about cattlemen who employed dummy entrymen to grab critical chunks of land bordering on water sources, lumbermen and minerals exploiters who used preemptions to strip public lands of their timber or coal and then abandon them, and California land barons who managed to accumulate enormous acreages within a few families. As Donaldson put it, "One hundred and sixty acres was determined upon after many years as the true unit of disposition for a home. Upon this are the country settled. The abuse of this [is now documented]; 1,120 acres to a person under the several laws is now the rule, and a million acres at $1.25 per acre, if you have the money, in the South. It is of the highest national importance that not another acre of the public lands shall be sold outright for cash, warrants, or scrip." Notice that Donaldson's concerns are almost entirely about other methods of disbursing public land: the Timber Act, nominally affiliated with homesteading, was widely acknowledged to be a magnet for abuse (and was soon repealed), but land sales, use of military warrants and agricultural college scrip, and commutations opened the door for speculators to accumulate large tracts. Donaldson's pleas for reform failed to find favor in the Congress.[33]

GLO Commissioner Sparks also worried about fraud leading to theft of public land. As he described it, "The prevailing idea running through [the land offices] was that the government had no distinctive rights to be considered and no special interests to protect; hence, as between the government and spoilers of the public domain, the government usually had the worst of it." This notion combined with the willingness to cheat: "Men who would scorn to commit a dishonest act toward an individual, though he were a total stranger, eagerly listen to every scheme for evading the letter and spirit of the settlement laws, and in a majority of instances I believe avail themselves of them." Indeed, there was often a sense that cheating the government (chiseling as it was known) was not really dishonesty. The land laws, and in particular relinquishment, commutation, and preemption, seemed to encourage cheating. As Roy Robbins described it, "To defraud the government of a few acres of valuable land was not considered a very grave crime during the formative period of American history. Such defrauding, however, can hardly be blamed upon the frontiersmen as a class, for among them were also to be found honest and enterprising citizens."[34]

Paul Gates in his 1963 paper recognized that defrauding government of land had a long pedigree, but in his 1968 *History of Public Land Law Development* he maintained that the widespread willingness to cheat was something new and specifically related to the new land laws: "The chief difference between [earlier] scandals and the misuse and gradual breakdown of the land system after the Civil War was that it was no longer people of influence who were responsible. Instead, many ordinary people (one hesitates to say all westerners) were showing a willingness to perjure themselves when testifying on land matters."[35] The General Land Office had very limited funds to employ antifraud agents (sixty-one in 1890, for example), and the local land offices and even GLO headquarters in Washington were often overworked and disorganized, so commissioners knew that official enforcement was slack.

After Donaldson and Sparks, evaluation of homesteading passed to twentieth-century historians, who by and large accepted their predecessors' gloomy view of public land disposition. Benjamin H. Hibbard, the first great authority on public land law after Donaldson, published *A History of the Public Land Policies* in 1924 and benefited from having an additional four decades of the law's operation to observe. Though positive toward the idea of homesteading, he saw its operations as more nuanced, and he agreed that "fraud was invited and the challenge accepted."[36] The biggest loopholes, he believed, were the commutation provision and its cousin, the sale of relinquishments. As Donaldson had documented, during the first couple of decades of homesteading, few filers resorted to commutation: up to June 30, 1880, less than 4 percent of the homestead initial entries were commuted. But commutations soon came to play a bigger and bigger role. The Public Lands Commission reported that from 1881 to 1904, out of 96 million acres granted by patents, 22 million were via commutation—about 24 percent. A later report indicated that during the first decade of the new century in North Dakota, 5,781,000 acres were commuted compared with only 5,614,000 acres on which final proof was made; that is, more was commuted than settled. For Hibbard, the explanation was clear: "In the early years of the homestead law the settlers were genuine homesteaders. They settled upon the land because they wanted farms. Twenty years later the situation had changed greatly.... [Commutation] was the means whereby large land holdings were built up through a perverted use of the Homestead Act."[37]

Still settlers commuted for a variety of reasons, many of which were reasonable and clearly nonfraudulent (a title helped in getting a mortgage or could serve as collateral in purchasing additional land), so commutations are an unreliable index of fraud. Some "abuse" of the homesteading laws was in fact a creative and perhaps even socially positive response to the poverty of settlers, the 160-acre maximum claim, and other limitations. What must be added to the picture is that some, perhaps a significant amount, of the manipulation and cheating on land laws, including clear illegalities, might be termed "benign abuse" and reflected attempts by poor settlers to create viable farms within the harsh restrictions they faced, just as the Homestead Act intended.

There were two situations in particular that enticed settlers to skirt or violate the law. The first was simple poverty. In order to establish a viable farming operation, more was needed than just land, yet as many have pointed out, the Homestead Acts provided no assistance for the penniless settler. To obtain those things required for successful homesteading—many months' supply of food, labor to break the prairie, seed, farm equipment and animals, building materials for house and barn—might cost as much as $500 to $1,000, although for beginning farmers who traded tools, shared machinery, and exchanged labor, the start-up costs would have been less. Still, it was reported that some entrymen who had no capital chose to file claims and then, either by selling their homesteads as relinquishments or by making deals for commutations, walked away with the proceeds, perhaps to repeat (illegally) the process elsewhere.[38] Certainly some and perhaps many homesteading "frauds" were in fact part of an intentional strategy used by some poor settlers to accumulate sufficient capital to establish viable farms.

A second circumstance that encouraged illegal or shady dealing was the fact that, as settlement moved beyond the 99th or 100th meridian, a 160-acre farm was no longer sufficient to support a family. Farmers needed to expand their holdings, and some turned to schemes utilizing preemptions, multiple homestead filings by a spouse or other family members, and other possibilities. For example, since there was no restriction preventing homesteaders from owning preemption lands, a settler could file a 160-acre preemption and after six months pay up and take title, file on an adjacent 160-acre homesteading entry and also (after 1873) file on a 160-acre timber culture entry, thereby gaining control of 480 acres for the preemption price of $200. This creative use of the land laws, condemned by so-easily-scandalized later scholars, really represented a continuation of the spirit of squatting. Settlers with few resources were willing to bend or even break the laws to create viable farms for themselves. They saw the immense bounty of the public domain that the government had opened, and as Commissioner Sparks had put it, they felt that "a strict compliance with the conditions imposed is not essential."[39] As noted, the futility of farming a 160-acre place in the drier parts of the West was later addressed in the Kinkaid and Enlarged Homestead Acts.

Fred Shannon, Roy Robbins, and Paul Gates, three giants of public lands historiography writing in the 1930s and 1940s, followed

Hibbard. They were even more dubious about homesteading's benefits; they directly questioned whether the law had operated in the public interest at all and saw fraud as a major problem. Shannon set the tone for this criticism with his concern that the laws permitted speculators and corporations to acquire enormous tracts of public land: "The evidence of [speculators'] activities in monopolizing the public domain is abundant.... A premium was put on perjury." Shannon approvingly quoted the Public Land Commission: "In very many localities, and perhaps in general, a larger proportion of the public land is passing into the hands of speculators and corporations than into those of actual settlers who are making homes." In his landmark book, *The Farmer's Last Frontier: Agriculture, 1860–1897*, Shannon cataloged what he perceived as the homestead law's many flaws, including its failure to assist poor settlers, its enticing of poor settlers into "the arid stretches" where they had little chance to succeed, its encouragement for speculators and corporations to get control of the best land, and its invitation to widespread chicanery and virtual land theft through commutations.[40]

These writers and others repeated well-known anecdotes to illustrate the problem of land-grabbers and speculators getting too much land, using cases supplied by the various commissioners of the General Land Office in their annual reports, others recorded in the documents of the local litigation that homesteading engendered, and still others visible only after patient and smart research. Some local studies, such as those of Pierce and Gage Counties in Nebraska, have documented how these areas experienced a high level of cancellations and relinquishments of homesteads, evidence, according to Gates, "of the extent of the land business, the buying and selling of land, more than anything else." That is, it was evidence that homestead filings were not being used by actual settlers but rather by land dealers to gain control of public land.[41]

This line of scholarship reached its culmination in the work of Gates, who became the most influential of these mid-twentieth-century historians as a result of a string of important papers and monographs, capped off by his magisterial and authoritative *His-*

tory. In an influential early essay, he announced his concern: "The Homestead Act of 1862 is one of the most important laws which have been enacted in the history of the country, but its significance has been distorted and grossly misinterpreted." And what was the misinterpretation? As Gates saw it, earlier writers, including especially Hibbard, had viewed the Homestead Act in isolation and failed to see that "its adoption merely superimposed upon the old land system a principle out of harmony with it, and that until 1890 the old and the new constantly clashed. . . . Speculation and land monopolization continued after its adoption as widely perhaps as before." As with Donaldson, Gates's concern was less with the Homestead Act per se than with the other land giveaways with which it was entangled: he condemned the profligate granting of lands to railroads and to the states for various purposes (after which most of it was quickly sold off), the continuation of cash sales, preemptions, the prodigal granting of military land warrants and agricultural college scrip, and the exclusion of homesteading from Indian lands.[42]

Although he started as a critic of the homesteading law, by the 1960s Gates had deepened his analysis and changed his views. He signaled the change in 1963 in an essay in which he noted that revelations about bonanza farms, illegal enclosure of public lands using dummy entrymen, huge land acquisitions by timber companies, and other abuses "have led historians to misunderstand and underestimate the role of the Homestead Law and related settlement measures. Recent textbook writers," he wrote, "have declared that the Homestead Law was 'not a satisfactory piece of legislation'; it was a 'distressing disappointment'; 'farmers only benefitted slightly from it'; it ended 'in failure and disillusionment'; two-thirds of all 'homestead claimants before 1890 failed.'" These characterizations were overblown and wrong, he thought, complaining that they were *too* negative. He continued: "I must confess that I may have contributed to this misunderstanding some twenty-six years ago when I wrote a paper, 'The Homestead Law in an Incongruous Land System.' . . . The article was intended as a corrective for some of the ideas then prevalent concerning [homesteading]."[43]

Gates's *History* summarized and brought to a conclusion a long line of research and writing on homesteading. It was careful, authoritative, and comprehensive, but it also necessarily incorporated many of the limitations and flaws of the prior research as well: a dependence on close reading of the laws and legislative history, reliance on anecdotes, meager statistical analysis, and perhaps most debilitating, dependence on the hugely flawed official statistics of homesteading. But Gates's final overall evaluation was clear: the homestead laws' "noble purpose and the great part they played in enabling nearly a million and a half people to acquire farm land, much of which developed into farm homes, far outweigh the misuse to which they were put."[44]

Despite Gates's patiently documented argument for his change of heart, historians continued to be more swayed by Donaldson, Robbins, and Shannon than by the 828-page *History*, which was mostly ignored.[45] No new quantitative analysis appeared to support this choice, and instead a narrative of extensive fraud, often exaggerated beyond even the original work, has been established. A typical account, appearing just fourteen years after the *History* and often reprinted since, was written by Yale University's Alan Trachtenberg: "The promise embodied in the idea of the West as a yeomen's garden had seemed so much closer to fulfillment with the passage of the Homestead Act by the Civil War Congress in 1862...., But from the very beginning of the administration of the Homestead Act, it was clear that a society of small homesteaders in the West was not its functional goal. The act did not provide necessary credit.... And its clauses permitted land grabbing by speculative companies and the eventual concentration of large tracts in private hands."[46] Thus we find a modern consensus about pervasive fraud in homesteading built on a foundation of frequently repeated anecdotes, unreliable data, old studies, conflation with other land laws, neglect, and lack of interest.

How much fraud was there in fact? The next chapter seeks to answer that question.

Estimating the Extent of Fraud

4

In this chapter we continue our examination, begun in the last chapter, of the third stylized fact:

- The homesteading process was rife with corruption and fraud.

Under the Homestead Act, the government gave away a huge amount of federal land by anyone's measure, somewhere around 285 million acres. Like any such program of federal largesse, it attracted crooks, law-abusers, sleazy manipulators, perjurers, thieves and liars, quick-buck artists, and various other types of self-aggrandizing villains. Even so, the *extent* of fraud matters. Just how pervasive was it? Was it, for example, on a scale with the vast swindle of the railroad land grants, recognized at the time and ever since as among the most corrupt and disgraceful giveaways in U.S. history? That's apparently what Fred Shannon thought, asserting that there were an "astonishing number" of homestead frauds, and later writers have agreed with him and followed his lead. Or was homesteading more like, say, today's Medicare program? It is occasionally plagued with scandals of theft or embezzlement, which are sensational, wrong, disturbing, and lamentable for sure, but hardly surprising in a program providing such massive benefits. We recognize that Medicare fraud is actually quite limited in scope compared to the overall size of the program. In the case of homesteading, how much fraud was there?

Modern writers such as Trachtenberg, Hines and Faragher, Warren, and Danbom, as well as virtually all current American history textbook writers, have adopted the view that the homesteading process was rife with corruption and fraud; however, they have provided little new evidence. Instead, they have tended to rely on the statistics and findings of a prior generation of scholars, none more so than Fred Shannon. Shannon is the one who downplayed homesteading's importance, claiming "less than a sixth of the new homes [farms] ... would have been on land that came as a gift from the government," an assertion we have examined and found to be grossly misleading and wrong. He also attached another claim to it, this one about fraud: Shannon declared that "an astonishing number of homesteaders were merely the hired pawns of land monopolists who took over the land as soon as the final patents were received, thus reducing free farms [from less than a sixth] more nearly to an eighth, or possibly a tenth of the increase for the forty-year period."[1] Although he provided no data or calculations to support this assertion, Shannon's claim has been repeated by later writers who grounded their own views on it.

Let us examine Shannon's claim. Although he seemed not to recognize it himself, his assertion contains an implicit rate of fraud. Once we calculate his implied fraud rate, we can evaluate it by comparing it to other data on fraud. For example, consider first his claim that fraud reduced free farms from a sixth to an eighth of all new farms. We can calculate the fraud rate implicitly contained in this assertion as follows: We know (using the same figures from the decennial censuses Shannon used) that there were 2,000,000 farms in the United States in 1860 and 5,737,000 farms in 1900, so 3,737,000 new farms had been formed during the forty-year period. The GLO reported that it had issued 599,402 patents on proved-up homestead claims during the period, which is how Shannon got the figure he used to declare that free farms accounted for "less than a sixth" (16.0 percent, as calculated in chapter 2) of new farm formation. But if valid or nonfraudulent free farms truly only constituted "an eighth" or 12.5 percent of all new farms, then the valid homesteads would number 467,125 (that is, 12.5 percent of 3,737,000). With 599,402 patents having been issued and only 467,125 being valid, the remainder, 132,277, would be the claims

Shannon identified as fraudulent. The implied fraud rate is then 132,277 divided by 599,402, or 22.1 percent. A parallel calculation for Shannon's claim of "possibly a tenth" yields an implied fraud rate of 37.7 percent.[2]

Thus Shannon's "astonishing number ... of hired pawns" turns out to be a claim that the fraud rate was between 22 percent and 38 percent. Is this claim reasonable? Is Warren's claim of "half" reasonable? Later in this chapter we will compare it to new data we have collected.

The Project Study Area

To examine the extent of homesteading fraud more closely, we developed a database using the recently digitized homestead records; this chapter and chapters 6 and 7 report results obtained from this new data. Most previous studies of homesteading have been severely limited because researchers found it difficult to access the physical homestead records. Short of traveling to the National Archives or ordering costly paper copies of individual case files, scholars lacked easy access to the documents, and obtaining paper copies to construct a large database has often not been feasible. As a result scholarship has primarily employed anecdotes or the poor quality homesteading data reported in the General Land Office's (GLO) annual reports, assembled by severely overworked land office clerks.[3]

We use the digitized homestead records for Nebraska made available through a consortium that is digitizing all the case files of finalized homestead claims that are currently housed in paper form at the National Archives and Records Administration (NARA). Nebraska, the state with the first homestead claim, was also the first to be digitized. The consortium includes NARA, the Homestead National Monument of America, University of Nebraska, Fold3.com (later Ancestry.com), and FamilySearch.com. Fold3. com and Ancestry.com are making these records available (for a subscription fee) to the public for the first time; the University of Nebraska is providing additional metadata for scholarly research on the Nebraska records.

We developed a study area of five townships each in Custer

Number of entries

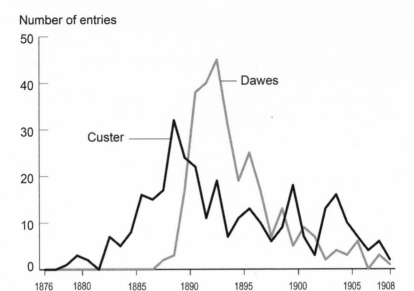

FIG. 4.1. Homestead final entries in Custer and Dawes Counties, by year.

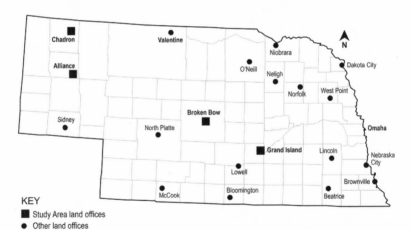

FIG. 4.2. Nebraska land offices, with those used in study area identified. Map created by Katie Nieland based on data from Robert Shepard.

County (central Nebraska) and Dawes County (western Nebraska). The bulk of homesteading in the Custer County townships occurred between 1885 and 1904, whereas in Dawes County homesteading occurred mainly between 1890 and 1899, both with their last claims occurring in 1908 (fig. 4.1).

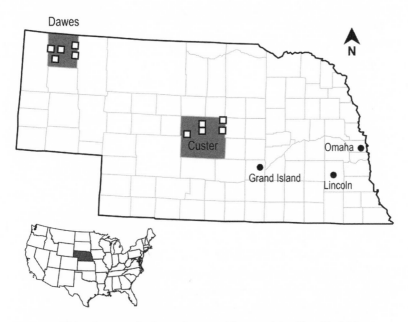

FIG. 4.3. Nebraska counties in study area with townships identified. Map created by Katie Nieland based on data from Robert Shepard.

At the time we began our research in the summer of 2013, the digitization of the main land offices servicing these counties, Broken Bow for Custer County and Chadron for Dawes County, was complete. During our processing, we realized that the Broken Bow office, which was open from 1890 to 1908, and the Chadron office, open from 1887 to 1894, did not in fact process all the records for our counties. The Grand Island office, open from 1869 to 1893, and the Alliance office, open from 1890 to 1908, also served homesteaders in our townships. The Broken Bow office opened in response to regional demand, while the Alliance office eventually replaced the more remotely located Chadron office to serve the sparse western Nebraska population better.

Independent scholar Russell Lang from Craig, Nebraska, meticulously classified all Nebraska townships based on the "methods of land transfers from the public domain to private and governmental entities."[4] Using his map, we identified five townships each in Custer and Dawes Counties in which the majority of the land was transferred via the Homestead Act. We defined these ten townships as our study area; five in Custer County (T17N, R24W; T18N, R17W; T18N, R21W; T19N, R21W; and T20N, R17W) with 324 claims, and five in Dawes County (T30N, R51W; T31N, R47W; T32N, R50W; T32N, R52W; and T33N, R47W) with 297 claims.

We created a database of all 621 successful homesteaders in these townships, recording application number and date, name, legal description of land, acreage claimed, gender, country of origin and citizenship application date (if applicable), state of origin (if applicable), age, and other information included in affidavits such as acreage broken, improvements made, and any absences from the land. Our database is thus not a sample but rather a full census of these townships. Where relevant, we also collected information outside the records on claimants' land transfer, military, and census records. The military and census records are available through Fold3 and Ancestry.com; the land transfer records required us to go to the historical societies for both counties. In addition to collecting demographic data, we mapped the homestead claims. To fully explore the particulars of the homesteaded lands, we tracked down original survey maps for each township and overlaid them with modern geospatial data. We also recorded all four witness names included in each Proof of Posting for every homesteader in order to generate sociolegal networks of the community within each township.

And what kind of land did they find? The first homesteaders arrived in our five Custer County townships in 1878, sparking a robust period of settlement that would see 324 successful claims proved up by 1908. These homesteaders found themselves situated on the rich, silty soils near the South Loup and Central Loup Rivers in land that had already been used by big-scale cattle ranchers. The landscape provided a view of rolling prairie equally suited for farming and ranching. Its 22- to 24-inch mean annual rainfall and rich soil made the region attractive to would-be farmers, but long periods of drought between bountiful years provided an uncertain rhythm to farming life.[5] Even more than farming, this land

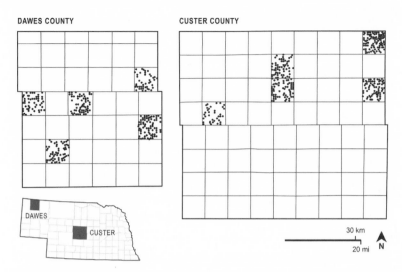

FIG. 4.4. Location of homesteads in study area. Map created by Katie Nieland based on data from Robert Shepard.

was long considered natural grazing land due to the abundance of hills and canyons.

Custer County homesteaders in our townships ranged from 25 to 83 years of age, with 55.6 percent filing their final claims between the ages of 25 and 39. There were 292 men and 32 women who filed claims. A majority, 253 of the 324, or 78.1 percent, had been U.S. citizens before making their claim. Of these 253 citizens, 85, or 33.6 percent, migrated to Custer County from Iowa and other parts of Nebraska with the rest coming from the other states. Of the 71 noncitizens, 38, or 53.5 percent, came from central European areas of Austria, Bohemia, Poland, and Moravia.

In our five Dawes County townships, farther west than Custer County, the 297 successful homesteaders found flat grasslands cut by erosion and geological curiosities and bordered on the north by the pine ridge. A mosaic of mixed grasses covered a blend of sand, clay, and silt earth. These soils, along with the county's 18 to 20 inches of rain per year and long periods of drought, made farming even more difficult than in Custer County, though it clearly did not stop homesteaders—domestic and foreign—from trying.

Homesteaders settled the area between 1887 and 1908, and 80.8 percent came during the 1890s alone. Their ages ranged from 21 to 87, with 54.5 percent of them proving up when they were between the ages of 25 and 39. There were 265 men and 32 women, the same number of women as in Custer County. Of the 297 homesteaders, 238, or 80.2 percent, were citizens; the remaining 59, or 19.8 percent, were noncitizens. Citizen claimants in Dawes County came predominantly from states stretching from the interior to the east coast, including 168, or 70.6 percent, of the 238 coming from Illinois, Iowa, New York, Ohio, Pennsylvania, and Wisconsin; and 33, or 55.9 percent, of the 59 immigrant claimants came from Germany and England.

Homesteaders in both counties faced environmental disasters that complicated their progress. Grasshoppers plagued the state between 1874 and 1877. Hot winds scorched the crops. Drought hit the region for a hard twelve years between 1884 and 1895 and again between 1906 and 1913.[6] The ten-year reprieve lured more settlers into the region; 197 individuals homesteaded in the study area between 1895 and 1904, demonstrating the enduring hope and short-term memory of those who dreamed of owning their own land.

New Estimates of Fraud in Homesteading

As we saw in chapter 3, fraud was sometimes difficult to define and its operational definition shifted over time. Moreover, understanding what constituted fraud sometimes depended upon local community ethics. Over several decades the GLO developed and refined its definition of fraud and its regulations for combatting it. Three behaviors—speculation, stolen soldier identity, and marriage fraud—emerged as particular concerns. We analyzed all successful homestead entries in our study area, 621 cases, for the presence of fraud, paying attention to these three categories. For speculation, we developed quantitative filters to identify all "suspicious" cases and then studied those cases in detail. For stolen soldier identity and marriage fraud, we examined all eligible cases.

We should note that our examination of possible marriage

TABLE 4.1. Characteristics of homesteaders in study area

	Custer	Dawes	Study area
Total	324	297	621
Men	292	256	557
Married	221	186	407
Single	53	62	115
Other*	18	17	35
Women	32	32	64
Citizens	253	238	491
Noncitizens	71	59	130

*Includes men widowed, divorced, separated, or marital status not stated.

fraud also includes elements of improper residency and claims exceeding 160 acres. Marriage fraud sometimes involves improper residency, as when a man and woman claim separate homesteads but in fact reside together; these claims also exceed 160 acres. Aside from the cases of marriage fraud, no one in our study area had more than 160 acres without paying for the additional acreage.

We also note that there is a potential undercounting bias in the records, because if for example an entryman was absent from his or her claim for more than six months without the GLO's permission or knowledge, and four witnesses were willing to give false testimony on that point, then the absence might have left no record in the file. However, we found no evidence of improper residency, and as we discuss in chapter 7, neighbors in the surrounding community of entrymen appeared to be quite vigilant about cheaters. Finally, we did not look for fraud via commutation. Commutation was an entirely legal procedure, so the land office transaction was not fraudulent unless, for instance, false affidavits were filed. Although both the GLO and some critics believed commutation to be a bad policy, it was typically not fraud as such.

The results of our detailed investigation of all 621 cases are discussed below.

Speculation

Public land scholars like Shannon and Cochrane focused on speculation in part because the land offices, the GLO commissioners' *Reports*, and nineteenth-century newspapers were obsessive about speculators on public lands. In 1875 the *New York Times* published part of a letter from the GLO commissioner to the chairman of the Senate Committee on Public Lands arguing that preemption laws and homestead laws are "two laws of which speculators avail themselves to fraudulently secure . . . lands." Similarly the *Los Angeles Times* argued in 1901 that by lessening the requirements to obtain a homestead the government had "nullified the original intention of the law by making it subservient to the purpose of land grabbers and speculators."[7] From coast to coast this type of public discourse expressed the very real distress over people claiming lands for speculation, but it does not provide much guidance for how to measure the extent of fraud.

There are inherent problems with searching for fraudulent speculation; unfortunately, speculators rarely announced their intention to violate the law. Even in cases where a landowner made money by quickly selling his or her homestead, there are no notes from that seller explaining whether at the beginning of the claim process his or her intent was to become an "actual settler" or simply to speculate on the land. But while there is little way to determine beyond a doubt if a sale was fraudulent, deep investigation into suspicious cases typically exposes sufficient evidence to make a sound, reasonable judgment.

We began by looking for any obvious cases of fraud in which a speculator, land agent, or cattle baron used dummy entrymen to file claims that would be transferred to the speculator, agent, or cattleman after proving up. Parroting nineteenth-century discourse, Shannon claimed that "homesteaders were merely the hired pawns of land monopolists who took over the land as soon as the final patents were received." We identified cases in our study area where the entryman used a prominent cattle rancher or land aggregator as a witness. The most important cases to investigate were seventeen Custer County homesteaders who listed William G. Comstock as a potential witness between 1880 and 1898. Comstock, a notorious bonanza cattleman whose career we explore in more detail in chapter 7, was convicted of illegally fencing the public domain in 1905 and 1906. But he was never charged with any wrongdoing related to homesteading in our study area. His appearance as a witness is hardly surprising, given that for many years he was a well-regarded and influential rancher whose testimony would likely prove helpful to an entryman. All but three of these homesteaders who listed Comstock actually called him to testify. We investigated all seventeen entrymen, but scrutiny of their individual cases offers no suggestion that the homesteaders acted as dummy "hired pawns" for Comstock. His crimes lay elsewhere, and we do not include these seventeen claims as fraudulent.[8]

To cast the widest net in our search and create a general screen or procedure to identify speculative fraud, we examined all cases where the claimant sold his or her land shortly after receiving patent. In effect, we operationalized Shannon's complaint that "land monopolists ... took over the land as soon as the final patents were received" by assuming "as soon as" could be given specific quantitative expression as homestead sales within the first month after receiving patent, the first two months after receiving patent, or, in the most conservative reading, the first year after receiving patent. We labeled all such cases in our study area as "suspicious and possibly fraudulent" and marked them for deeper investigation.

As we examined these cases, we realized that application of these criteria resulted in the identification as "suspicious and possibly fraudulent" of a number of cases that almost certainly were not fraudulent. For example, if a woman's husband died during the required five-year residency and their original plan for a married partnership to farm the land now necessarily changed to her having to farm it alone, a quick sale of the claim after proving up was hardly unlawful in any meaningful sense; yet that quick sale would be identified using our method. So cases labeled as suspicious required further examination to separate the clearly non-

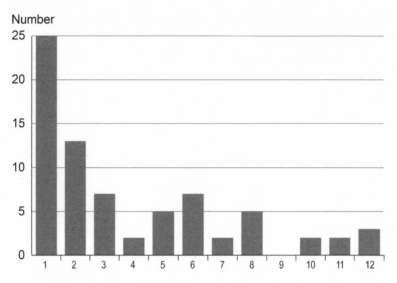

FIG. 4.5. Study area claims sold within one year after receipt of patent, by month.

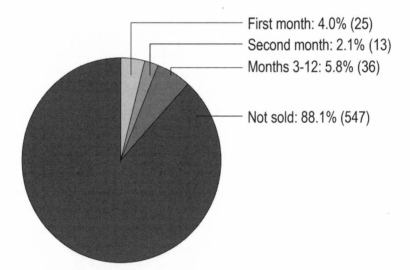

First month: 4.0% (25)
Second month: 2.1% (13)
Months 3-12: 5.8% (36)

Not sold: 88.1% (547)

FIG. 4.6. Study area claims sold in first month, second month, and months three to twelve after receipt of patent, and claims not sold.

fraudulent cases like that described above from cases of actual fraud by "hired pawns" or others.

We identified twenty-five homestead claims, or 4.0 percent of all proved-up claims, as "suspicious" and deserving of further scrutiny using the one-month-sale criterion (figs. 4.5 and 4.6). There was a burst of sales during the first month after receiving patent, and then we see a sharp decline, suggesting that most claimants who intended to sell would not wait around but would do so as soon as they could.

If we employ the sale-within-two-months criterion, 38 homestead claims, or 6.1 percent of all proved-up claims, were identified. By the end of the second month, more than half (38 of 74, or 51.4 percent) of all sales that would occur in the first year had already been made. When we extend the "suspicious" category all the way out to include sale of any claim within one full year of the patent, the number of suspicious claims grows to 74, or 11.9 percent of all proved-up claims.

The one-year criterion seems to us dubious as an index of fraud, because by the time the entryman received the patent, he or she had already spent at least five years on the land. If his or her intent from the time of the initial filing had been to serve as a "hired pawn" of a land monopolist, why would either the pawn or monopolist want to wait significantly longer than the law required? And indeed, the burst of sales during the first and second months supports this skepticism. Willingness to stay and work on the land for a full year after proving up, rather than making them suspicious, would seem to mark them instead as persistent settlers who tried hard to stay on unforgiving, semiarid land.

As it turned out, none of the seventeen claimants who listed Comstock as their witness were identified by our one-month, two-month, or even our one-year criterion as having disposed of their claims quickly. Apparently these homesteaders did not surrender their land to Comstock, reaffirming our decision not to include these seventeen claims as fraudulent.

As noted, our next step was to examine each of the seventy-four identified "suspicious" cases to determine whether the sale appeared to be fraudulent—that is, a quick conveyance to a bonanza rancher or land grabber—or was due to other circumstances evidently indicating no fraudulent intent. In the latter category, *hardship* was the most common nonfraud cause for a quick sale. As we examined the cases, many early sales involved drought, ruined crops, accident or injury, loss of a key family member, and other unforeseen catastrophes. These cases become more tragic than suspicious. For example, thirty-four-year-old Herbert Edgerly moved to Dawes County from Maine. He ultimately built two stables, cultivated and fenced his land, and planted fruit trees. Edgerly left his farm to work at Fort Robinson (also in Dawes County) for two or three months in 1889, 1890, and 1891, years during the prolonged drought of 1884 to 1895. He proved up his claim and immediately took out a mortgage. Edgerly's behavior, mortgaging his land while leaving to work at Fort Robinson, hardly suggests the profile of a speculator greedy for a quick profit; more likely, he moved because he could not make a living from his land.[9]

Thomas Isaacs of Custer County also settled during this period of drought. He built a sod house and stable and cultivated twenty acres of land. This work was for naught as his crops failed due to "drouth and hot winds," and he raised "no crops whatever." The climate's betrayal forced Isaacs to move with his family to Kansas City for the winter where he could work for a living.[10] Crop failures during a period of prolonged drought forced some to farm within a different context from what they had expected when they jumped at the prospect of free land.

Like crop failure, death changed the context of keeping a homestead. Joseph Jackson claimed 160 acres in 1887 and died in 1890 before perfecting his claim. Joseph's death left his wife, Catherine, to bring the land to patent. Catherine had not planned to cultivate land without a husband. It is hardly a surprise that after her husband's death she waited the remaining year and four months to make final proof and then sold at the first opportunity.[11]

Among those listed as "suspicious" but not removed due to hardship are cases like that of Sarah Lynch. The records do not

TABLE 4.2. Likely hardship cases among homesteaders in study area who sold their claims within one year of receipt of patent

Name	County	Sold within	Reason for hardship
Adrick Boome	Dawes	1 month or less	Family: abandoned by spouse
Thomas Isaacs	Custer	1 month or less	Failed crops
Catharine Jackson	Custer	1 month or less	Family: widowed
Henry Klienenberger	Custer	1 month or less	Left land to earn living
Thomas McDonell	Custer	1 month or less	Left land to earn living
Mary E. Steinman	Custer	1 month or less	Family: abandoned by spouse
Alexander Stepney	Dawes	1 month or less	Failed crops
Elwood J. Thomas	Custer	1 month or less	Left land to earn living
Mary Wells	Dawes	1 month or less	Family: widowed
Andrew Atwood	Dawes	2 months	Elderly (age 62)
Elmus Barron	Dawes	2 months	Elderly (age 70)
Fred C. Friberg	Dawes	2 months	Failed crops
John McMannus	Dawes	2 months	Left land to earn living
Frederick W. Muller	Dawes	2 months	Elderly (age 66)
Ellen R. Abbott	Dawes	3 months	Family: widowed
Daniel Burns	Dawes	3 months	Disability
Charles F. Foster	Custer	3 months	Left land to earn living
Frank P. Knox	Custer	3 months	Left land to earn living
Samuel Hoshaw	Cuter	6 months	Failed crops
Russell Sweat	Dawes	6 months	Elderly (age 78)
Herbert F. Edgerly	Dawes	8 months	Left land to earn living
John I. Montgomery	Dawes	8 months	Failed crops
Stephen W. Carpenter	Dawes	11 months	Left land to earn living
Frank E. Brown	Custer	12 months	Left land to earn living
William E. Harding	Dawes	12 months	Family: sickly child

reveal enough about her to permit us to remove her on hardship grounds, but we do know that Lynch, of Dawes County, had left Indiana with her six children to homestead in Nebraska. She was a fifty-six-year-old widow at the time of final proof and sold her land to Elihu Bond in May 1900, the same day she received patent. Given the trouble single men and women, and even married couples, had eking out a living on the arid plains, it should come as little surprise that the land apparently failed to sustain Lynch and her family. But lacking more information, we retain her in our "suspicious and possibly fraudulent" category.

Another case, that of John W. Mathews, illustrates the difficulty of drawing hard distinctions between fraudulent and valid. Mathews homesteaded in Section 22 of T18N, R21W in Custer County and proved up in 1887. Because he sold his claim within the first month after receiving his patent, we marked him as a suspicious case to be investigated further. We discovered that during his five-year required residency he got a job on the railroad to make a living for himself, his wife, and three kids, although he also regularly raised crops on his claim. Initially we considered him a possible hardship case, but digging deeper we learned that he had finalized his claim and within ten days had taken out two mortgages and five days after that sold his land. His actions bear some resemblance to a well-known form of fraud in which the entryman receives his or her patent (which was required for getting a mortgage), immediately mortgages the land and (not telling the bank) also sells the claim; then he skips town, absconding with the proceeds from both the land sale and the mortgage. Such a person both defrauds the government and defaults on the bank loans, perhaps reappearing in another state under a different name.[12]

Was this Mathews's plan? It does not appear so, because he paid off his mortgages, accrued more land, and sold that land back to the person he bought it from; moreover, he continued to live in Custer County. Mathews had relatives in the adjacent township, T19N, R21W, including Charles R. Mathews, a long-serving postmaster and judge in that community.

We are left with two plausible interpretations of John Mathews:

He originally intended to be a farmer ("actual settler") but either wasn't very good at it or had hard luck, so he was forced to get a railroad job; he discovered he was better at other jobs than farming and changed occupations; no fraud was committed. Or Mathews never intended to be a farmer, took the opportunity to work on the railroad instead, and monetized his homestead claim (and defrauded the government) as soon as it was legal to do so. Applying our rule of using the most conservative interpretation, we categorized Mathews's claim as fraudulent, although this is clearly a "boundary" case. More important, his case demonstrates the robustness of our methodology, first flagging suspicious cases that we follow up with deeper investigation.

We were able to identify twenty-five clear hardship cases, homesteaders who shared experiences similar to Edgerly, Isaacs, and Faimon (table 4.2) and who sold their claims quickly due to hardship; despite early sales, these claims were not fraudulent. In the statistics reported below, we omit these cases from the "suspicious" category.

Stolen Soldier Identity

An 1872 law gave Civil War veterans the right to claim additional land if they had not initially settled the full 160 acres. Land grabbers sought out veterans (or their widows or other heirs) who had not used their right to a second homestead. Purchasing such rights (illegally), they then filed fraudulent claims using the veterans' or heirs' names.

Those attempting to buy homestead rights sometimes even found a nonveteran who shared the same name as a soldier, not worrying too much whether there was an actual connection. An example of such a case began when Mrs. A. P. Bungard sent a letter to her nearby land office in Lincoln, Nebraska, inquiring about her husband's service in the Civil War. She said she did not think that her husband had served in the war; however, a gentleman had offered her money in exchange for the right to claim a supplementary veteran's homestead. The land office clerk replied to Mrs. Bungard that the GLO had discovered "a great deal of fraud" concerning such matters. The clerk cautioned the woman not to sell this right if she did not think her husband had served, and he informed her that "several convictions have been secured against persons guilty of such practice."[13]

The incentive in stolen-soldier-identity fraud was that the person perpetrating the fraud could typically purchase the right to a homestead for less than it would cost to buy the land. Like every good defrauding scheme, they chose willing targets. Women in Bungard's situation probably would not bother digging too deeply into the matter because they received money for a right which they did not know they were entitled to claim (and perhaps were not entitled to claim). Furthermore, at first defendants charged with this crime were charged with forgery, but the schemers argued that they did not forge a document and that instead they had simply made a mistake. This logic survived initial court battles and created a loophole in which those perpetrating the fraud did not fear the legal penalty. However, the forgers' luck ran out in 1913 when, in *United States v. Davis*, the Supreme Court ruled that a fake document was the same as a forged document and constituted a crime against the U.S. government.[14]

To examine the incidence of stolen-soldier-identity fraud in our study area, we identified all those claimants who used Civil War soldiers' (or widows' or heirs') benefits to make their claim. Out of 621 claims, we identified 20 people who made their claims using a soldiers' benefit (table 4.3). We then used the adjutant general's records to check whether each soldier who had made a claim or whose heir had made a claim had actually been in the army or navy.

Our detailed investigation found that none of the twenty homesteaders who used soldiers' or soldiers' widow benefits in the study area had done so falsely. There were no identity thieves.

Marriage Fraud

We next turned our attention to collusion within marriage. We examined in detail the marital and land transfer records of all 621 homesteaders in our study area. We found four cases of land fraud via manipulating marriage status.

TABLE 4.3. All soldiers' benefit claimants among homesteaders in study area

Homesteader	County	Military service
John W. Brewer	Custer	Company D, 48th Indiana Infantry
Charles H. Chamberlain	Custer	Company H, 177th Pennsylvania Drafted Militia
William B. Coffey	Dawes	Company F, 5th Connecticut Infantry
John Connell	Dawes	Company F, 51st Missouri Infantry
Samuel H. Davis	Dawes	Company K, 5th Iowa Infantry
William Deffenbaugh	Dawes	Company D, 89th Indiana Infantry
John H. Gaylord	Dawes	149th Pennsylvania Infantry
John S. Holtz	Dawes	Company K, 5th Ohio Cavalry
Thomas L. Jeffers	Dawes	Company J, 7th Missouri Cavalry
William H. Kaiser	Dawes	Company D, 73rd Indiana Infantry
William H. Kates	Custer	Company D, 180 Ohio Infantry
Cornelius L. Moore	Dawes	Company D, 176th Ohio Infantry
Ralph Morton	Dawes	Company F, 111th Pennsylvania Infantry
Joseph C. Mowry	Dawes	Company F, 46th Pennsylvania Infantry
John R. Nunnally	Custer	Company E, 150th Indiana Infantry
Thomas J. Parrott	Custer	Company A, 2nd Iowa Infantry
Robert Pomeroy	Dawes	Company C, 87th Illinois Mounted Infantry
Robert W. Shafer	Custer	Company G, 29th Iowa Infantry
Eugene Stupplebeen	Custer	Company J, 91st New York Infantry
Delila Wells (inherited widow claim, Edgar Wells)	Custer	Company B, New York 1st Light Artillery

Marriage fraud was a concern of the GLO, as we saw in chapter 3. In proving up, all claimants had to "solemnly swear ... that my application is honestly and in good faith made for the purpose of actual settlement and cultivation, and not for the benefit of any other person, persons, or corporation."[15] The GLO struggled with how to reconcile the law's intent with the realities of family relationships and marriage. The incentive was clear: homesteading created an opportunity through which a woman could individually bring her own land and economic base to her marriage.[16] The Wyoming homesteader Elinore Pruit Stewart became famous through her letters to the *Atlantic Monthly*, emphasizing her pioneering spirit. Elinore filed a homestead claim as a single woman and married Clyde Stewart, also a homesteader, the next week. Many years later, historian Sherry Smith, after some sharp sleuthing, unraveled Elinore's story. Smith argues that Stewart was worried enough about a possible contestation of her dubious claim that she relinquished the claim to her mother-in-law, who later received patent and promptly sold it to Clyde. Although never detected by the GLO or its agents, Elinore's abuse of the homesteading marital rules shows how marriage could be used to gain excess land.[17]

The Homestead Act limited a single homestead to 160 acres but included nothing specific about married couples, but the GLO began addressing this issue in 1889 (see appendix 1). In 1895 the GLO decided that:

> A single woman who makes a homestead entry and marries before making proof does not by her marriage forfeit her right to make proof and receive patent for the land, provided she does not abandon her residence on the land to reside elsewhere. Where two parties, however, unite in marriage, each having an unperfected homestead entry, both entries can not be carried to patent.[18]

In spite of this prohibition, some couples in Dawes County claimed and kept multiple homesteads. For example, Bina M. Thein married Mathias Thein in 1891; four years later she received patent on a 160-acre homestead.[19] Then, nine years later, in 1904,

Mathias homesteaded an additional 40 acres. While only exceeding the prescribed maximum by 40 acres, this extra homestead still violated the law. We adopt the highly conservative premise that any couple that acquired a second homestead once married committed fraud.

One could argue that since Bina homesteaded the original 160 acres and the 40 acres were claimed under Mathias's name, the couple did not exceed the 160-acre maximum (per person), and could still have homesteaded an additional 120 acres; moreover, they were not concurrent claims. But this interpretation ignores the prevailing marriage law in the nineteenth century which treated the couple, once married, as a single entity or, rather, the husband absorbed his wife. Moreover, the Homestead Act also required the entryman to promise that the land would not be used for the benefit of anyone else. If Mathias and Bina constituted a single legal entity, they could not file for two homesteads. If they were separate individuals planning to use their homesteads in common, they could not truthfully swear that the homesteads would not benefit another (i.e., each other). Indeed, if one recognizes a wife as an individual property holder apart from the husband, it is difficult to argue that husband and wife are a single entity. Nineteenth-century laws regarding women's rights were rife with contradiction. Even so, the Theins, at the very least, are suspicious, and we will count their case as fraud.[20]

We move to a more clearly fraudulent case when we examine John Kurt. Kurt was born in Switzerland in 1858 to a farmer and factory hand. He served in the army and then learned the cheese and butter-making trade. He arrived in the United States in 1880, settling first in Ohio, then moving on to Dawes County, Nebraska. Kurt claimed a homestead in 1898. A local history notes that Kurt's "persistent industry has placed this gentleman among the prosperous agriculturists of Dawes County," commenting further that "his home in section 6, township 33, range 47, has been gained through the strictest economy and excellent management." Further investigation suggests that along with strict economy and excellent management, however, prosperity also came through fraud.

TABLE 4.4 All cases of identified marriage fraud in study area

Name	Year of application	Year of final patent	Year married
Bina and Matthias Thein	Bina: 1889, Matthias: 1899	Bina: 1895, Matthias: 1904	1891
Simon and Lillian Wright	Simon: 1887, Lillian: 1889	Simon: 1892, Lillian: 1896	1893
John and Maggie Kurt	John: 1892, Maggie: 1900	John: 1898, Maggie: 1905	1901
Lillie and Lawrence Bacon	Lillie: 1888, Lawrence: 1896	Lillie: 1893, Lawrence: 1902	1888

After his marriage in 1901, John Kurt's wife, Lillian, also claimed a homestead. Within a year of his wife claiming her own homestead, Kurt sold his original claim to his father-in-law only to buy it back in 1915, suggesting he knew that having two homesteads could cause him legal problems. Mr. and Mrs. Kurt defrauded the federal government.[21]

Similarly, the Simon Wright family claimed multiple homesteads totaling well in excess of 160 acres. In 1892 Simon Wright homesteaded 166 acres and then married Lillian Palmer in 1893. In 1896, Lillian homesteaded 163 acres. In a matter of four years, the Wrights had managed to acquire 329 acres through the Homestead Act, nine of which they paid for at the standard rate of $1.25 per acre.[22]

Investigating all cases in the study area for marriage fraud, we discovered the Thein, Kurt, and Wright cases as well as a similar case involving Lillie Bacon and her husband, Lawrence. As we show in table 4.4, there were eight patents issued to the four married couples; we count these as four cases of fraud, because each couple was legally entitled to one claim, the second one being fraudulent. Among 621 proved-up homesteads, the four cases of marriage fraud accounted for 0.6 percent of all examined homesteaders.[23]

Even in cases that are clearly fraudulent, it is possible that they were accidentally fraudulent because laws regarding women's homesteads changed often during the late nineteenth and early twentieth centuries. Then, too, although the government never granted married women the right to claim their own homesteads outside of desertion or divorce, the Kurts and others may have seen their extra homestead as a small violation no different from that of other men and women who delayed marriage in order to double their landholdings. Perhaps their neighbors agreed with this assessment, because they did not report the Kurts for committing fraud.[24]

Bringing the Elements Together

We examined all 621 proved-up homesteads in the study area. First we applied the one-month criterion to examine these cases for possible speculation fraud. We found sixteen suspicious nonhardship cases (disqualifying the nine hardship cases) which we include as possibly fraudulent. We found zero cases of stolen-soldier-identity fraud, and we identified four suspicious cases of likely marriage fraud. Thus altogether there were twenty cases of possible fraud using the one-month criterion, amounting to 3.2 percent of all homesteaders (fig. 4.7).

Using the two-month criterion, we find twenty-four suspicious nonhardship cases of possible speculation fraud (disqualifying the fourteen hardship cases) plus zero stolen-soldier-identity cases and four suspicious marriage-fraud cases, for a total of twenty-eight cases of possible fraud, resulting in an overall fraud rate of 4.5 percent (fig. 4.8). Even if we extend the "quick-sale" period to one full year, we find there are forty-nine suspicious nonhardship cases, plus four marriage-fraud cases, for a total of fifty-three suspicious nonhardship cases, or a fraud rate of 8.5 percent (fig. 4.9).

We label these cases as "fraudulent" although we cannot prove they were fraudulent; in that sense, the estimates give us an upper bound for the fraud rate. Take, for example, an entryman who was not clearly a hardship case, that is, who left no record of an accident or devastating crop loss; if this person sold his or her claim a week after receiving patent, he or she could have either been a speculator or simply someone tired out from five years of hard farming—our data do not allow us to distinguish between them.

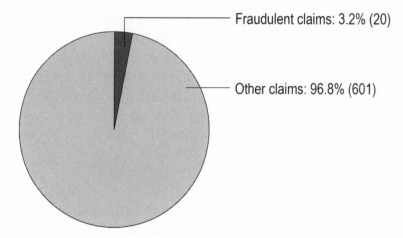

FIG. 4.7. Homestead claims marked as "fraudulent" using the one-month criterion, excluding hardship and including marriage fraud.

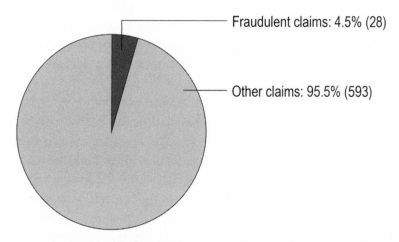

FIG. 4.8. Homestead claims marked as "fraudulent" using the two-month criterion, excluding hardship and including marriage fraud.

Despite this caveat, *for purposes of being extremely conservative in our estimate of fraud* (that is, including as fraudulent all possible cases of fraud), below we will label as fraudulent all "possibly fraudulent" cases as though they were definitely fraudulent; moreover, we will adopt the extremely conservative fraud estimate based on the full one-year criterion.

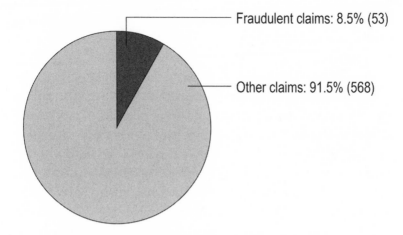

Fraudulent claims: 8.5% (53)

Other claims: 91.5% (568)

FIG. 4.9. Homestead claims marked as "fraudulent" using the one-year criterion, excluding hardship and including marriage fraud.

After careful analysis, our most conservative (i.e., highest) estimate is that in the study area, 8.5 percent of proved-up homesteads may have been gained through fraud, and we derived plausible estimates of roughly half that rate. In these ten townships in the last decades of the nineteenth century, it appears that more than 91 percent of homesteads went to bona fide or "actual" settlers.

The evidence from Dawes and Custer Counties requires us to take a second look at the scholarly consensus regarding fraudulent homestead claims. Fred Shannon asserted an implicit fraud rate of between 22 percent and 37 percent; later scholars have contended that half of all homestead entries before 1900 were fraudulent or even that half of *all* homestead entries were fraudulent.[25] Our evidence makes those conjectures appear absurdly high.

Rather than the homesteading process being rife with corruption and fraud, the results reported here suggest that the overwhelming majority of homestead patents on claims filed in the nineteenth century were probably valid; perhaps as many as 8.5 percent of patents issued may have been based on some form of fraud. The government granted a total of 80,103,409 acres as homesteads during the period 1868–1900. If we assume our estimated fraud rate of 8.5 percent applies to all these homesteads, then fraudulent claimants wrongly obtained approximately 6.8 million acres; alternatively, more than 73 of the 80 million acres were obtained by bona fide homesteaders.

So was homesteading more like the railroad giveaways or the modern Medicare program? The government gave 131.2 million acres to the railroads, and as Richard White has so eloquently demonstrated, much of this subsidy was unneeded and corrupt, simply a transfer of public assets to private individuals and corporations. Indeed, concerning just one transaction involving one railroad, and by no means the greatest fraud, financier Jay Cooke boasted that he gained "at once over 5 million acres between the Red River and the Missouri intact, not an acre of it lost. This of itself is worth a good deal more than the cost of the [rail]road on both coasts all the expenditures up to this date to say nothing of our other larger grant on the Pacific and in Minnesota & the completed railroad." Cooke's one land grab of 5 million acres was only slightly less than the 6.8 million acres that would have been lost to all fraudulent homestead claims (at the 8.5 percent rate) over the entire forty-year period.[26]

By contrast, recent studies of improper payments and fraud in Medicare put the swindle rate at about 8.3 percent—extremely close to our most conservative estimate, 8.5 percent, of fraud in homesteading.[27] Any loss of public land (or Medicare funds) to fraud is of course regrettable and wrong, but the exaggerated claims of Shannon and others of "an astonishing number" or "half were fraudulent" appear to have no basis in fact.

5

Homesteading and Indian Land Dispossession

In this chapter we examine the scholarly homesteading literature's fourth stylized fact:

- Homesteading caused Indian land dispossession.

What was the relationship between homesteading and Indian land dispossession? Did homesteading cause dispossession?

The relationship between homesteading and dispossession is a highly sensitive topic. For scholars who frame the white settlement process as one of settler colonialism, homesteading was but one of many colonial elements and strategies used to subdue the West. In this formulation, specific evidence linking homesteading with dispossession is not required, because homesteading is categorized as part of colonization, and colonization clearly dispossessed Indians, so the relationship between homesteading and dispossession appears obvious. Still, it seems apposite to ask: what exactly was the connection between homesteading and dispossession? It is remarkable that there have been few attempts to answer this question, that is, to identify the actual or empirical connection between homesteading and dispossession. By submerging homesteading in the larger colonialist premise, scholars have presumed it was complicit. Was it?

Dispossession cleared Indian land titles in American law, resulting in land being "restored" (to use the contemporary term) to the public domain and thus making it available for white settlement. It was rarely a smooth or simple process. The legal system declared

Indian land titles to be extinguished, whether on the basis of treaty, sale, or proclamation, when whites declared them to be so. This was clearly a one-sided process in which the affected individuals sometimes but not always agreed to the outcome. Indians were pressured by military force, conflicts with other tribes, intrusion of white traders and migrants, infiltration by land seekers, the effects of disease and hunger, and many other factors, all of which limited and distorted their options. So, too, factions or chiefs within the same tribe sometimes disagreed or could be suborned to disagree, making it unclear who (if anyone) legitimately spoke for the tribe. Finally, two or more Indian nations sometimes claimed ownership of the same lands, resulting in some tracts being ceded to the government multiple times.

What role did the Homestead Act and homesteaders play in this process? It is clear that white settlement of the vast lands west of the Appalachians had been the nation's ambition at least since President Thomas Jefferson sent his Corps of Discovery to the Pacific coast. This aspiration was implemented both by federal policy, including military intrusions, and by land seekers and squatters incessantly entering these territories. President Andrew Jackson pursued the national aim via the Indian Removal Act, and New England and Virginia farmers carried it out on the ground when they moved into the fertile lands of Kentucky, Ohio, and Illinois. Mormons migrating to Utah; forty-niners seeking their fortunes in California; miners digging for gold, silver, and copper in Colorado, the Black Hills, and Montana; railroads laying track across vast distances; and bonanza cattle barons seeking to exploit the enormous grasslands once the bison were exterminated— all contributed to this massive human wave. Whether driven by notions of Manifest Destiny or religious conviction, by simple self-interest or more elevated ideas of national development, the migration was unstoppable, surmounting all obstacles, physical, climatic, and human. Inevitably these newcomers and their activities, even just their presence, disrupted and came into conflict with the Native peoples of the region, restricting their range, bringing disease and debilitating goods like alcohol and guns, driving out or destroying the game, and encroaching upon hunting grounds and sacred places.

Homesteaders too were part of this vast movement and social disruption, and so it can be asked, what part did they play, or more specifically to what extent did the demands and needs of homesteaders drive the federal program of dispossession, and was it similar across all western homesteading states? In the profusion and confusion of actors, interests, and causes, was homesteading simply an indecipherable one among many? Or can we ferret out the extent to which homesteading was responsible for dispossession?

In this chapter we attempt to assess homesteading's role in dispossession, but we do not assess the process, validity, and fairness or unfairness of the dispossessions themselves.[1] We write of the government "settling" or "extinguishing" or "clearing" Indian land titles, but we mean those terms to carry no implication of "just settlement" or "amicable extinguishing." However we might judge the final results, we know the process was filled with violence, deceit, double-dealing, and much human suffering. Here we focus instead on homesteading's part in dispossession, and we do so by comparing the timing of dispossession with the timing of homesteading. Our main focus is on the three states and one territory with the greatest homesteading activity: Nebraska, Colorado, Montana, and Dakota Territory (table 5.1). We also do a quick look at several other homesteading states and Indian Territory. We conclude with some observations about the patterns that occurred in other homesteading states.

There appear to be different answers to the question of homesteading's role in dispossession depending upon the time and place, and it is not surprising that such a significant social process should have multiple stories. In Nebraska, most Indian land titles were cleared before 1862, and forces other than homesteading produced virtually all the dispossessions. Here, the homestead law served mainly to regulate who among whites (and a few blacks) obtained land, proving to be an equalizing corrective to most other federal land policies. In Colorado and Montana, dispossession preceded homesteading by several decades, and the primary drivers of dispossession were mining interests, railroads, land speculators, and big cattle ranchers, with homesteading playing a very minor role. In Dakota Territory and Indian Territory, by contrast, homesteading was an important driver of dispossession. Thus in much of the prairie region, including Nebraska, Colorado, and Montana, homesteading played little role in Indian dispossession; by contrast, in Dakota Territory and Indian Territory it played a central role.

Homesteading in the Dispossession Process

In any homesteading state, the federal government needed to clear Indian land titles prior to opening land for homesteading. Homesteaders could only legally file on land that was part of the public domain. But in some states the federal government achieved its goals long before the homesteading process reached their borders, making it implausible that demands by (future) homesteaders or their advocates for homesteadable land were a significant factor pushing the government to clear the land titles. Here other interests and agents constituted the primary force. In other states, homesteaders began seeking land and the federal government forced dispossession; the political weight that potential homesteaders and their advocates placed on government decision-makers contributed to the political process leading to dispossession.

There were three basic patterns in the relationship between homesteading and dispossession. The Nebraska pattern occurred where the federal government settled major Indian land claims before the Homestead Act was even passed, eliminating homesteading as a possible cause of dispossession; this pattern characterized eastern and central Nebraska as well as some other homesteading states. The Colorado pattern occurred where, although the government settled Indian land claims around the time of or after passage of the Homestead Act, homesteaders did not begin entering these lands until decades later, long after the federal government had extinguished Indian land titles, making it implausible that homesteaders' demands for eligible land were a significant incitement of the government's actions; this pattern characterized Colo-

TABLE 5.1 States with the most homesteading

	Ranked by acres of final entries	Ranked by number of final entries
Dakota Territory (later ND + SD)	1 (33 million acres)	1 (249 thousand entries)
Montana	2 (32)	2 (151)
Nebraska	3 (22.3)	4 (104)
Colorado	4 (22.1)	3 (107)

Note: Rank in millions of acres or thousands of entries among thirty homesteading states.

Source: Department of the Interior, "Homesteads" (Washington: Bureau of Land Management, 1962), 2.

rado, Montana, and some other states as well. The Dakota pattern occurred where would-be homesteaders actively agitated for further dispossession; this pattern characterized both Dakota Territory (later North Dakota and South Dakota) and Indian Territory (later Oklahoma). In states that followed the Nebraska and Colorado patterns, it was others—railroaders, mining companies, cattle barons, through-haulers going to the West Coast, and the U.S. Army—and not mainly homesteaders who forced the pace of dispossession. In the Dakota pattern states, homesteaders actively participated in the dispossession.

As noted, the analysis that follows compares the timing of dispossession with the timing of homesteading. For each state or territory, we provide three arrays of data: First, a graph that displays for each year the total remaining Indian acres on the left-hand scale and the number of final homestead entries on the right-hand scale; when entries were filed is a good measure of homesteading's *timing* or *activity*. Second, a state map showing Indian land cessions by decade. And third, a graph that for each year again displays the total remaining Indian land acres on the left-hand scale and the cumulative total of homesteading acreage on the right-hand scale; the cumulative total is a good measure of homesteading's *scale* or *impact*. What emerges is a more complex story of western settlement than we typically see. This closer examination allows us to start linking the places where homesteading did or did not contribute to dispossession.

The Nebraska Pattern

In some ways Nebraska is homesteading's iconic home. It is the state with the largest proportion (45 percent) of its land transferred via homesteaders' claims, the site of the officially recognized first homesteader, Daniel Freeman, the fictional locale of Willa Cather's *O Pioneers!* and *My Ántonia*, and the present-day site of Homestead National Monument of America. Yet here homesteading appears to have had a marginal role in dispossession, mainly because the federal government had already largely dispossessed Nebraska's Indians before the 1862 Homestead Act was even passed. Nebraska Indians had seen their traditional means of support destroyed, their societies disorganized and demoralized, and the major forces for their removal well advanced before the homesteading era. This timing was not true of Nebraska's northwest corner, where dispossession occurred as an outcome of the Great Sioux War, and it was not true of the Ponca removal in the 1870s. But elsewhere the Homestead Act primarily regulated the distribution among whites of already cleared public (formerly Indian) lands, reducing the share of such lands going to speculators, land companies, banks, big ranchers, and investors in favor of "actual settlers."

Homesteading in Nebraska's eastern and central portions, the Nebraska pattern, occurred between roughly 1863 and 1894; a second boom, in northwestern Nebraska, occurred between 1905 and 1917 and is discussed later as part of the Colorado pattern. As can be seen in figure 5.1, the government had extinguished Indian land titles on roughly 30 million acres (of Nebraska's 49 million) by 1860; that is, most Nebraska Indians had already been dispossessed before the Homestead Act was passed and, *a fortiori*, before the first homesteading boom occurred in these regions. By the time Nebraska's first homesteading boom began, around 1870, non-Indians in the state already outnumbered Indians, 122,993 to about 7,000, or by more than 17 to 1.[2]

David Wishart, in his meticulously researched and passionately

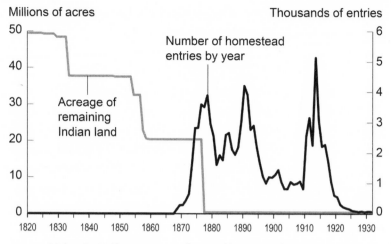

Millions of acres   Thousands of entries

FIG. 5.1. Nebraska Indian acreage and annual homestead entries.

argued *An Unspeakable Sadness: The Dispossession of the Nebraska Indians,* describes the process whereby the Omaha, Ponca, Otoe-Missouria, and Pawnee first lost most of their lands and then were removed by the federal government to Indian Territory. As Wishart tells the story, it was a long process involving many elements. He notes, "The world of Nebraska Indians had never been stable, but before 1800 change had generally been slow. ... By the beginning of the nineteenth century, however, the changes were occurring virtually overnight, and the shock waves were increasingly difficult to absorb." The introduction of horses, the growing volume of the fur trade, the penetration of trade goods (especially guns and alcohol), the pervasiveness of new diseases, and the intrusion of other groups, especially the Brulé Sioux (a Lakota band), disrupted traditional life and culture. Among other consequences, the use of horses by the Brulé, Dakota, and Cheyenne opened Nebraska Indians to much greater danger from raids and in particular made the bison hunt extremely dangerous. Simultaneously, the voraciousness of the fur trade quickly depleted the game. Bison became scarce, so bison hunts ranged much further west, and Wishart observes that these changes "increased the likelihood of meeting enemies on the bison range. Defensive warfare became more common, putting the lives of the chiefs in jeopardy. ... Attacks on villages had to be avenged, and so an endless cycle of defense and retaliation was set in motion." Gene Weltfish notes about the Pawnee that by "the 1830s, when the Pawnees were living in the western part of their territory . . . the direct effects of the many historic pressures of the time began to bear down on them."[3]

These various forces produced rapidly worsening conditions for all four groups of Nebraska Indians. Hunger became a persistent and unrelenting feature of life. Wishart writes: "When starvation became the normal condition of life, particularly in the 1840s, groups of Indians camped near the missions and begged for corn and potatoes."[4] In 1854 the Kansas-Nebraska Act promised the opening of new lands to white settlers, and individuals and families crossed the Missouri River even before politicians had worked out all the details. The resulting influx of settlers increased the pressure on the Indians' traditional ways of life, especially the bison hunt. By 1860 the traditional forms of life for Nebraska Indians no longer produced enough food to sustain them.

Nebraska Indians began trading their land, under increasing degrees of coercion, as early as when the Kansa (Kaw) tribe ceded land along the Big Blue River in 1825 in a treaty signed in St. Louis. Figure 5.2 maps Indian land cessions in Nebraska by decade. In 1830 several groups of Sioux, Otoe, Missouria, and Omaha peoples ceded land along the Republican River in the Treaty of Prairie du Chien. A series of treaties followed as the federal government sought to find homelands for other Indians (the Kickapoo, Delaware, Potawatomie, Chippewa, and Ottawa), who were pushed westward by white settlement further east. In 1833 the government signed treaties with the Otoe-Missouria and the Pawnee.

Hungry, living in dread of continuing attacks by the Brulé or other Lakotas, and desperately poor, Nebraska-resident Indians attempted to trade their one asset—land—for better conditions. Wishart notes, for example, "The Ponca . . . wanted the Indian Office to act. From 1855 on they repeatedly expressed their willingness to sell their lands in return for a reservation and annuities. . . . All the other Nebraska Indians had annuities, they pointed out, and they wanted the same treatment." He also writes, "By 1858 all

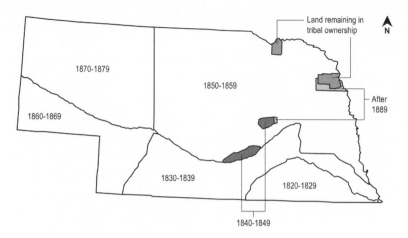

FIG. 5.2. Indian land cessions in Nebraska, by decade.

four [Nebraska] Indian societies had sold the last of their ances-
tral lands except for small reservations."[5]

The Pawnee provide a revealing example. Traditionally dominant in a huge swath of land in what is now central Nebraska
and Kansas, they were pushed out of Kansas by the Osage and others, decimated by smallpox, attacked by Lakotas, disrupted by the
increasing traffic along the Oregon Trail, and faced with declin-
ing game. Under these pressures, in 1833 they ceded by treaty all
their lands south of the Platte River, some 13,000,000 acres. But the
forces destroying their way of life continued to press on them—
between 1836 and 1844 they suffered debilitating attacks by the
Sioux, plundering of food and robe caches by the Oto, poor har-
vests, and unproductive hunts. As Wishart notes,

> The spring of 1844 found all the Pawnee bands without food. The
> Indians living around the mission had raised a good crop of corn the
> previous fall, but in their eagerness to leave on the winter hunt they
> stored it before it was dry, and the entire harvest rotted. The Skiri [a
> Pawnee band] had been so harassed by the Dakota that they were not
> able to work in the fields and had raised no corn at all. The Dakota
> also preyed on the Skiri and Pitahawirata [another Pawnee band]
> while they were out on winter hunt and prevented them from getting
> any meat. None of the Pawnee bands had a good hunt that winter.[6]

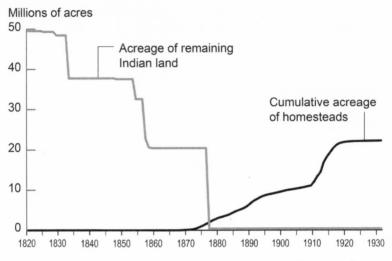

Millions of acres

Acreage of remaining Indian land

Cumulative acreage of homesteads

FIG. 5.3. Nebraska Indian acreage and cumulative acreage of homesteads.

Perhaps most devastating of all was the growing through-traffic by whites. Each year hundreds of emigrant wagons—more than 2,500 in 1848—traveled along the south side of the Platte, joined by the Mormon exodus, which mostly followed a new road on the north side of the Platte. All this traffic traversed Pawnee lands, scaring away the game, exhausting the pasturage, and creating endless minor conflicts with nearby Pawnee villages. In 1857 at Table Creek the Pawnee agreed to another treaty in which they ceded most remaining lands and accepted a small reservation on the Loup Fork of the Platte River. Having started the nineteenth century more than 10,000 strong, by midcentury they were reduced to about 2,000. As one observer put it, "By 1854 . . . the Pawnees were a beleaguered people."[7]

In the 1860s Nebraska Indians lived on small reservations where they were vulnerable to both Brulé attacks and harassment by white settlers. The Ponca and Pawnee became increasingly desperate. Wishart notes, "The main problem for the Pawnee in these troubled years [the 1860s] . . . and the main failing of the government's reservation policy was the lack of protection provided against both Indian and American [white] enemies. Their nemesis, the Brulé, raided the reservation every summer, and their war parties were never far away on the bison hunts." Conflict with whites, much of it provoked by the settlers and for which the Pawnee had little recourse, likewise demoralized and distressed them. As Wishart observes, "There would be no peace or effective protection for the Pawnee as long as they remained in Nebraska."[8]

The Ponca, Omaha, and Otoe-Missouria likewise suffered hunger and debilitating living conditions. Each group was stressed. The Omaha and Otoe-Missouria were surrounded by increasingly dense white settlement (perhaps including homesteaders), and settlers, speculators, and politicians all clamored for opening up part of the remaining Indian lands. The government forced the tribal nations to sell much of the small reservation lands they had retained and eventually removed them to new reservations in Indian Territory. The demands of the Ponca chief, Standing Bear, to return to Nebraska resulted in the famous court case, *Standing Bear v. Crook*, in which a federal court declared for the first time that an Indian was indeed a "person" within the meaning of the law and therefore could seek habeas corpus redress from the court. Remaining in Nebraska were Standing Bear and a small group of Ponca, who became known as the Ponca Tribe of Nebraska (or Northern Ponca) in contrast to the majority of Ponca (the Southern Ponca) who moved to Indian Territory.[9]

Nebraska's Indians endured a process of dispossession aptly described by Wishart's phrase, an unspeakable sadness. It was not, however, a result of homesteading, as we see in figure 5.3. Most dispossession occurred before the Homestead Act was passed; approximately thirty of Nebraska's 49 million acres were alienated before 1860. (The sharp drop in Indian-held land in 1876 reflected the cession of the northwest corner of Nebraska following the Great Sioux War, discussed below). Much smaller tracts were stripped from already small eastern reservations; these lands were never opened to homesteaders, only to purchasers of land.

If homesteading contributed little to dispossession of most Indian land in Nebraska, it had a huge—and equalizing—influence on the distribution of available lands among whites and a small group of blacks. Before the homesteading law, and afterwards on public lands where the law did not govern, speculators, big investors, large ranching operators, and others frequently accumulated large tracts of the public lands made available. Studies of the great speculator empires such as those of William Scully, the Brown-Ives-Goddard group, and Ira Davenport reveal that they depended on the full range of public land laws to aggregate their holdings, especially using agricultural college scrip, military warrants, cash sales, and purchases of Indian allotments. More detailed studies of land transfers in specific areas such as Gage County, Nebraska, have reinforced these findings. Much of the public land in eastern Nebraska was locked up by these means before the major flood of homesteaders even entered the state starting about 1870.[10]

The constraints imposed by the Homestead Act generally did not govern the sale of those Indian lands in Nebraska and Kansas rendered "surplus" by the application of allotments to reservations, although the system was later revised for lands in Dakota Territory and Indian Territory. For example, Wishart describes the sale of the remaining Pawnee reservation in 1878 resulting from their removal to Indian Territory: "Sales began by auction in 1878. . . . By 1883 the entire reservation had been sold and reorganized as Nance County. There was no limit to the number of tracts that could be bought, no residence requirement, no restrictions on resale, no stipulation that improvements be made; in other words, this was an open invitation to speculators. More than half of the total area went to only fifty-five purchasers. . . . Most of the land purchased by the major buyers was resold at great profit in the boom years of the 1880s." By contrast, the overwhelming bulk of homesteaded land—even with the various abuses that generated so much contemporary press notice and subsequent scholarly attention—wound up in the hands of individual families. The Homestead Act's principal consequence in Nebraska was thus directing much public land, whose Indian titles had already been cleared, away from large landowners and speculators and into the hands of "actual settlers," many of them poor or near-poor when they started. Here homesteaders did not need to participate in or agitate for the clearing of Indian land titles.[11]

The Colorado Pattern

In Colorado, Montana, and the northwest corner of Nebraska, Indian cessions occurred around the time of the Homestead Act or later, but homesteaders only became interested in those lands long after the federal government had extinguished the Indian land titles. This process, referred to as the Colorado pattern, is thus distinguished from the Nebraska pattern by the fact that dispossession as well as homesteading occurred after 1862. In the Colorado pattern, the timing (i.e., homesteading lagging dispossession by several decades) suggests that homesteading played little role in the dispossession, and instead the Homestead Act primarily governed the distribution among whites and blacks of lands already "restored" to the public domain.

Colorado experienced its homesteading boom toward the end of the national homesteading period (fig. 5.4). Homesteaders such as those Katherine Harris and David Wishart studied started filtering into far eastern Colorado in the 1880s, as homesteading prospects across the border in Nebraska and Kansas dried up, accounting for the small final filings peak in 1894. Filings were relatively few before 1900, however, and the big Colorado boom occurred later, with initial claims filed between 1903 and 1922 (and proved up between 1908 and 1927). This activity was concentrated in eastern Colorado, as can be seen in the very rapid population increases in eastern Colorado counties during these years. Kiowa, Kit Carson, Washington, Yuma, Lincoln, and Cheyenne Counties recorded big increases, the smallest being Kiowa's 313 percent increase and the largest being Cheyenne's 635 percent. In these regions the land had been transferred to the public domain thirty or more years before homesteading.[12]

By the time significant numbers of homesteaders began entering Colorado, it had already become a state with a large white population and well-established industries. White settlement in Colorado began as early as 1851 with the establishment of San Luis on the Culebra River. But it was the discovery of gold in 1858, and the subsequent Pike's Peak gold rush that brought the first large influx of

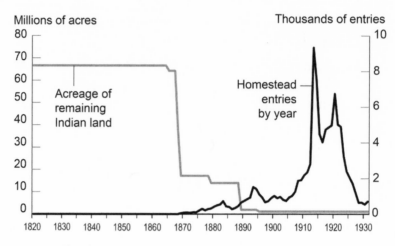

FIG. 5.4. Colorado Indian acreage and annual homestead entries.

whites. Perhaps as many as 50,000 miners rushed to the gold fields in 1859. An even bigger boom followed the discovery of silver in several locations in the mid-1860s and the big strikes around Leadville in the 1870s, bringing thousands more whites into the state. Bonanza cattle ranchers also discovered the lush grassy valleys. As whites moved in, they often intruded on Indian lands and scared away game, and quarrels between small groups of whites and Indians flared up. Indians sometimes retaliated by stealing cattle, and whites demanded that the U.S. Army or territorial authorities protect them. In the most infamous case, a group of loosely organized territorial troops under Col. John Chivington surprised and massacred a Cheyenne and Arapahoe village at Sand Creek in 1864.[13]

Denver recorded a population of 4,749 by 1860 and began developing as a major regional entrepôt in the following decade. By 1871 the Denver Pacific Railroad ran north, connecting the city to the Union Pacific's transcontinental tracks in Cheyenne, the Kansas Pacific line stretched east to Kansas City, and the Denver and Rio Grande, though not reaching the Rio Grande, did link to the southern part of Colorado and the burgeoning mining regions. After statehood in 1876, Denver served as the capital as well as the railroad, provisioning, finance, and cattle export hub. By 1890 Denver was already a large city with 106,713 people.

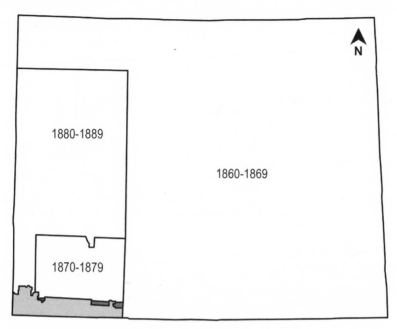

KEY

■ Land remaining in tribal ownership
■ Land ceded after 1889

FIG. 5.5. Indian land cessions in Colorado, by decade.

The federal government's efforts to clear Indian land titles in Colorado began with the Ft. Laramie Treaty (1851) between the United States and the Sioux, Cheyenne, Arapaho, Crow, Assiniboine, Mandan, Hidatsa, and Arikara nations. Despite that treaty and partially in violation of it, the government took more drastic measures in the 1860s and 1870s. The February 18, 1861, treaty between the United States and the Arapaho and Cheyenne removed their land titles covering nearly three-quarters of the state. When further agreements with the Arapaho, Cheyenne, and Kiowa were reached in October 1865, the federal government declared the entire eastern part of the state—all land east of a line passing somewhat west of Kremmling-Vail-Leadville—to have been "restored" to the public domain; figure 5.5 shows Indian land cessions in Colorado by decade. By 1865 the government thus considered these lands,

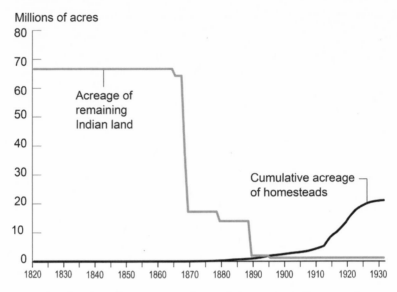

FIG. 5.6. Colorado Indian acreage and cumulative acreage of homesteads.

which would prove so attractive to homesteaders two generations later, to be cleared of Indian titles.

In western Colorado, the government sought to settle with the Utes and to a lesser extent with the Comanche and Kiowa. As early as the 1860s it had attempted to subdue the Utes and move them onto reservations. It achieved or enforced major cessions in the agreements of March 1868 and April 1874. In the fall of 1879, conflict at the White River Agency caused the U.S. Army to send an expedition against the White River Utes led by Chief Nicaagat (Jack). The ensuing battle at Milk River and killings at the agency inflamed white public opinion, which demanded, "The Utes must go!" As Dee Brown put it, the miners and politicians "wanted to push [the Utes] off those twelve million acres of land waiting to be dug up, dammed up, and properly deforested so that fortunes could be made in the process." The Army sent a larger expedition, the Utes surrendered, and most were marched 350 miles to a reservation in Utah, only a few remaining on a small patch in extreme southwest Colorado.[14]

Many interests were thus pressing for early clearing of Indian land titles in Colorado, including migrants passing through the area on the way to the coast, cattle ranchers on big spreads poaching on public lands, mining corporations and miners attracted by the gold, silver, and other mineral discoveries, and railroad companies seeking rights-of-way, land grants, and protection of their traffic. By 1881, according to Dee Brown, "Colorado was swept clean of Indians. Cheyenne and Arapaho, Kiowa and Comanche, Jicarilla and Ute—they had all known its mountains and plains, but now no trace of them remained."[15]

In 1890, before any significant homesteading began, Colorado had 191,126 whites, 2,436 blacks, and only 1,092 Indians, if the census is to be believed, or a ratio of 177 to 1. The resulting chronology of dispossession and homesteading is shown in figure 5.6. Long before significant homesteading began, the federal government had removed most Indians and settled the remaining ones on small reservations, transferred their lands back to the public domain, and overseen the establishment of a large resident non-Indian population. Major industries and transportation networks had grown up. Homesteading played little role in Colorado land dispossessions, and the Homestead laws seemed mainly to regulate who among the whites and blacks would gain title to already alienated lands in the process of public domain disposal.[16]

Montana largely followed the Colorado pattern of relatively early (but post-1862) clearing of Native land titles and relatively late homesteading (fig. 5.7). Homesteaders did not enter the state in significant numbers until the twentieth century, but the government had moved Indians to reservations decades earlier. The government's initial step, as with so many tribes in the region, began with the Ft. Laramie Treaty in 1851. But soon white miners began moving into the region, disrupting the treaty's arrangements. "Montana's foundation, like that of many other western states, stands on a golden cornerstone," note Michael Malone, Richard Roeder, and William Land in their comprehensive history of Montana. After the discoveries of 1859 and 1862, "The promise of gold first attracted significant numbers of whites to the area." Tens of thousands of white miners entered the region.[17]

Soon, however, it was "the more abundant resource of free grass

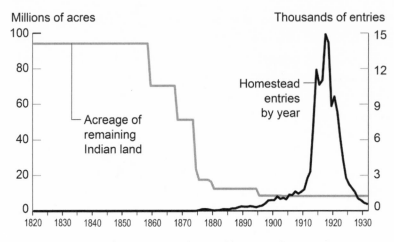

FIG. 5.7. Montana Indian acreage and annual homestead entries.

[that] first lured a permanent white population to the [Montana] eastern plains during the 1870s." When Generals Sheridan and Sherman toured the area in 1877, they marveled at the bountiful and nutritious grasses in the innumerable valleys in the Powder River, Big Horn, and Yellowstone River country. Capt. John Bourke, accompanying Sheridan, observed that the region "ought, inside of two years, to be filled with a population of herders and graziers, superintending hundreds of thousands of fat cattle."[18] By 1886 Montana ranchers did in fact graze roughly 664,000 cattle and 986,000 sheep on the grasslands. So too, copper mining, concentrated around Butte and increasingly monopolized by the Anaconda Corporation, soon outpaced gold and silver and grew to be the dominant industry in the state. Miners, ranchers, and the Northern Pacific railroad, which wanted to push westward from its railhead in Bismarck, demanded that the Army provide protection for their operations and restrict Indians to reservations.

In 1855 the Flathead, Kootenai, and upper Pend d'Oreilles ceded the extreme western part of the state (around today's Missoula). In 1868 the government forced the Crow, Cheyenne, and northern Arapaho to make major cessions in central Montana and placed them on reservations. In 1869 the government dealt with the Arikara, Gros Ventre, and Mandan, moving them to the Ft. Berthold

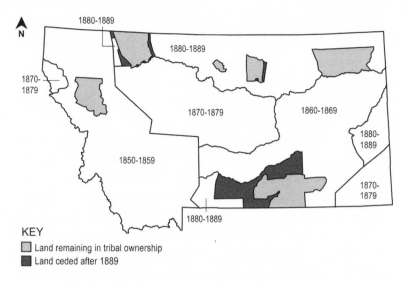

FIG. 5.8. Indian land cessions in Montana, by decade.

Reservation and obtaining cession of the territory in the south-eastern part of the state that had remained to them under the Ft. Laramie Treaty (fig. 5.8). In 1873 the government extracted major cessions from the Blackfeet, Gros Ventre, Piegan, Blood, and River Crow in the north-central part of the state as part of the agreement to settle them on reservations.

Fully opening the region awaited resolution with the Sioux and the outcome of the Great Sioux War. After Little Bighorn some chiefs, most famously Sitting Bull but also Crazy Horse and Morning Star, continued to resist federal authority, but other chiefs purporting to represent the Sioux, Northern Cheyenne, and Arapaho ceded the remainder of nonreservation land in the extreme southeastern part of Montana (anticipated in the treaty of April 29, 1868). The military had thus cleared the land, and as historian Paul Hedren writes, "With access, the Northern Pacific Railroad finally extended itself through Sioux Country to a completion in western Montana in 1883. With access and that railroad, hide hunters took aim at the millions of buffalo still roaming the newly wrested countryside. And with access and a prairie without buffalo, cattle ranchers filled Sioux Country—or in their lingo, portions of the Open Range—to a state of overflowing."[19] In 1880 a presidential executive order "restored" to the public domain a significant tract in east-central Montana southeast of Glendive. By 1890 Indian land holdings in Montana had been reduced mainly to reservations in south-central Montana and scattered others along the northern border.

There was also in Montana a process involving homesteading on reservations, however, in which homesteading played a more contributory role to dispossession. Implementing the Dawes Act (discussed below in the "Dakota pattern"), the government entered the Flathead, Crow, Blackfeet, and other reservations to locate Indian families on family or individual plots; it then took the unallotted or "surplus" land that had earlier been pledged to the tribes and "restored" it to the public domain, thereby opening it to homesteaders. Thus whereas nonreservation lands in Montana followed the Colorado pattern, "surplus" reservation lands followed the Dakota pattern.

Montana like Colorado saw homesteading occur after the state and its major cities and industries were already developed. By 1890, 127,271 whites lived in Montana, several times the remaining Native population; by 1910, when significant homesteading was just beginning, there were 360,580 whites and 1,834 blacks compared with just 10,745 Indians.

Homesteaders proved up more claims (14,891) in Montana in 1917 than in any other state in any year, and the 1918 Montana filings (14,178) were the third most ever.[20] Figure 5.9 displays the several-decades gap between Indian land cessions and the beginning of homesteading activity. The federal government had nearly completed its campaign of forcing Montana's Indians onto reservations and ceding their rights to other lands, and a large white and small black population had been established, nearly two generations before the influx of homesteaders. As in Colorado, the most popular areas for homesteading had been public domain for thirty or more years.[21]

The Colorado pattern focuses mainly on Colorado and Montana, but northwestern Nebraska properly belongs to this story as

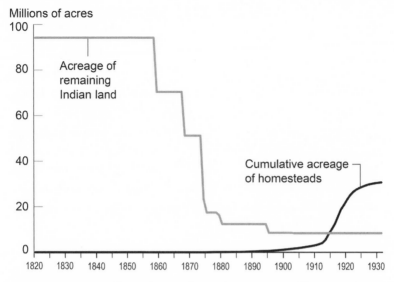

FIG. 5.9. Montana Indian acreage and cumulative acreage of homesteads.

well. The government extinguished Lakota title to roughly 19 million acres in the northwest corner of Nebraska in 1875 and 1876 as a result of the Great Sioux War. Indians retained some very small reservations in the east, but other Indian titles in Nebraska had been cleared (see fig. 5.2). A generation later homesteaders entered Nebraska's northwest region, an influx that resulted in Nebraska's second homesteading boom between 1905 and 1917 (shown as the second peak in fig. 5.1).[22]

The Dakota Pattern

A strikingly different process, here termed the Dakota pattern, emerges when we examine the relationship between homesteading and dispossession in Dakota (referring both to Dakota Territory and, after 1889, the states of North and South Dakota). Here homesteading was intimately tied up with dispossession. As Karen V. Hansen notes in her exceptional study of the Scandinavian immigrants in North Dakota, "The Dawes Act and its sequel, the Land Allotment Act of 1904, created the conditions that enabled homesteaders to settle on Indian land at Spirit Lake at the price of Dakota dispossession." Would-be homesteaders joined railroaders,

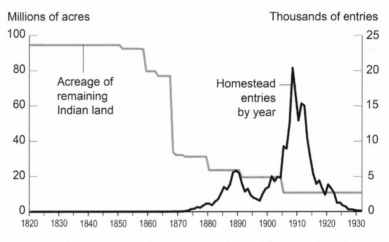

Millions of acres   Thousands of entries

FIG. 5.10. Dakota Territory Indian acreage and annual homestead entries.

mining interests, and other powerful forces to agitate for implementing the Dawes Act provisions requiring allotment of Indian
land. We cannot know what would have happened in the absence
of a homesteading law, of course, but it seems reasonable to assume
both that dispossession would have occurred without homesteading and that homesteaders' land hunger intensified, widened, and
speeded up the process of dispossession.[23]

Most of Dakota Territory—about two-thirds, or 61.5 million of
its 93.6 million acres, as shown in figure 5.10—followed the Colorado pattern. The federal government had coerced or induced
cessions from Indians that "restored" these lands to the public
domain by 1870; indeed, by 1880, long before much homesteading began, the Territory already had a non-Indian population of
135,177, four and a half times the Indian population of around
30,000.[24] In general, white settlement of the nonreservation lands,
including extensive homesteading after 1900, went smoothly and
without conflict. What was different in Dakota, justifying the cat-
egorizing of it as a separate Dakota pattern, was what happened
on the extensive reservation lands. Here homesteading advocates
were directly involved in the dispossession process.

Dispossession after 1880 proceeded in two stages: first, the government reduced existing reservations, which still encompassed

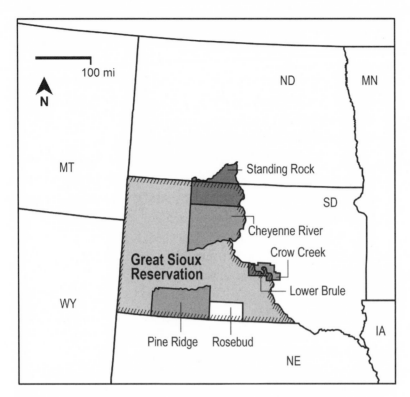

FIG. 5.11. The Great Sioux Reservation and subsequent reservations.

tens of millions of acres, and then it opened "surplus" land within reservation boundaries after allotment. Homesteading advocates actively agitated for both measures. The new course could be seen as early as July 13, 1880, when President Rutherford Hayes, by executive proclamation, extinguished Arikara, Gros Ventre, and Mandan land titles in far western (North) Dakota.

But Hayes's action was only a prelude to the more draconian alienation of Sioux land. An 1868 agreement, the "second Laramie Treaty," had reduced the Sioux's prior, somewhat undefined territory but established the Great Sioux Reservation (fig. 5.11), with clear boundaries, as their "perpetual home." Unfortunately the new reservation lay directly in the path of whites' developing plans. These were years when gold miners wanted access to the Black Hills, railroads planned new lines through the area, buffalo hunters, cattlemen, and through-haulers demanded protection, and the Army insisted on building forts in Sioux country and roads to connect them. As Richard White noted, by 1887 a fairly complete railroad net existed east of the Missouri River, but "the Great Sioux Reservation blocked expansion to the West." [25] The railroads viewed tracks running to the Black Hills and mining regions of Montana as potentially very lucrative.

Congressman William Holman of Indiana noted in the 1888 House debate on dividing up the Great Sioux Reservation, "This whole movement takes its origin from the necessity for the construction of railroads through that region of the country. The pressure for the right of way for the purpose of reaching the Black Hills region of country was irresistible. The motive in that direction is not so strong now as it was formerly. . . . But still every person must concede that roads running directly east and west are desirable." The railroads needed to obtain rights-of-way across Indian lands, but equally significant, they wanted land grants to subsidize track construction and sell their bonds. The land needed to be in the public domain, however, before the federal government could grant it. Richard White put the railroads' dilemma this way: "The peculiar configuration of the Great Northern was the first problem. In 1893 it ran through miles and miles of territory lacking literate inhabitants and U.S. post offices." The lack of post offices and letters to carry between them meant the line earned little revenue from the post office. Companies lobbied for the removal of Indian land titles, pressing Congress for resolution of "the Sioux Problem."[26]

There appeared to be broad agreement among Americans, especially after Little Bighorn, that leaving the Great Sioux Reservation in place created an obstacle to the advancement of civilization and commerce.[27] This was the region where Theodore Roosevelt established his Elkhorn Ranch in 1884, and like other land investors, speculators, hide hunters, and ranchers, he viewed the region as excellent ground for the next big bonanza ranches; homesteaders were among the gathering forces promoting Sioux dispossession. Congressman Samuel Peel of Arkansas in 1888 noted, "This bill [to divide up the Great Sioux Reservation] has been before Congress for eight or ten years. . . . The whole country is expecting passage of the bill. They have been anxiously waiting for years for some such measure. The effect of the bill . . . is to open up a large amount of the public domain, from which settlers are now excluded, to settlement under the homestead law at 50 cents an acre, and confine the Indians to a very small reservation." Even Senator Dawes in 1884 had attempted to persuade his Senate colleagues to pass an earlier bill, S. 1755, by noting that "I want to say to the Senate that this opens to actual settlers ten million acres of land. There is an immense pressure everywhere, especially in Dakota to get this bill through."[28]

In 1887 Congress passed the Dawes Severalty Act to establish a new policy on most reservations throughout the country, moving Indians from holding and using their land communally (by tribe or band) to individual ownership of properties, termed allotments. It required the government to settle Indian families on separate allotments of 160 acres for each head of household, 80 acres for single persons over eighteen and orphans under eighteen, and 40 for other children under eighteen. After setting aside the lands required for the allotments, the remaining reservation land was declared a "surplus" eligible to be sold to settlers. The revenues from sale were to be held in "trust" and used for the benefit of the tribes.[29]

On March 2, 1889, Congress addressed Sioux land explicitly, passing "An act to divide a portion of the reservation of the Sioux Nation of Indians in Dakota into separate reservations and to secure the relinquishment of the Indian title to the remainder, and for other purposes." It moved the Sioux onto six smaller reservations and transferred the remaining land to the public domain. Nor would the 1889 law be the last: between 1889 and 1910, Dakota Territory Indians were forced or induced to make at least fourteen more major cessions, ten involving Sioux land. The effect of this legislation can be seen in figure 5.12. By 1890 the government had cleared Indian titles to nearly all of North Dakota and roughly two-thirds of South Dakota while still leaving the Sioux on reservations encompassing millions of acres.

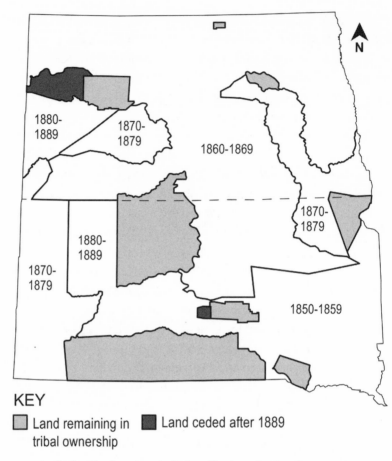

FIG. 5.12. Indian land cessions in Dakota Territory, by decade.

In his Presidential Proclamation 295 (February 10, 1890) implementing the statute breaking up "the Great Reservation of the Sioux Nation," Benjamin Harrison began by announcing that his commissioners had provided him with "satisfactory proof" of "the acceptance [of the new act] and consent thereto by [three-quarters of the males of] the different bands of the Sioux Nation of Indians" as required by the Treaty of 1868 and the statute; therefore, he proclaimed, the act "is hereby declared to be in full force and effect." The methods by which the alleged three-quarters approval was obtained were rank in the extreme. After listing some protections for Indian rights to "rations and annuities" and cleaning up some issues with allotments, railroad rights, missions, and other concerns, the Proclamation announced its main purpose: "it is therein [in the act] provided that all the lands in the Great Sioux Reservation outside of the separate reservations described in the said act . . . shall be disposed of by the United States, upon the terms, at the price, and in the manner therein set forth, to actual settlers only, under the provisions of the homestead law."[30] Thus the government declared such lands open to settlement and specified that it would be distributed under the provisions of the Homestead Act.

Homesteading advocates next turned their energies to opening the "surplus" lands remaining within the reduced reservations. Especially enticing were lands in the Lower Brulé, Rosebud, Fort Berthold, Devil's (later Spirit) Lake, and other reservations. The prospect of reservation lands being opened generated great enthusiasm among whites fevered by land hunger.

This then was the larger context in which homesteading proceeded in Dakota Territory. There was a small surge of homesteading in the late 1880s, mostly confined to the far southeastern corner of (South) Dakota, but intense homesteading of the region only began in 1901, peaked in 1908, and extended to 1915 (fig. 5.10). As noted, most homesteaders staked claims in the two-thirds of Dakota that had been ceded decades previously; for example, Mountrail County, whose land had previously been ceded and was confirmed by Congress on March 3, 1891, had virtually no white population in 1900, but by 1920 it recorded 12,140 residents. But that was not enough: intense pressure by whites for opening new land forced the government to open "surplus" reservation lands as well. We can't know how the pressures for opening these lands would have played out if there had been no Homestead Act; the evidence from elsewhere (such as Nebraska and Kansas) suggests that nonhomesteading forces—pressure from speculators, ranchers, squatters, railroads, big land investors, and others—would likely have been sufficient to remove Indian land titles by themselves. Nonetheless, the lure of homesteading added a new and powerful voice, and perhaps the strongest force, pushing for dispossession in Dakota.[31]

Homesteaders were placed at the center of this consortium of interests due to a change in federal policy regulating the disposal of the newly "restored" lands. In Nebraska and Kansas, restored Indian lands were sold, not opened as free lands to homesteaders, with the predictable result that large buyers, such as those who gobbled up most of the Pawnee surplus land in the 1878 auction, often gained most of the newly available land. Largely in reaction, Congress changed the rules so that the lands opened in Dakota Territory were typically opened only to homesteaders.

There was this twist: homesteaders would have to buy their land. Claimants on these lands were required to meet all the ordinary Homestead Act requirements—five-year residency, building a dwelling, making other improvements, producing witnesses, and so on—and in addition pay for their claims. Land was priced on a sliding scale from $0.50 to $6.00 per acre, depending on the quality of the land. In this respect homesteading on reservation land was a hybrid, but it precluded corporations and speculators from gobbling up large tracts, as they had on the Pawnee lands in the 1870s.

The new policy responded to white fears that the West was becoming closed off to the "poor man." Congressmen and senators from the region were particularly strong advocates. In debate on the Great Sioux Reservation bill, Congressman B. W. Perkins of Kansas introduced an amendment to permit squatters—"persons who . . . in good faith, entered upon or made homestead or timber-culture filing upon any part of the Great Sioux Reservation"—to be able to purchase their land at 50 cents per acre. Congressman George W. E. Dorsey of Nebraska observed, "I have had scores of letters complaining of the injustice [of squatters being evicted from Sioux land]."[32]

The scale of whites' land hunger can be judged by the popular response when reservation land was opened (fig. 5.13). On August 12, 1907, President Theodore Roosevelt issued his Proclamation 771, "Opening of Lower Brulé Indian Reservation Lands." To avoid the chaos, early entry, violence, and other problems experienced with the "land runs" in Indian Territory (Oklahoma), Roosevelt established a lottery system. Interested individuals were to travel

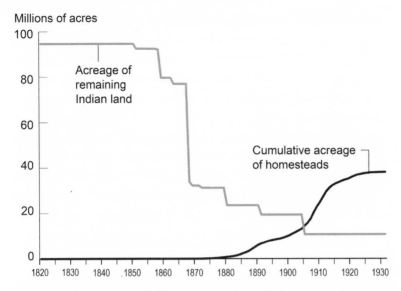

FIG. 5.13. Dakota Territory Indian acreage and cumulative acreage of homesteads.

to Pierre, South Dakota, and "execute in person" an affidavit showing that he or she was qualified to claim a homestead; his or her sealed envelope containing the affidavit was entered in the lottery. Roosevelt set 9:00 a.m. on October 14, 1907, as the time for the drawing. Officials were to draw only as many names as homestead claims could be accommodated on the available land; those whose names were drawn would choose their land in order of the drawing. They had two months, from October 20 to December 20, 1907, to stake their claims.[33]

Edith Eudora Ammons (later Kohl) was a twenty-three-year-old woman who witnessed the drawing and wrote about it in *Land of the Burnt Thigh*. She wrote, "Government posters and advertisements for the land opening were published in every section of the country. And along with the government publicity appeared the advertisements for the railroads. For them increased population in this area was a crying need." According to Kohl,

> Into the little town of Pierre they swarmed, by train, by stagecoach, by automobile, by wagon, on foot—men and women from every part

of the country, from almost every state. . . . Like a thundering herd they stampeded the United States Land Office at Pierre. . . . One day the little frontier town of Pierre drowsed through the hot afternoon, and the broad plains lay tenantless, devoid of any sign that men had passed that way. The next day the region swarmed with strangers. . . . Sturdy, ruddy-faced farmers, pale-looking city boys, young girls alert, laughing—all sons and daughters of America—not an immigrant peasant [i.e., a servile person] among them; plumbers and lawyers, failures and people weary of routine, young men from agricultural colleges eager to try scientific methods of farming and older men from Europe prepared to use the methods they had found good for generations; raucous land agents and quiet racketeers alert for some way of making easy money from the tense, anxious, excited throng.[34]

Kohl believed that many land seekers saw the lotteries as their last chance to establish themselves: "A generation before people had migrated in little groups in covered wagons to find new land. Now they came by automobile and railroad in colonies, like a great tidal wave." The little frontier town of Pierre had been completely unprepared for the avalanche of people who descended upon it during the Brulé opening.[35]

But as much as the opening of the Lower Brulé Reservation generated excitement, it was small potatoes compared with the Rosebud Reservation land rush. In answer to pressures to open more land, President Roosevelt issued Proclamation 820, "Rosebud Indian Reservation" on August 24, 1908. He proclaimed that "all of the said lands which shall remain unallotted to Indians, unselected by any state and unreserved for townsite purposes, be disposed of under the general provisions of the homestead laws of the United States, and be opened to settlement, entry and occupation." He thereby released nearly a million acres for homesteading; again a lottery would be used to distribute the 1,500 square miles of territory. The drawing was to begin at 10:00 a.m. on October 19, 1908.[36]

Government officials did a better job this time around of preparing for an influx of people on a gigantic scale. The government

FIG. 5.14. Land seekers flood into Gregory, South Dakota, to file their
affidavits for opening of Tripp County lands in the October 1, 1909, lottery
drawing. Courtesy *South Dakota Magazine*.

employed a small army to staff the various registration points and
notarize the affidavits. "Free Land! Free Land! It was like the tune
piped by the Pied Piper," Kohl wrote. "This is the chance of the poor
man. The Rosebud has been throwed open!" Newspapers and others estimated that somewhere around 115,000 claimants registered
for the drawing, but with only 4,000 affidavits to be drawn, the
probability of winning was slim. While the land seekers mobbed
the registration towns like Presho, Chamberlain, and Gregory,
others saw the end of the existing regime of land use. "The stock-
men were shocked," Kohl wrote. "They had not dreamed of anything like this invasion. Their range was going and they owned
none, or little, of the land." And, she observed, some "old Indians
looked on, silent and morose."[37]

In 1911 thousands of land-seekers registered in Gregory, South
Dakota, for the lottery for Rosebud land in Tripp County (fig.
5.14). One of them was a failed twenty-seven-year-old Missouri
farmer named Harry Truman. Truman's affidavit was not drawn
from the barrel—"I could never draw anything," he wrote to his
fiancé, Bess Wallace—and he returned to St. Louis. Individuals

like Truman who failed to get a homestead worried that the supply of free (or cheap) land was about gone, leaving the poor man little hope of owning land. "If they had only stopped immigration about twenty or thirty years ago," Truman wrote, "the good Americans could all have plenty of land."[38]

Karen Hansen described a similar land boom in 1904 on the Spirit Lake Dakota Reservation in east-central North Dakota. Hansen studied Norwegian homesteaders who claimed land within the reservation boundaries where the federal government had imposed Dawes Act allotments and then opened the remaining "surplus" land to white settlement. The people Hansen studied (including her own ancestors), in contrast to those who homesteaded lands elsewhere in the state not on reservations, were literally on the front lines of dispossession. As in South Dakota, the federal land agents used a lottery system; 15,076 people, including many women, entered their affidavits. The agents would draw 600 winners, who could select their land in order of their being chosen from the 100,000 acres being made available. In less than a year, about three-quarters of the claims had been made, with homesteaders whose names had been drawn early getting the best land, those nearer to 600th getting poorer sites.[39]

The infiltration of white homesteaders onto lands inside reservation boundaries produced—as it did on Rosebud, Pine Ridge, and elsewhere—a checkerboard pattern of holdings (not shown in fig. 5.12) that defeated any attempts to manage tribal land, even Indian-owned allotted land, in communal ways, a problem that continues to the present. In Spirit Lake, homesteading was intrinsically connected to dispossession. Hansen quotes her grandmother, speaking about her homesteading great-grandmother, as saying that "she took homestead on the Indian Reservation" and "we stole the land from the Indians." As Hansen points out, "In point of fact, Dakotas had to agree to sell unallotted land before it was homesteaded, so it was not stolen, but rather taken legally." (Hansen's point is not justification but rather a subtle one about memory.) Still, as Hansen shows, voluntary exchange in a market can occur under varying degrees and kinds of coercion.[40]

The crowds of land seekers were simply confirmation of what representatives and senators had reported when deliberating on the dispossession statutes. The promise of homesteading generated intense pressures for "restoration" to the public domain of Indian lands in Dakota Territory. It would be impossible at this stage to disentangle homesteading as an *independent* force for dispossession from homesteading as simply one among many forces pressing for opening the land. Public land had already been granted to railroads, set aside for townsites, or otherwise encumbered. But the "surplus" Indian lands in North and South Dakota remained unclaimed, and by 1900 the public demands left the government with little option other than doing what it wanted to do anyway, opening it to homesteaders. Thus homesteading began in Dakota quite dissociated from dispossession and ended as a prime driver of dispossession.[41]

The Other Homesteading States

What of the other homesteading states? In ongoing research we have been able to find comparable data for six other states. California, Kansas, and Minnesota appear to follow the Nebraska pattern; in southwestern Minnesota, the U.S.-Dakota War in 1862, with its tragic aftermath of the Mankato hangings, extinguished Indian land titles before the Homestead law became effective. New Mexico and Wyoming follow the Colorado pattern. Thus of the eleven states analyzed (counting North and South Dakota), in eight of them homesteading appears to have played little role in dispossession.

By contrast Indian Territory (Oklahoma) generally followed the Dakota pattern. Its particular history as the depository for Indian tribes from elsewhere, including the Five Civilized Tribes, imparted peculiar circumstances to the dispossession process, but clearly would-be homesteaders played a central role in dispossession.

The original inhabitants of what became Indian Territory were the Osage, Plains Apache, and to some extent the Comanche. Early in the nineteenth century their land titles were effectively extinguished to make way for other Indians, that is, to create Indian Territory (fig. 5.15). This original dispossession was

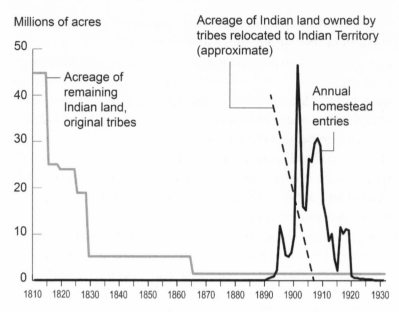

Millions of acres

Acreage of Indian land owned by tribes relocated to Indian Territory (approximate)

50

Acreage of remaining Indian land, original tribes

40

Annual homestead entries

30

20

10

0

1810 1820 1830 1840 1850 1860 1870 1880 1890 1900 1910 1920 1930

FIG. 5.15. Indian Territory (Oklahoma) Indian acreage and annual homestead entries.

unrelated to homesteading and predated it by several decades. There was, however, a *second* dispossession in Indian Territory that occurred when homesteaders and other whites desired the land of the resettled Indians.

As Rennard Strickland observed, "Oklahoma Indian tribes in a real sense were still sovereign—'domestic dependent nations,' in the words of Chief Justice John Marshall. Until that fateful year [1889], although subject to many federal regulations, Indians owned all the land that was to become Oklahoma. Whites within their domain were there on Indian sufferance or were government or military officials. Illegal intruders were subject to expulsion."[42]

Between 1870 and 1890 the population of Texas nearly tripled and the population of Kansas nearly quadrupled, and the land lying between them became increasingly alluring to whites. Cattle drives north through Indian Territory brought whites into the region. Railroads, land agents, and others, including Elias Boudinot, member of a distinguished Cherokee family, agitated for opening unoccupied Indian Territory lands. C. C. Carpenter, a "Boomer"

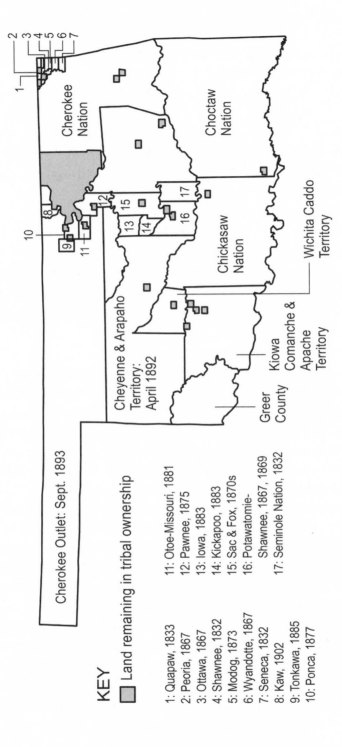

FIG. 5.16. Indian land cessions in Indian Territory (Oklahoma).

KEY

■ Land remaining in tribal ownership

1: Quapaw, 1833
2: Peoria, 1867
3: Ottawa, 1867
4: Shawnee, 1832
5: Modoc, 1873
6: Wyandotte, 1867
7: Seneca, 1832
8: Kaw, 1902
9: Tonkawa, 1885
10: Ponca, 1877

11: Otoe-Missouri, 1881
12: Pawnee, 1875
13: Iowa, 1883
14: Kickapoo, 1883
15: Sac & Fox, 1870s
16: Potawatomie-
     Shawnee, 1867, 1869
17: Seminole Nation, 1832

Cherokee Outlet: Sept. 1893

Cheyenne & Arapaho Territory: April 1892

Cherokee Nation

Choctaw Nation

Chickasaw Nation

Wichita Caddo Territory

Kiowa Comanche & Apache Territory

Greer County

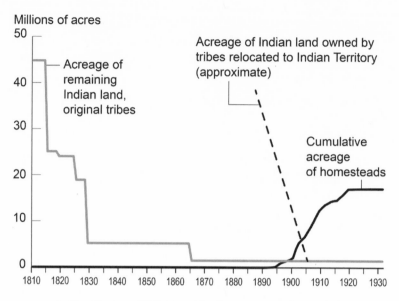

Millions of acres

Acreage of remaining Indian land, original tribes

Acreage of Indian land owned by tribes relocated to Indian Territory (approximate)

Cumulative acreage of homesteads

FIG. 5.17. Indian Territory (Oklahoma) Indian acreage and cumulative acreage of homesteads.

(homesteader) leader, assembled a group of farmers in 1879 on the Kansas border with the intention of settling in the so-called Unassigned Lands in the middle of the territory (fig. 5.15); only the stationing of federal troops in nearby Kansas towns prevented the threatened invasion. Other expeditions of settlers organized and entered the territory with varying success. Meanwhile advocates for opening parts of Indian Territory organized a national publicity campaign to change federal policy, and it soon had success. By 1885 President Chester A. Arthur had declared in favor of opening Indian lands, and on March 23, 1889, President Benjamin Harrison, during his third week in office, issued a proclamation authorizing eligible persons to enter identified lands for the purpose of making homestead claims.[43]

In a relatively brief span from late 1889 to roughly 1906, these by-then-well-established resident tribes were given allotments or otherwise moved to small reservations and their "surplus" lands opened to white settlement (fig. 5.16). The most common method of opening Indian Territory lands was by "runs": homesteaders were excluded from the opened tracts until a specific date and time, at which point the settlers literally raced to their desired plots, with the first to arrive winning the claim. Figure 5.17 shows the great increase in homesteaded acreage that was unleashed by the second dispossession, represented (approximately) in the figure by the dashed line.

Would-be homesteaders had repeatedly organized illegal and provocative white intrusions onto Indian lands and lobbied Congress and the national executive to extinguish Indian land titles. They succeeded.

Homesteading and Dispossession

Although homesteading occurred in thirty states, this chapter has focused on the process in the Great Plains, its center of gravity. As we have seen, the relationship between homesteading and dispossession differed depending on place and time. In the Nebraska pattern, which held for eastern and central Nebraska, the federal government had largely cleared Indian land titles even before passage of the Homestead Act, and homesteading mainly served as an equalizing corrective to other federal land policies that had grossly favored speculators and other large operators. California, Kansas, and Minnesota appear to mostly follow the Nebraska pattern, though more detailed studies would likely reveal more nuanced local patterns. In Colorado, dispossession preceded homesteading by several decades, and homesteading simply came too late to have been a significant cause of dispossession. Montana followed the Colorado pattern, as did the northwest corner of Nebraska and seemingly New Mexico and Wyoming as well. The Dakota pattern, by contrast, which characterized both Dakota Territory and Indian Territory, was driven by land seekers and their advocates becoming noisy and powerful advocates pressuring their federal representatives to open Indian lands to white settlement. In Dakota Territory and Indian Territory, homesteaders were not the only ones working to "restore" Indian lands, but their actions speeded up dispossession and emboldened federal leaders to open larger tracts of Indian lands for white settlement.

This concludes our reexamination of the four stylized facts adopted by the scholarly consensus on homesteading. In analyzing the first three stylized facts, we find the consensus wrong or deeply flawed. In examining the fourth stylized fact, which links homesteading to dispossession, we arrive at a more nuanced conclusion than its simple statement allows. It is both wrong and right. Taken together, the consensus facts provide an altogether misleading interpretation of homesteading.

6

Women Proving Up Their Claims

Having completed our analysis of the four stylized facts, we turn now to explore how we can use the study area data to reveal other significant aspects of the homesteading experience. In this chapter we focus on the 64 women who successfully filed homesteads in their own names in our townships in Custer and Dawes Counties. To place our findings in context, we first review how female homesteaders have been portrayed by historians and others. We then explore what our study area data can tell us about the demographic characteristics, community connections, gender customs, and other aspects of female homesteaders' lives and environment. In particular, we look at who they were and why they succeeded or failed. In these explorations we combine quantitative analysis with deeper scrutiny of individual cases to gain a fuller view of women's participation in homesteading. We do not deviate far from the homestead and land transfer records, but the depth of information in those records is surprising, as we will see, allowing us to reconstitute important aspects of female homesteaders' lives.

Before we begin that deeper examination, however, we should note that there were in fact many more than 64 women in the study area using the Homestead Act to build homes, farms, and futures. We have data on the marital status of the 557 male homesteaders in the study area in table 6.1.

Thus there were at least 407 other female homesteaders who are not counted because of the nineteenth-century convention that in a marriage, men were the heads of household and hence the

TABLE 6.1 Marital status of male homesteaders in study area

	Custer	Dawes	Total	%
Married men	221	186	407	73.1
Single	53	62	115	20.1
Widower	8	10	18	3.2
Separated	0	2	2	0.4
Divorced	0	1	1	0.2
Not stated	10	4	14	2.5

homesteader. We have little information about these 407 women, although we know from many other accounts that wives were usually critical to the success of homesteads. Women brought complementary but equally crucial skills to the homestead operation, including more "domestic" tasks such as food preparation and preservation, vegetable gardening, poultry and egg production, making and washing clothing, tending the injured and sick, and of course giving birth and looking after the children. Their cash income from sales of butter and eggs often saved the family from starvation when the crops failed or prices were low. In many cases they also joined men in the heavier work in the fields (fig. 6.1). As Mari Sandoz put it, "Nothing happened [on the farm] after [the wife] arrived that did not vitally touch her. Particularly important was her place in accident or sickness, with doctors so few and far between. . . . When drouth and hail and wind came, it was the housewife who set as good a table as possible from what remained and sustained the morale of her family."[1] Altogether women provided huge contributions to the survival and success of homesteads. Thus, while we focus on the 64 women who homesteaded *in their own names*, we should not lose sight of the larger group of married women who also struggled to succeed at homesteading.

Homesteading Women in Myth and Reality

The gender-neutral Homestead Act of 1862 was part of a contemporary movement toward recognition and acceptance of a range of increased rights for women, including the right to own land. When Wyoming officially became a territory in 1869, its legislature became the first to grant women the right to vote and hold public office. Its action reflected not only the understanding that women were due these rights but that the country needed women and their "civilizing" influence to move west. The 1850 Oregon Donation Land Act encouraged American settlement of Oregon Territory by providing 320 acres free of charge to single men and 640 acres to married couples. In effect, the wife obtained her portion of the free land as an adjunct to her husband rather than in her own right.[2]

In contrast to the Oregon law, the 1862 Homestead Act directly recognized women's right to own land by opening settlement to any single person over the age of twenty-one, equalizing men and single women, or women who were otherwise heads of household, as potential property holders in the West. As for married couples, the GLO issued a series of clarifications (see appendix 1) stating that a husband and wife could both have claims, but they had to have been single at the time of initial filing. Further, if they wed during the proving-up period, the GLO assumed they would begin residing together on the husband's claim, and hence the wife would fail her residency requirement. The GLO expected that if they both had unfinished claims, one of the parties would need to relinquish his (or more likely her) claim. Thus the Homestead Act, by permitting some women to claim free land, did recognize their right to own land, but it still limited that right for married women whose husbands were present. The number of women moving west increased slowly, but once the forerunners demonstrated their success, more and more women followed suit. According to historian Susan Hallgarth, women continued to move west in large numbers via the Homestead Act through World War I.[3]

Women homesteaders became emblematic of the freedoms of the West, but the pervasive myth of the passive, reluctant wife or the local harlot often muffled their stories. In other words, early male-centric scholars and the public alike tended to view women as secondary characters who lived in the West only to serve male needs and as male helpmeets. The women in O. E. Rølvaag's classic 1927 homesteader novel *Giants of the Earth* illustrate this view. As historian Sheryll Patterson-Black observed, Rølvaag's women follow a common pattern: "helpless women who have been brought west against their better judgments, nesters who are dependent upon their husbands for almost everything, women who anxiously and helplessly await the return of their husbands." So, too, Everett Dick's 1966 article "Sunbonnet and Calico: The Homesteader's Consort," a history of a Nebraska female homesteader, drew upon the image of women as reluctant husband-followers. Dick's history told of the harsh realities and lived experiences of homesteading, but his interpretation did not veer far from the popularly held stereotype. In these fictions and histories, women lack agency, courage, and enthusiasm for starting new lives on the plains.[4]

Sandoz, a keen observer mostly unaffected by myth and image, began the push-back against these views in her 1934 paper "Pioneer Women," in which she called for the dismantling of the image of women as frontier drudges or dancehall girls. She noted that the story of the pioneer woman had yet to be written. But a persuasive rejection of the traditional views, and its replacement with interpretations that did not ignore female agency, awaited "second-wave" feminist scholars, who decisively dispelled the myth. For instance, historian Barbara Handy-Marchello argued that male homesteading scholars used the common image of the western woman as drudge "in a kindly way, intending to show sympathy for the woman who appears to be overburdened with work and family." She added that "the word 'drudge' suggests that farm women had no control over their work and no management role on their farms," when in fact the opposite was true.[5]

Within our study area, Hetty A. Houge of Custer County, sixty-two years old when she filed her claim, reported that she hired laborers to do the heavy work such as plowing. Hogue's farm was small, worth approximately $202. She only plowed three acres, as the remainder of the land was far more suited to grazing and ranching, but it—and the control over it—were hers. She listed her profession as "Housekeeping and overseeing my farm."[6]

FIG. 6.1. Woman binding wheat shocks, North Dakota, ca. 1910. Courtesy North Dakota State University.

Another woman peripherally associated with our study area (she was listed as a witness for one of our male homesteaders), Elvira Vore, also hired most of the labor on her farm worth $710. She oversaw her fifty acres of broken land and planted more than six hundred trees. While she and Hogue are the only women who reported hiring labor, they surely were not alone; the form did not ask for this information, but hiring, exchanging, and bartering labor was common in the homesteading economy. As western literature scholar Marcia Meredith Hensley noted, by the time Congress ratified the Nineteenth Amendment, women homesteaders had already successfully staked their claims in the West and were "independent from male authority and self-supporting, women who exercised control over their personal, social, and economic lives."[7]

Beginning in the 1970s, women scholars have revisited homesteading and revealed a more complicated, nuanced history of women homesteaders across many regions and time periods. The Homestead Act, they argue, represented far more for women than just the legal capacity to acquire land. Dee Garceau asserted that "homesteading fell into that compelling region where the mythic

West—and opportunity for reinvention of the self—was grounded in actuality." For women, she continued, the law straddled "the seams between homesteading as concrete reality and as a literary metaphor for gender role change." Homesteading allowed women to cast off the thralldom of Victorianism and challenge the mores of traditional gender roles. Some female "literary homesteaders," as Garceau called them, produced newspaper stories for East Coast readers and other reminiscences or memoirs, but these women reflect only a small part of female homesteaders' typical experience. More broadly, as Katherine Harris noted in her study of women homesteaders in Colorado, homesteading imbued women with self-determination not typically available to them back east.[8]

Women Claiming Homesteads in Their Own Names

In our study area, the 64 female homesteaders represented 10.3 percent of all study area homesteaders. This proportion is roughly similar to women's percentage in other data sets. Sheryll Patterson-Black's early study of women homesteaders in Colorado and Wyoming found that women claimants comprised 11.9 percent of total entrants; sociologist H. Elaine Lindgren's study of 306 women in North Dakota found that women comprised 12 percent of the total homestead entries; and Paula Bauman's study of six Wyoming counties between 1888 and 1943 also determined that women accounted for 12 percent of all successful entries.[9]

There appears to have been a significant increase after 1900 in women's percentage of all homestead claims, perhaps adding another dimension to Paul Gates's idea that homesteading had two distinct phases. No one in our study area filed claims after 1908, so we cannot provide a good test of the thesis that the female home-steader percentage increased during the second phase. However, Lindgren's North Dakota data show a jump in the percentage of female claimants after 1900, from 6 percent in Pembina County in the 1870s and 1880s, to 20 percent in McKenzie County after 1900. Katherine Harris, in her study of Logan and Washington Counties, Colorado, likewise found that whereas prior to 1900 female homesteaders averaged 12 percent and 10 percent, respectively, of

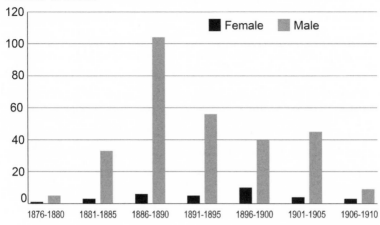

FIG. 6.2. Number of female and male homestead final claimants, by five-year span, Custer County.

Number of entries

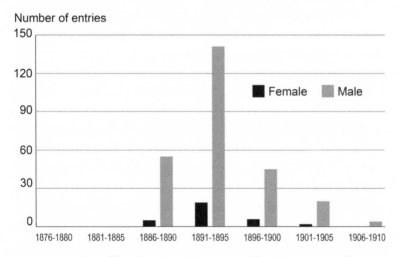

FIG. 6.3. Number of female and male homestead final claimants, by five-year span, Dawes County.

total entries in her two counties, after 1900 they averaged 18 percent of total entries.[10]

The two counties in our study area show a somewhat divergent pattern. In Custer County, as figure 6.2 shows, female homestead final claims peaked a decade after the male claims reached their maximum. Male proving-up was highest between 1886 and 1890, a five-year span accounting for 35.6 percent of all claims filed by men. By contrast, the largest number of final claims by women were filed a decade later, between 1896 and 1900, a period that accounted for 31.3 percent of all women's claims. Here women homesteaders followed men onto the land, apparently only home-steading en masse after men had already established communities. In Dawes County by contrast, as figure 6.3 shows, homesteading by men and women occurred in closer proximity: both the largest number of men making final claims, constituting 52.8 percent of all male claimants, and the largest number of women making final claims, representing 59.4 percent of all female claimants, were filed between 1891 and 1895.

Current scholars' studies have tended to reinforce what the public had already accepted, that single women filed homestead claims at high rates. By 1915 enough single women staked claims that a *Denver Times* headline read, "Women Are Taking Up Much Land in Colorado," and reported that "almost 50 percent of the homesteads are now taken up by women." So many single women filed for a homestead under the Kinkaid Act of 1904, an act that expanded homestead claims in Nebraska's arid areas to 640 acres, that they developed national reputations, entering Sandoz's liter-ature as "'Boston old maids' (retired school teachers) or 'Chicago widows' (the lone women 'too gay for quiet ways')." They exercised their rights under federal land law in high numbers, spurring on their own social and legal liberation. For all the debate over whether or not the Homestead Act and its subsequent expansions benefited bona fide settlers, it had tangible results for women.[11]

In most existing studies, single women account for the bulk of claims filed by women. In one of the most sustained studies of women homesteaders, Lindgren found that 83 percent of female homesteaders in her North Dakota sample from the 1880s through the 1930s were single and 15 percent were widows. They were also young: 59 percent were under twenty-five when they filed their claims, and only 9 percent were over the age of forty. Harris found similar numbers in her study of Colorado women homesteaders, reporting 78.4 percent of her sample as single and only 18.9 percent as widows prior to 1900. However, neither Lindgren's nor Harris's sample was scientifically drawn, and how representative they are is unclear. In her study of the single women homesteader literature, Hensley notes that they often wrote about independence, economic security, and neighborly cooperation. Their voracious appetite for writing reinforced the public perception that young, single, and literate women dominated the frontier.[12]

Our study area is characterized by a somewhat different pattern for the marital status and age of women homesteaders. The GLO created categories of marital status reflected in the homestead records, drawing a distinction between unmarried ("Single") and widowed women ("Widow"). Though today we might interpret both these categories as "single," the distinction can be revealing. In table 6.2 we separate categories by the woman's marital status at the time of initial filing and at the time of final proof up; hence "Single/Single" refers to a woman who was single when she filed her initial claim and also single when she proved up. Within our study area, twenty-one women were single when they made their initial claims (adding together the Single/Single and Single/Married categories); they comprised 32.8 percent of all initial claims by successful female homesteaders. However, only nine women stayed single during the required residency period; they constituted 14.1 percent of all female homesteaders. By contrast, there were twelve Single/Married who started homesteading single but married before proving up, constituting 18.8 percent of all female homesteaders.

What were these women's intentions? Hensley in *Staking Her Claim* challenged the idea that single women were homesteading solely to find a husband, and Lindgren reported that 57 percent of the women in her study who filed as single did not marry by the time of final proof.[13]

In our study area, a somewhat smaller proportion, nine of twenty-one (42.8 percent) of single women did not marry during the residency period and twelve (57.1 percent) did. Thus our data seem to support Hensley's point—many women homesteaded

TABLE 6.2 Female homesteaders' marital status at initial filing and time of final proof

Marital status at initial claim / final claim	Custer County	Dawes County	Total	Median age
Single / Single	6	3	9 (14.1%)	33
Widow / Widow	6	10	16 (25.0%)	59.5
Single / Married	3	9	12 (18.8%)	29.5
Married / Widow	11	5	16 (25.0%)	53
Widow / Remarried	1	1	2 (3.1%)	53.5
Other*	4	4	8 (12.5%)	40
Unknown	1	0	1 (1.6%)	54
Total	32	32	64 (100%)	

*Includes two desertions, two divorces, one separation, and three nonspousal inheritors.

for reasons other than marriage, such as economic prosperity and independence, or if marriage was their aim, they were only indifferently successful. Given that 115 men (20.6 percent of all male claimants) were unmarried, this seems unlikely; however, our data cannot account for love.

Widows constituted a large proportion of successful female homesteaders in the study area. At time of initial filing, eighteen widows (Widow/Widow and Widow/Remarried) made claims, nearly as many as single women (21) and constituting nearly a third (28.1 percent) of all female homesteaders. As table 6.2 shows, sixteen of these remained widows (Widow/Widow) and only two remarried (Widow/Remarried). However, there was a second way in which being a widow came into play: some married women's husbands died during the residency period, and the wife inherited the claim. Their loss transformed these women, who entered homesteading expecting to be part of a married team, into widow claimants (Married/Widow). And indeed, as the figure shows, women who became widowed constituted a full quarter (25.0 percent) of all women homesteaders. Thus if we include women who either entered homesteading as widows or proved up their claims as widows (or both), fully thirty-four, or 53.1 percent of all women homesteaders, homesteaded as widows during some part of the process. In this sense, there were more widows than single female homesteaders.

Let us now consider the ages of female homesteaders in the study area. The median age for the eighteen widows who filed initial claims, counting both Widow/Widow and Widow/Remarried groups, was 59.5; for the Married/Widow women, it was 53.0. This is not an enormous difference. More revealing is the age range: widows who filed initial claims as widows were typically older, ranging in age from thirty-six to seventy-five, while Married/Widow women ranged from twenty-one to sixty-three. Perhaps unsurprisingly, women who lost their husbands during the required residency period were younger than Widow/Widow and Widow/Remarried claimants. Intent differentiates these two categories and adds nuance to our understanding of the large percentage of widows among our women homesteaders.

Despite the perception of the law as a single-woman's law, Nebraska widows also took advantage of the Homestead Act and the new legal space for property ownership that the law afforded them. Widows filed initial entries in nearly equal numbers to single women; however, because of high mortality among husbands, many married women who didn't expect to homestead as widows did. Moreover, married women lost husbands at a much higher rate than widows found husbands—in the study area, sixteen wives lost husbands, whereas only two widows found husbands. Hence widows—intentionally or not—played a much larger role in the homesteading process than would be suggested by viewing the Homestead Act as a single-woman's law.

Women's Tenure on the Land

How long did the women homesteaders stay? Lindgren originally posed this question in 1989: "Did these women ever dispose of their land? Did they sell it to relatives or to strangers? Did they keep it throughout a lifetime?"[14]

Some recent feminist scholars have creatively examined how women used their claims, citing financial security and familial expansion as key reasons for women to homestead. They argue that women used the free homestead land to gain economic independence. These women typically did not work the land; rather, they held a variety of positions in their communities including accountants, doctors, nurses, secretaries, and teachers. In fact, as Deborah Fink asserted, it was far more expensive for a single or widowed woman to run a farm in Nebraska because she typically needed to hire the farm or ranch hands, as in the case of Hetty Hogue mentioned previously. Instead of farming or ranching, a female claimant was more likely to lease out her land. After receiving title, she could either continue to lease the property or sell the land to neighbors. Isabel Proctor, discussed in chapter 1, filed on a claim in Montana, and after receiving her patent, she rented out her land until she died sixty years later.[15]

Examining the land transfer records for women of four counties in Wyoming from 1900 to 1929, Garceau found that many of the women took their claims "to enlarge their family's property," citing the need for more range and to secure water rights in the arid environment. She continues, "In this respect, single women homesteaders demonstrated cooperation, not individualism; they filed claims to support a family ranch rather than to establish individual property ownership." Lindgren found that 81 percent of the women homesteaders in her area settled near relatives.[16]

Some women in Nebraska, too, filed claims to enlarge a family farm, the most publicized case being the four daughters of Joseph Chrisman. Joseph, a rancher, was worried that the influx of homesteaders in his region would decrease the amount of land available to his cattle operation. To aid him, his daughters each filed claims when they came of age, with Lizzie, the oldest, filing first and acquiring land in 1886 via the Preemption Act. Each of the sisters in turn filed three claims under the Homestead Act, the Timber Culture Act, and the Preemption Act when they came of age. Figure 6.4 shows the four young women standing in front of Lizzie's house.[17]

FIG. 6.4. The Chrisman sisters, Harriet, Elizabeth, Lucy, and Jennie Ruth (left to right), on Elizabeth's claim, Goheen settlement, Custer County, Nebraska, ca. 1886. RG2608 PH 0 1053. Courtesy Nebraska State Historical Society.

But to get a more general picture of how long female homesteaders stayed on their claims and finally provide an answer to Lindgren's questions, we compared the homestead records with land transfer records for claimants in the study area. We followed the female owners until they sold their property or died. In figure 6.5 we show the proportions of land transfers classified by category of the purchaser: "Family," "Local Homesteaders" (i.e., cases in which we could document the buyers' homestead status), "Local Nonhomesteaders," and "No Known Relationship," which included sales to banks, mortgage companies, or people whose surnames did not match any local homesteading family. Those claims labeled "Not Sold," totaling 15.6 percent, were retained by the claimant; another 28.1 percent of the women sold their claims to family members, including sons, daughters, or parents. The fact that 44 percent of women's homesteads were retained in the family suggests that homestead land, once acquired, became an important building block for the extended family's farming enterprise.

Ella Bohy, for instance, appears to have filed a claim for the sole

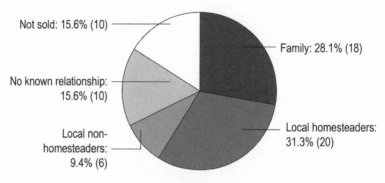

Not sold: 15.6% (10)

Family: 28.1% (18)

No known relationship:
15.6% (10)

Local homesteaders:
31.3% (20)

Local non-
homesteaders:
9.4% (6)

FIG. 6.5. Recipients of sales of claims by female homestead claimants at any time after claimant received patent.

purpose of expanding her father's landholdings in Custer County. Her French immigrant father, Gustave Bohy, received American citizenship in 1876, two years prior to Ella's birth in Iowa. The Bohys soon moved to Nebraska, and in 1888 thirty-nine-year-old Gustave proved up his homestead claim. He filed a timber culture claim for supplemental acreage and received patent in 1889. He continued to expand his landholdings by purchasing adjacent parcels from his neighbor in 1913. To help with his expansion, Ella filed a homestead claim on 80 acres adjacent to her father's property at her first opportunity, when she was twenty-one or twenty-two, and in 1905 proved up on it at the age of twenty-seven. Ella, by then married, sold her land to her father in 1913. Ella did not receive a copy of her patent until 1931, perhaps through GLO incompetence, yet her father mortgaged her property as early as 1926. In essence, Gustave bought and assumed ownership of the property with recognition from the local land office even though the patent hadn't been issued. Since many family land sales were not contentious, perhaps the physical title mattered less to the land office than oral confirmation. Only when Gustave entered his eighties did the Bohys recognize that they had never received Ella's patent. Ella ordered a copy in anticipation of settling her father's estate, a long process that lasted until 1945.

Stories like that of the Bohys demonstrate that women homesteading to expand the extended family's farm did occur in our

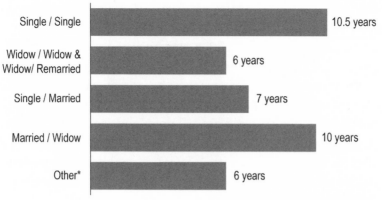

Single / Single		10.5 years
Widow / Widow & Widow/ Remarried		6 years
Single / Married		7 years
Married / Widow		10 years
Other*		6 years

*Other includes abandonment, desertion, and divorce, but excludes three inheritances from non-spousal family members.

FIG. 6.6. Women homesteaders' median length of residency, by marital status at time of initial filing and time of final proof.

study area, but while 43.7 percent of land stayed in the family, 40.7 percent of female homesteaders sold their claims to neighboring homesteaders or other locals. Many women homesteaders in the study area thus sold their land, and they typically sold it to local individuals. According to the land transfer records, few of the No Known Relationship purchasers retained the land, instead often reselling it within the local community soon after acquiring it. Women, then, were an essential part of farm and ranch formation and the success of their local communities regardless of whether or not they continued to hold title to their land.

In figure 6.6 we show female homesteaders' median length of residency after finalizing their claims classified by their status at the time of initial claim and the time of final proof. The claimants most inclined to sell immediately were the Widow/Widow claims, though five of the eighteen women from this group remained on their property after receiving their patents until they died. Of the five deaths recorded, four of them were Widow/Widow claim-ants, one Unknown, demonstrating that perhaps these typically older women intended their homestead claims to be their final grand effort and estate. As we saw in table 6.2, Widow/Widow claimants, with a median age of 59.5 years at time of final proof, were the oldest marital category as well, another factor perhaps in their shorter residency. The "Single/Single" women, as intentionally single homesteaders with a median age of 33.0 years, had the most staying power and mettle to succeed on the Nebraska plains.

What comes as a surprise is that the women who started their lives in Nebraska as married partners and ended as widows (Married/Widow) typically did not sell their land soon after receiving patents despite their loss. Certainly, some packed up and moved after the deaths of their husbands, as for example the youngest of this group, Lucy A. Wells of Dawes County, who was twenty-one at the time of final proof. Her husband died in 1891 during the required residency period, presumably prompting her to move back to her family in West Waterloo, Iowa. She received patent in 1892, and by 1905 she had remarried and sold the land.[18]

In another instance, Ellen R. Abbott, age fifty, had to testify to the death of her husband the previous year and her residency during her final proof in 1889: "[We] made said tract of land our home and resided there continually up to his death and I have continued to reside there ever since." Abbott sold her farm worth $890 the year she received her patent. If unmarried at the time of the claim, Abbott's rapid land transfer would seem a suspicious attempt to defraud the government for free land with no intent to stay. However, her additional testimony bemoans the work involved in the upkeep of such a large farm. It appears that she wanted to sell her property before it lost value from disrepair, and then she disappeared from the homestead records like so many other women. Both Wells and Abbott sold their deceased husbands' claims, giving them inheritances through the sale of what they and their husbands likely invested in the land. Presumably their cashing in on their claims provided them with a different form of financial independence.[19]

Still, nearly half of the recently widowed women (46.1 percent) stayed on their land even after the deaths of their husbands. Anna Faimon, thirty-one, of Custer County, lost her husband in the summer of 1886. Left with five children, a cave, a dugout, granary, sod henhouse, sod stable, and seventy cultivated acres, she remained on the land for approximately fifteen years before selling her land to her neighbor. Lueretia J. McQuiston of Custer County lost her husband and proved up at the young age of thirty-four, yet remained on her land for forty-one more years. She and her nine children stayed in their eighteen by thirty foot sod house with their forty cultivated acres, though she did ultimately remarry.[20]

These examples reveal the myriad considerations that new widows faced, once they received their patents, in deciding whether to keep their land or not. For some, the cost of staying was too high. For others, the thought of parting with their land so arduously gained was simply unfathomable. The variety of experiences and the difficulty of keeping a farm going give glimpses into the lives of these otherwise silent women homesteaders.

Building Community on the Plains

Another dimension of women's homesteading experience is the nature and character of the community ties they forged. As figure 6.5 demonstrates, 84.4 percent of women homesteaders' land stayed in local hands, improving the chances of success of their family and neighbors. Communal effort settled the plains, and women tended to form their own communities, often living in clusters. This held true on a small scale in both Custer and Dawes Counties, with no clusters exceeding five women—hardly the immense "Ladyville" settlement Sarah Carter describes occurring decades later in Montana, but significant within our study area nonetheless.[21]

Women formed their community ties in four distinct ways: through ethnic settlement, employment, local cooperation, and by mutual witnessing for one another in homestead affidavits. Relying on cooperation and neighborly kindness, sixty-four women finalized their homestead claims.

Ethnic Settlement

In chapter 7 we will examine ethnic settlement in more detail, but here we consider how it affected female homesteaders. Blake Bell, former historian at the Homestead National Monument of

America, interprets the Homestead Act as a progressive immigration law because anyone declaring intent to become a United States citizen could claim land, though he or she had to officially become a citizen by time of final proof.[22] The welcoming nature of the law fostered the intentional creation of several ethnic settlements within Nebraska, and immigrant women were no small part of their formation. Within the study area, 13 women (20.3 percent of female claimants) and 117 men (21.0 percent of male claimants) immigrated to the United States, naturalized as citizens, and received their patents.

Lindgren suggests that, for some of the ethnic groups, immigrant women homesteaded at much younger ages than American women homesteaders. This did not hold true in our study area. Immigrant women had a median age of 53.0 years at the time of their finalized claim; non-immigrant women homesteaders were much younger, with a median age of 39.0 years. If we narrow our results to the central European immigrant women, the median age is still 52.5 years. Lindgren's conclusion that German-Russians "were more likely to be . . . planning to take land because of a pending marriage or were older widows without dependents" caused us to ask a similar question of the marital status of immigrants versus U.S. citizens. Of the twelve women who filed as single and then married during their residency period, only two were immigrants. One woman sold her land after several years, and the other's husband moved onto the property with her.[23]

Eight of these women, or 61.5 percent of immigrant women, intentionally homesteaded in Nebraska either as single or widow claimants, while five lost their husbands during the residency period, ostensibly leaving them alone to finalize the claims. The median time, where known, they spent on their homesteads after the deaths of their husbands was 8.0 years. Only one woman sold her land immediately after proving up (she is counted as a hardship case), indicating that these women generally had the pluck to succeed even after such loss. Their length of residency was comparatively close to the immigrant women who intentionally filed their claims as single or widowed and had a median length of residency of 9.5 years. As another point of comparison, nonimmigrant women who were widowed, separated, or deserted during the required residency period also stayed on their land for a median length of 8.0 years. Women, immigrant and non-, are not merely a blip in the homestead records. They had staying power. Neither the immigrant nor American Married/Widow claimants (or claimants otherwise separated or deserted) simply packed up and returned to their prior home country or state. Perhaps living so closely with the land redefined how these women understood home.

Employment

Women homesteaders, whether or not their marital status changed over the course of the five-year required residency, relied on more than just the land for support and economic stability. They worked in their local communities and reciprocally provided economic opportunities for local workers. Though the final affidavits from witnesses and claimants did not explicitly ask for alternate employment information, the land agents did ask how much land they cultivated or improved for ranching, which provides us with a fairly clear assessment of women as farmers and ranchers. Women broke a median of 26.2 acres. Thirty-one female claimants (48.4 percent) broke 30 acres or more. Nine, or 14.1 percent of the women, claimed to have substantial timber on their lands, ranging from a low of ten fruit-bearing trees to seven hundred "forest trees." Although low, the percentage is unsurprising considering how arid the region is. The vast majority of women indicated that their land was primarily suited for grazing or haying.

Two women claimed they broke no acreage. Sarah E. Copeland (née Butler) of Custer County married during the proving-up period, but stayed on her land for seven years before selling to her father, Ezra M. Butler. The other, Amanda M. Hughes, age seventy-five, testified, "I did not cultivate any of the land [and] it is not fit for cultivation." Hughes finalized her claim in 1907 and remained on the land until her death four years later. Since both Butler and Hughes could have earned no money from crops, they must have either found other employment or relied on their fam-

TABLE 6.3 Median acres cultivated by female homesteaders, by marital status, excluding heirs

Marital status	Median acres cultivated
Single / Single	10 acres
Widow / Widow and Widow / Remarried	20 acres
Single / Married	27.5 acres
Married / Widow	33 acres
Other	30 acres

ilies for sustenance. When Hughes's witness Christopher Payton was asked if she resided continuously on the land, he replied, "Settler could not make her living on the land and she was away to earn money." Salathiel Dutton similarly testified, "I [cannot] give dates of her absence. She was away at different times to keep house for her son. She was never away for long at a time." As an elderly homesteader, Hughes's situation points to one potential alternative for homesteaders to expand the estates they could bequeath, though this was not common in our study area.[24]

Did marital status affect a woman's ability to earn a living on the land? For example, were single women homesteaders more or less successful than others? We can examine the number of acres broken by different categories of marital status. As table 6.3 demonstrates, Single/Single women cultivated a median of ten acres. Only Catharine Standlea cultivated more than thirty acres, indicating that Single/Single claimants likely worked other jobs.

We identified three off-land occupations of women in our study area that illustrate the variety of jobs outside of farming or ranching. Lizzie Gilshannon, thirty-seven and a dressmaker, tried to earn a living on her land, but drought stymied her efforts. She subsequently applied for a leave of absence from the land on November 6, 1889:

> Affiant further says that she is a single person and earns her own support and has no one to provide for her wants. Affiant further says that

the drouth the past season destroyed all her growing crops and she did not harvest anything. Affiant further states that she is unable to support herself from said tract the coming winter.

Eliza Wescott could not make her farm viable either, so she sought employment as a teacher. Elizabeth Karnes, a homemaker, reported that she worked for her parents to earn a living. She did not invest much in her land, selecting a homestead that already had a cabin and some improvements, presumably from a failed settler. As the experiences of these three women suggest, single women often worked *off* the land in order to survive *on* the land.[25]

On the other hand, Widow/Widow and Widow/Remarried claimants cultivated a median of 20.0 acres, twice as much as Single/Single women. These women frequently had children living at home available to help with farm labor. For instance, Mary A. Hickman cultivated 30 acres for six seasons with the help of a grown son who still resided with her. Matilda F. Wescott, a self-proclaimed "widow lady," had the largest cultivated area of 75 acres, and her son and daughter both lived with her. Having children made cultivation and general farm labor far more productive, but not uniformly so. For instance, widow Mary E. Steinman, age forty, appears to have left her land for a time in order to support herself and her children: "I was temporarily absent from claim about 3 months last winter. I was compelled to be away for the purpose of earning money to live on." Still other widows lamented that their children were all of age and did not reside with them on the land. Christian Buchanan, seventy-one, of Dawes County stated, "I am a widow and my children are all of age and have homes of their own." Her winters proved difficult as a result: "I have staid each winter with my children about three months. I am old and cant stay alone in the winter time." This formula seemed to work for Buchanan. She received her land patent in 1891 and retained the property until her death thirteen years later.[26]

Women who filed as single and then married during the proving-up period are of particular note because they typically cultivated more land than their counterparts who remained single or were widows at the time of initial filing. Single/Married claimants cultivated a median of 27.5 acres. Examination of the differences in cultivation acreages based on marital status indicates that women had significantly better economic success in farming their land when they had assistance from husbands or children. Further demonstrating this point, the women who began their homesteading adventures as married recorded the highest median acreage broken, 33.0 acres.

But with additional cultivation came additional dangers, including agricultural disaster. Drought destroyed Ellen R. Abbott's crops in the 1890–91 seasons, forcing her to work elsewhere. The same drought affected Helene K. Rasmussen and her husband: she testified in support of her request to the land office for a leave of absence that her 25-acre crop was "a total failure." The land agent wrote, "That this affiant and her husband are without means of support and must procure employment in order that they may provide the necessities of life for themselves and family. That such employment can not be had in the vicinity of this tract of land." In another record, Delila Wells stated that she and her husband grew three acres of corn, potatoes, and a garden, only to report later, "Hail destroyed everything." Josephine Denio and her husband lost 11 acres of corn and an acre of garden in the grasshopper infestation of 1875. The following year, when the grasshoppers rehatched, they lost 9 acres of corn and just shy an acre of garden, as well as one hundred of their trees.[27] Women homesteaders suffered along with male homesteaders from the often hostile natural environment. Weather had an equalizing effect, making close-knit communities even more important for individual success.

Local Cooperation

For women as for men, homesteading was a deeply interdependent experience. Cooperation between male and female homesteaders fostered community and was often essential for their success. Hallgarth's study of homesteaders highlights the group dynamic of cooperation upon which they built conceptions of independence. She explains, "Theirs was not the rugged individualism of the trapper and mountain man, or the aloneness associated with 'lonesome' cowboys. Settlers—male and female—survived not by going it alone, but by joining together." Garceau similarly argues that this "interdependent independence" accounts for single female homesteader success. It is difficult to glean how well any one homesteader fared on the isolated plains solely from the records; however, their testimony and the testimony of their witnesses upon final proof reflect this ubiquitous communal independence. Within our study area, the local community often rallied to support nontraditional women's homestead claims, particularly inheritance and desertion, and improved their chances of success.[28]

Inheritance and desertion claims contain an interesting set of records that straddle a legal gray area for women. Since their husbands or other male relatives made the initial claims, the questions and testimony generally pertain to the original male claimants, and the GLO system was set up on the presumption that the entryman was male—for instance, the earliest witness-statement form asks about voting, a right that most women were denied at the time. Women often had to go to unusual lengths to prove their right to the claims and the original identity of their husbands, and in so doing we see the critical role their neighbors and community played in helping to secure their homesteads.

Perhaps the most peculiar Married/Widow claim in the study area is also one of the earliest, and the lack of an established protocol for inherited claims is clear. Josephine Denio and her husband, Edgar, moved onto their Custer County homestead in July 1874, before the land office in Broken Bow even opened. There they essentially squatted for three months. The Grand Island land agent noted in October 1874:

> [Edgar] has dug a cellar and prepared the material for building a house, and have about four acres of said land broken. The reason he is not now living upon said land is that he was not able to build his house on account of not having the money to hire it done and he was physically unable to do it himself. Also for the want of money he has not been able to apply for the same Homestead until the present time.

Edgar died two years later on September 26, 1876, and approximately eight months afterward his widow, Josephine Denio, finalized their claim. Her case is unusual for several reasons. Witnesses were supposed to give separate testimonies, but Denio's witnesses, Thomas and Mollie Darnall, used a combined affidavit; perhaps the land agent did not consider Mollie Darnall a legal entity separate from her husband; perhaps he was granting Denio some leniency. More revealingly, however, Denio's case illustrates the primacy given to the original male claimant, because all the land agent's questions pertained to Edgar, not Josephine. Indeed, she did not even give any testimony.[29]

Similarly, Elizabeth Cramer's husband died in October 1886, and a year later she sought to prove up the claim she had inherited. Her statement and those of her witnesses pertained to her deceased husband, not to her own right to the claim. Cramer further had to prove to the Land Office (via her male witnesses) that she was in fact the widow of Paul Cramer and therefore had a legal right to the claim. Her witness, Oscar Smith, testified, "I believe [Paul] intended to remain on his land and that [his] widow intends to remain there." Complicating matters, she was also unable to reach the land office on her scheduled date due to a severe storm, provoking yet another sworn statement regarding her delay. Without the testimony of her neighbors as to her identity, intent of claim, and reason for her tardiness, she might well have lost her claim. Cramer identified her profession as "Keeping house & farming for self alone," but we also catch a glimpse of the importance of her community: she made additional money after her husband died keeping house for a neighbor. Her neighbors apparently rallied around her during her time of need to ensure a steady income and her right to the homestead. Unfortunately this was not enough to keep her afloat. She received patent on December 31, 1887, and mortgaged it by March 1888. In 1893, at the age of sixty-seven, she sold the land to her relative, John Cramer.[30]

As Cramer's story indicates, recently widowed claimants needed to provide substantial proof of their husbands' deaths and their own identity. Taking a female claimant on good faith only worked if she had men to confirm her testimony. The case of Delila Wells falls on the extremes of this trend. Edward J. Wells, a blacksmith in Broken Bow, homesteaded in the Arnold neighborhood and kept boarders at his home for additional income. He fell ill in early December 1887, the same month he was scheduled to finalize his homestead claim. On December 5 his two witnesses appeared at the land office to testify that he was unable to attend the hearing. Abner D. Brown stated of Edgar, "He now requires constant daily nursing—he is not able to lie down and sleep but must sit in a chair to sleep—cannot wear anything but large slippers on his feet." The land agent pushed the hearing back until December 15. On that day Delila Wells appeared in his stead and testified that her husband had died. Her witnesses had to verify her statement. Thomas J. Parrott, a witness and boarder on their property, said that he

> knows from personal knowledge that the Claimant said Edward J. Wells is now dead, that he was personally present in the house of said Claimant on above described land at the time of the death of said claimant—that said claimant died sitting in a chair, at 3 o'clk and 15 minutes P.M. on Friday, December 9th A.D. 1887 in the said house on their said land—that he has been personally acquainted with said Edward J. Wells since the year 1881 and that he is positive, and cannot be mistaken, that the person whom he saw die as aforesaid was the identical person who made original Homestead Entry No. 9497.

When Wells signed her X on her final claim, the land agent signed the final affidavit "Edward J. Wells by Delila Wells his wife," but then heart-wrenchingly smudged out "wife" and wrote "widow" instead.[31]

The last days of Edward's life were hard on Wells and complicated even more by the necessity of complying with the GLO's bureaucratic timeframes and appointments. Because of the clear hardship she endured in losing her crops to hail and husband to illness, Wells's male neighbors and friends came together to help finalize her claim. Her testimony speaks to determination as well as sadness. When asked about her residency on the land, she responded, "Actual & continuous—Have had no other home or place to live." She continued, "I want this land for my own personal home—this is all the home I now have."[32] The level of detail in Wells's records is rare and compellingly demonstrates both the power and necessity of community support.

As these cases show, support from neighbors and others in the local area was often crucial for a claimant to secure her patent, despite otherwise clear entitlement to it. Often cooperation extended beyond the official acts, as neighbors and friends helped get the crops in, care for livestock, and assist in other ways. As we see in chapter 7, cooperation had another side, too: it formed an essential part of the community policing of fraudulent claims. The absence of such support, or the unwillingness of known local witnesses to testify that a (fraudulent) claimant had met all the residency requirements, could doom a claim.

The second category of inherited claims, desertion, occurred in only two instances within the study area, and each case presents unique features underscored by the necessity of male community support. As with the Married/Widow claims, these deserted women had trouble asserting a right to the land because of both misinformation and land transfer roadblocks. They depended on the advocacy of their male neighbors to secure their land. In the first case, Mary Candee and her husband, Russell, built their homestead in Dawes County in 1887. Twenty-seven years old at the time, Candee found herself running the homestead alone after Russell abandoned her and their four children in April 1891. Candee continued to reside on the land and make improvements in compliance with the law, but she failed to understand the legal nuances.

Candee knew that without finalization, her husband's claim to the land expired after seven years, but she wrongly concluded that she had to wait until 1894 to refile on the land, then wait five more years to prove up and earn the title in her own name. According to the law, however, if she could simultaneously demonstrate her husband's failure to prove up and her own success, she could count all the years of residency after 1887 toward her own claim. In fact, because of her previous years of residence, she would be unable to refile beyond 1894 because she would have exceeded the seven-year limit to finalize a claim. She realized this only in the seventh year, most likely again because of the help of her neighbors. As such, her testimony to the land office in 1894 reads:

> Affiant further says that Russell B. Candee deserted myself and family April 28, 1891 and has not since been up said tract and that affiant and family have continuously resided upon and improved said tract and that Russell B. Candee has not in any way assisted affiant with improvements and cultivation of said tract since April 28th 1891.

Two men—Lincoln and William Shove—testified on her behalf that her residence was continuous, her husband did indeed desert her and her children, and her improvements were legitimately hers alone. Candee undeniably worked hard to improve her claim, which included a buggy shed, cave, frame barn, hen house, and log house worth approximately $350. Without the support of her neighbors and the leniency of the land agent, however, Candee easily could have missed the window to file and lost the claim (and her improvements) to another settler.[33]

In the other desertion case, Mary E. Steinman of Custer County found herself both the only adult on her claim and overwhelmingly supported by her community after her husband, William W. Gardner, died, probably in 1881. Left with the inherited homestead and four children to care for, she married Jacob Steinman in 1882. By 1883 Jacob had abandoned her, and thanks to her second marriage, Jacob's name was now on the claim as well. Steinman was alone again and further isolated in her own neighborhood as a result of her and Gardner's early settlement: "When I settled on the above described tract of land the country was new and settlers far between. And when I got ready to make proof I found that there was no settlers living in the neighborhood that had been living there for more than three years." Not to be stymied by two marriage failures, Steinman swore an affidavit at the land office on her own behalf: "For the last two years my husband . . . has deserted me and has not contributed to myself or family."[34]

In order to attain the necessary witnesses, she used people who did not know the full extent of her residence: Morgan S. Parks (a merchant in Arnold) and Asa S. Booton (a real estate agent in Gothenburg). Significantly, these two men both testified that she was "formerly" the wife of Jacob, and further testified to her status as "head of a family," shifting her claim status from Widow/Remarried/Abandoned to Head of Household in order to prevent him from returning to claim the property. In other words, her neighbors helped her accomplish a legal status that she would otherwise have been denied. Steinman's case demonstrates not only the power of community but also the necessity of it.[35]

The land transfer records reveal even more about the legal complexities of Steinman's claim. The GLO officially transferred patent to her in 1885. She sold the land on the same day to Theresa E. Wheeler. But Jacob did not officially relinquish his marital right to the land after he deserted his wife (though Steinman's witnesses would have argued otherwise). The land transfer records subsequently document a quitclaim deed for Jacob in 1890, which relinquished any claim he previously held. Despite the legal hoops Mary Steinman jumped through to retain right to her property (including alienability), her community advocated for her claim above that of her deserter husband.[36]

Establishing community among male neighbors played a clear role in securing land for women homesteaders, but the women also provided valuable services for the community in return. Women worked as housekeepers, seamstresses, and schoolteachers, and the homestead records suggest a deeper social interaction as well. Catherine Ross of Custer County proved up on her homestead claim in 1886 and subsequently deeded 2.5 acres of her land for the construction of a cemetery. She evidently felt sufficiently integrated into the community to make this investment in its longevity.

Women as Witnesses

Another revealing aspect of how women interacted with the official apparatus of homesteading is their role as witnesses. Out of 557 male claimants, only in two instances did men use women as witnesses. Women called upon other women as witnesses much

TABLE 6.4 Women's use of women as witnesses among 64 female claimants in study area

	Female claimants who listed female witnesses	Female claimants who used female witnesses	Total female claimants
Custer County	3 (9.4%)	1 (3.1%)	32
Dawes County	10 (31.3%)	6 (18.7%)	32
Total	13 (20.3%)	7 (10.9%)	64

TABLE 6.5 Men's use of women as witnesses among 557 male claimants in study area

	Male claimants who listed female witnesses	Male claimants who used female witnesses	Total male claimants
Custer County	6 (2.1%)	1 (0.3%)	292
Dawes County	4 (1.5%)	1 (0.4%)	265
Total	10 (1.8%)	2 (0.4%)	557

more frequently, at over ten times the rate of men, though even so, the majority of women used one female and one male witness to finalize the claim.

The GLO required individuals who intended to prove up to list and advertise in their Proof of Posting four potential witnesses who could testify that the entryman had met the residency and other requirements, and during proving up itself to choose two of them to actually provide testimony. In tables 6.4 and 6.5, we list all the cases where women and men listed and used female witnesses.

With little exception, women witnesses provided the same information in the same vernacular as male witnesses, leaving no discernible difference between male and female testimony. Part of this similarity results from the formulaic questions in GLO documents that left little room for personality in the answers. However, since there was virtually no difference between male and female testimony, whether to use a male or female witness would seem to have been decided by social norms, perhaps including what was publicly seen as "proper" versus "improper." Additionally, local land agents may have preferred male testimony over female testimony.

A small number of women used women as witnesses, but men almost never did. As tables 6.4 and 6.5 indicate, 13 of 64 (20.3 percent) female homesteaders in the study area listed women as their possible witnesses, and 7 (10.9 percent) actually called on women to testify. By contrast, only 10 of 557 (1.8 percent) male claimants in the study area listed women as potential witnesses, and 2 (0.4 percent) actually used women to testify. In short, women were rarely listed as possible witnesses, and even more rarely were they called to testify.

Dawes County contains the only instance in which women served as both of the witnesses. Josephine A. Lane asked Martha A. Bowdish and Ellen R. Abbott to testify on her behalf and used them rather than the two men listed in her Proof of Posting. While there is no discernible difference between the testimony of Bowdish and that of Abbott, they testified on behalf of Julius, Lane's husband who had died on April 19, 1891, before he could finalize his claim. As his widow, Lane, fifty-eight, inherited her husband's claim worth $1,500, including all the improvements.[37] The witnesses discussed "his" improvements for "his" family on "his" land. Rather than acknowledging the property as inherited by Lane, the women (presumably for the sake of the land agent) gave testimony for the deceased.

Lane, Bowdish, and Abbott are examples of the practice of women homesteaders in the study area calling upon their closest female acquaintances to testify on their behalf (fig. 6.7). In these situations, female claimants often bypassed geographically closer male neighbors in favor of their female friends who were clustered nearby. For example, Bowdish and Abbott testified for one another. They finalized their claims approximately three years apart, so these were not testimonies of convenience but rather of choice. Abbott had six male neighbors who had lived in the area at least as long as Bowdish, yet Abbott chose to use her friend over these male neighbors. Bowdish similarly preferred Abbott's testimony over

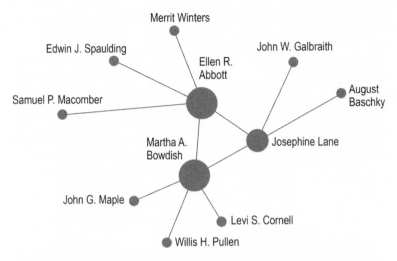

FIG. 6.7. Network of listed witnesses for Ellen R. Abbott, Josephine A. Lane, and Martha A. Bowdish.

that of her immediately adjacent male neighbors. Lane was the last of the three women to settle in the township, and despite the fact that her husband apparently maintained good relationships with their neighbors, Lane chose to use her two female friends.

In another instance, Amanda J. Plymate and her friend from an adjacent township, Harriet L. Mellinger, used each other as witnesses at the Alliance land office. They planned the finalization of their claims on the same day, presumably as a social event to commemorate a proud moment with a close friend. They also enlisted the testimony of a nonhomesteader, John Harrington. While Harrington's lack of a homestead record makes him difficult for us to track, he was likely the same J. J. Harrington who served as a prominent district judge, well known in the north central section of Nebraska. The women chose Harrington in advance probably because he was related by marriage to the Alliance land office receiver.[38]

Despite the bureaucratic standardization of witness testimony that forced relatively uniform witness statements, only 2 of the 557 men who proved up called on women to testify. Men *listed* women slightly more often, probably based on convenience: these

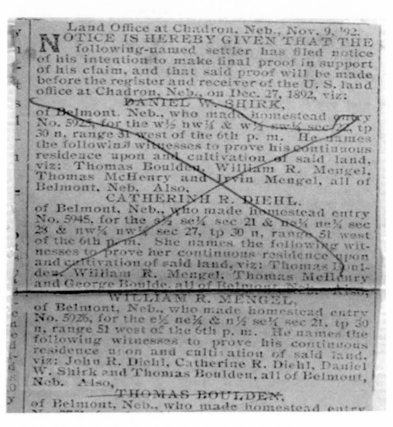

FIG. 6.8. Proof of Posting for Catherine R. Diehl and William R. Mengel. Courtesy Fold3.

women were their closest individual homesteader neighbors or the wife of a male neighbor they also called to testify. The day of the land office appointment, however, male claimants overwhelmingly chose men to testify. For example, William R. Mengel listed Cathrine R. Diehl as a witness to appear on December 27, 1892—the same day Diehl listed him as a witness for her claim (fig. 6.8). While Mengel testified for Diehl, he did not enlist her services as a witness, calling instead on another man. That is to say, Mengel and Diehl were evidently in the same office at the same time for the same purpose, yet Mengel did not use Diehl's testimony. Significantly, women also favored men as witnesses. For example, Amanda S. Wilson was twice listed as a witness, first for Joshua

Cavin and then for Melissa Emerson; both Cavin and Emerson opted for male witnesses instead.

In the two cases in which men in the study area used female witnesses, the testimonies are almost an exact match between the claimant's male and female witnesses. When Hazel Williams testified on behalf of Thomas Isaacs, however, one abnormality stands out. When asked, "Are you interested in this claim; and do you think the settler has acted in entire good faith in perfecting this entry?" Hazel answers, "No. We do." Elsworth Dutton, on the other hand, answers, "No. I do." Who is Hazel's communal we? Was she being prompted to answer the questions, or was she merely responding to the communal act of witnessing for a neighbor? Clerical error or not, the difference in pronoun seems revealing.

Whereas women as homesteaders represented an increasingly liberal federal policy and legal sphere, the use of women as witnesses in the claim process, even though rare, indicates social as well as legal change, spurred on *by* women *for* women. Women homesteaders— not just the 64 who claimed land in their own names but the 407 other women who were married to homesteaders—often formed the heart of social activity on the Great Plains, but they hardly occupied an equal place in the legal sphere. They rarely testified for individual homestead claimants, in part due to the restrictions the larger society placed on the legal activities of women. When they did testify, it was because women were carrying each other forward through camaraderie and friendship. Outside of mutual female support systems, cooperation and success were tied to women's ability to reciprocally join the rural economy through employment opportunities. Women pressed the bounds of their own economic, social, and legal limitations, with and sometimes without the help of their male counterparts. The women homesteaders in the study area also press the bounds of current homesteading scholarship, suggesting that widowed women may have more commonly taken advantage of a presumed single woman's law than previously thought.

7

Mapping Community Formation

Homesteaders created communities that provided for their needs, supported them in hard times, celebrated with them in good times, and sustained them emotionally. These communities played a key and unexpected role in how the homesteading process operated. Land-seeking Americans and immigrant homesteaders not only established towns across the plains but also created smaller places, variously called settlements, villages, townships, communities, or neighborhoods.

How did these smaller settlements function, and how did homesteaders go about establishing such communities? For some, shared nationality or ethnic identities shaped settlement. For example, in northeastern Custer County, a long, winding gravel road, Alps Road, snakes along sparsely forested hills, connecting the town of Comstock to the North Loup River eleven miles north; it hints of the lasting central European influence in the region. Only a couple of miles east of Alps Road, in Burwell, lies the Bohemian Brotherhood Cemetery. Elsewhere, in eastern Nebraska, the region's Czech immigrants found the rolling hills reminiscent of their central European homelands and named them the Bohemian Alps. Towns like Wilbur and Clarkson continue to hold annual parades and festivals commemorating their Czech heritage. Most homesteaders, however, did not settle in ethnic clusters, and they had to find other associations and means to create community.[1]

This chapter uses the study area data to map the dynamics of community formation to understand how communities came together and how their leaders emerged. Mapping reveals that some neighborhoods were formed on the basis of incidental, random settlement, while others, such as the central European immigrant communities, intentionally settled together and in that sense more consciously developed neighborhoods. Strong leaders emerged in nearly every community, usually based on longevity of residence, and they shouldered the majority of the civic duties required to create a social and economic infrastructure.[2]

Methods

We mapped geographically the legal descriptions of all 621 homestead claims in the study area using ArcGIS, and we created social networks of homesteaders based on the listed witnesses for each homestead claimant. Using witness lists does not map all social relationships—notably, women are poorly represented, given how rarely they witnessed—but it can nonetheless reveal important connections among leaders and among families. Legal descriptions identify each claimed parcel within the context of the U.S. Public Land Survey System (PLSS), providing a township, range, and section for the claim, as well as a specific description delineating the boundaries of the parcel within that section. The original act restricted claimants to a quarter section or its equivalent of 160 acres, and most homesteaders chose to claim the legal maximum. But the law did not require homesteaders to select a single quarter section; they could instead choose multiple smaller pieces of land that totaled 160 acres. For example, they could choose four adjacent quarters of quarter sections (40 acres each, 160 acres total), which might allow the homesteader to maximize his or her potential land value, for example by claiming land that ran along a river or creek.

The task of identifying individual homestead claims geographically was made more difficult because the GLO frequently used legal descriptions that only indicate which quarter section an entryman claimed (e.g., southwest quarter of section fifteen). Moreover, at the edges of townships, the GLO occasionally created irregular parcels that resulted in something other than 40-acre lots, which it simply numbered in ascending order, "Lot 1," "Lot 2," et cetera. This type of labeling provides no information to use in reconciling the lots with the contemporary PLSS, but fortunately original survey maps clearly indicate the location of the lots in relation to the townships. We obtained digital copies of original land survey maps, georeferenced them, and combined them with the written legal descriptions of each land claim in order to accurately locate and delineate the boundaries of all successful homestead claims.

Next we turned to the social connections among all of the homestead claimants, looking at the relationship between leaders and other members of their community; here we applied network analysis. Network theory is based on the premise that relationships forged among social actors are significant on both individual and local levels and that they shape the way in which a community forms or does not form. Within the context of Great Plains homesteading, network analysis reveals the important community leaders, and it identifies those who were socially distant from the community. Like geospatial mapping, it reveals group formation, except it is based on cultural, social, and legal affinity and network location rather than geography.

Relatively new to the humanities, network theory has never been applied in homesteading scholarship. Our analysis relies on two fundamental assumptions. First, the importance of individual homesteaders varies within the network; some homesteaders appear to be *keystone individuals*, central to the community's functioning, and others are *outliers*, weakly affiliated with the community. Second, homesteaders did not just move onto their 160 acres and remain isolated; rather, they interacted with their neighbors, kin, and others.

Our key innovation concerning data is that we harvest the information contained in witness lists that homesteaders submitted when they proved up. Each homesteader was required by the GLO to submit a list of four possible witnesses—two would actually testify and provide affidavits—in their Proofs of Posting. Digitization of the homestead records has made this kind of analysis achievable on a large scale, reducing our reliance on anec-

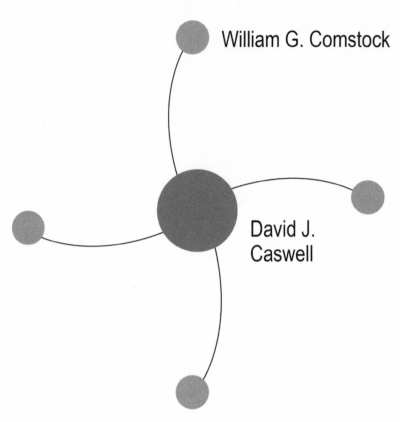

William G. Comstock

David J.
Caswell

FIG. 7.1. David J. Caswell's "out-degree" connections contained in his Proof of Posting in T18N, R17W, Custer County.

dotes. The Proof of Posting notice was a brief item printed in the newspaper containing the claimant's name, legal description of the land being claimed, and a list of four people who agreed to testify on the homesteader's behalf. We know a key fact about these four potential witnesses: they had an important social and legal connection to the entryman, sufficient for the entryman to trust them to testify to the validity of his or her claim. The posting thus identifies for us four confirmed and significant social and legal connections between each homestead claimant and his or her neighbors.

To create the networks, we used software called Gephi, in which we entered all four possible witnesses for each claimant. For exam-

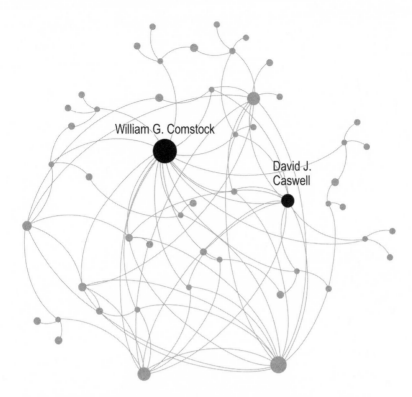

FIG. 7.2. David J. Caswell's direct and indirect connections contained in his Proof of Posting in Township T18N, R17W, Custer County.

ple, in figure 7.1, homesteader David J. Caswell is linked to his four listed witnesses; we call these connections his "out-degree" connections, because they map witnesses he called upon to testify for him. But of course Caswell himself also served as a witness for other claimants; those we term "in-degree" connections. To put this in another way, in- and out-degree connections are like phone calls; the incoming calls are people asking for the favor of witnessing, while the outgoing calls are the homesteader asking others for help. In-degree connections are the more useful metric for identifying community leaders because they identify someone's prominence in the network based on his or her frequency of being listed as a potential witness by would-be homesteaders.

In figure 7.1, Caswell appears to be the only connection among

FIG. 7.3. The entire network of listed witnesses for T18N, R17W, Custer County.

his witnesses; however, homesteaders and other locals witnessed for each other with great frequency, meaning that his witnesses had other connections that were indirect to Caswell. Figure 7.2 is a visualization of these connections as they build outward from Caswell. The network becomes much larger, and William Comstock emerges as the most prominent person in the network. Comstock, the cattle baron discussed in chapter 4 and later in this chapter, was listed as a witness for seventeen people, while Caswell was listed for eight. Replicating this process for the remainder of the township generates a vast network of homesteaders and their witnesses, seen in figure 7.3, which shows all the connections for the entire township and represents lives interwoven both directly and indirectly through the Homestead Act.

To identify keystone individuals, we selected the three persons in each township with the highest in-degree connections, including any third-place ties.[3] Out of 621 homesteaders in the study area, this process identified 33 keystone individuals. No townships shared keystone individuals.[4] Leaders stayed local, tied to their land and their community much as the Homestead Act intended. Identifying keystone individuals provides us a portal through which to begin qualitative investigation into the lives of crucial leaders and ask more pointed qualitative questions.

We recognize that using the homesteading Proof of Posting witnesses does not capture all of the important relationships within a community. Nonhomesteaders such as bankers, barbers, doctors, merchants, midwives, postmasters, teachers, and tavern owners also could have had multiple connections and exercised power within the community. To the extent that they were called upon to be listed as witnesses, they appear in our networks. But if they appeared less commonly in the lists of witnesses than their full role in the community would merit, they would be underrepresented in the network. Even more limiting is the fact that as we saw in chapter 6, women were rarely listed as witnesses, and so our analysis identifies no women as keystone individuals. Given the extensive recent scholarship on female homesteaders, including women married to male homesteaders, and on women's significant role in establishing communities, their exclusion here is a serious limitation. Despite these gaps, Proofs of Posting yield important insights into the networks that linked homesteaders to their nearby communities.

Neighborhood Formation

For many Great Plains homesteaders, the absence of nearby established towns often made purchasing goods and services difficult. As a result, homesteaders typically required extensive cooperation from their neighbors to succeed, and so they formed close-knit communities characterized by significant borrowing of implements,

Number of entries

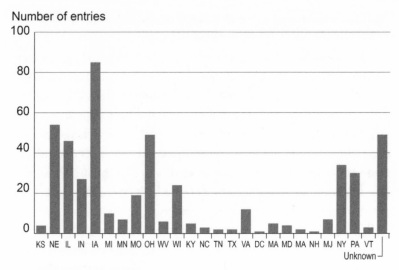

Note: Includes natural-born claimants and immigrant claimants
naturalized prior to filing of initial claim

FIG. 7.4. Number of citizen homesteaders in study area by state of origin.

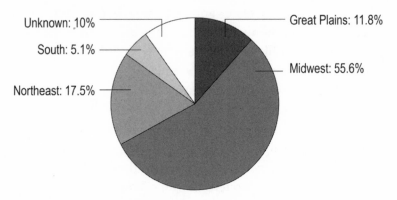

Note: Includes natural-born claimants and immigrant
claimants naturalized prior to filing of initial claim

FIG. 7.5. Region of origin for citizen homesteaders in study area.

exchanging of labor, and other trading and sharing. Revealing
these networks by traditional methods (e.g., by trying to connect
people with similar names) often fails in neighborhoods that
were formed through incidental settlement, because such neighborhoods were mostly populated by people with no biological,

cultural, or region-of-origin relationships. Using witnesses from Proofs of Posting is thus a superior method because it allows us to identify those connections.

To start, we should note that most homesteaders in our study area came from other regions of the United States (figs. 7.4 and 7.5). At the time of their initial claims, 79.1 percent were either native-born citizens or immigrants who had already achieved citizenship, and 20.9 percent were nonnaturalized immigrants. The overwhelming majority (66.2 percent) of the U.S. citizens were from the Midwest or Great Plains, 17.5 percent migrated from the Northeast, and only 5.1 percent came from the South (fig. 7.5). There were no identifiable non-European immigrants in the study area.

Homesteaders coming from other parts of the United States formed incidental, not intentional, communities, at least as far as our data reveal. If, for example, they settled in groups based on common membership in a church congregation or extended families, those patterns would not appear in our data. But to judge from county histories, personal accounts, and biographies, most homesteaders migrated as individuals or in family groups unconnected to larger affiliations and found themselves living near unrelated neighbors. For instance, Amos W. Young of T19N, R21W, Custer County, settled adjacent to Perry Coffman. They were from different states and had no known relationship. Yet when Young proved up in 1893, he listed his neighbor, Coffman, as a witness, demonstrating the typical incidental formation of nonimmigrant communities.

These individuals most likely drew upon public sources of information such as newspaper accounts, land company advertisements, and state publications, as well as informal sources including word of mouth. Often the *land locator* was a key player; he or she was a highly knowledgeable local resident who knew about what parcels remained available and their desirability, including soil quality, access to water, and distance to market. For a fee, the land locator (like a modern real estate agent) showed new arrivals available tracts; the new entrymen then chose their sites. Jules Sandoz, for example, whose biography is recounted in Mari Sandoz's *Old Jules*, worked as a land locator among many other pursuits in Sheridan

County, Nebraska, adjacent to Dawes County. Jules located many families of diverse backgrounds in the region.

We can identify from among all claimants those who were immigrants because of the Homestead Act's citizenship requirements. Immigrants could file initial claims so long as they declared their intent to become U.S. citizens. To implement this rule, the GLO required homesteaders to renounce allegiance to their nation of origin as part of the paperwork, which for our purposes provides the data needed to track nationality. We constructed maps based on nation of origin to examine community clusters and the development of ethnic communities. Ethnicity and nation of origin, however, were sometimes tricky attributes. For example, many central European immigrants identified themselves as Bohemians or Moravians, even though their citizenship would have been in the Austro-Hungarian Empire. Similarly, many immigrants from Ireland identified themselves as Irish, even though they would have been subjects of the British Crown. For this reason, we use the immigrants' self-stated nationality (table 7.1), producing categories that are a mixture of nations and regions, in the analysis that follows.

With the shifting boundaries of European nations and empires during Nebraska's homesteading period, we find it more useful to place these immigrants in regions rather than in individual nations. In figure 7.6, we group immigrants into three broad categories: central Europeans (from Austria itself, Bohemia, Germany, Moravia, Prussia, and Switzerland), western Europeans (from Belgium, England, France, Holland, Ireland, and Scotland), and Scandinavian settlers (Denmark and Sweden). We also show homesteaders from other parts of the United States and Canada, and some homesteaders' origins were unstated. Central Europeans comprised 9.7 percent of claimants in the study area, making them the most dominant foreign settler group, while western Europeans accounted for 5.5 percent and Scandinavians just 2.4 percent of all claimants.

We found two distinct settlement patterns among immigrant homesteaders: central Europeans tended to separate themselves

TABLE 7.1. Self-declared nation of origin for immigrant homesteaders

Nation of origin	Number of claimants	Percentage of all immigrant claimants
Austria	28	21.5
Belgium	2	1.5
Bohemia	6	4.6
Canada	2	1.5
Denmark	2	1.5
England / Great Britain	23	17.7
France	2	1.5
Germany	19	14.6
Holland	2	1.5
Ireland	4	3.1
Moravia	1	0.8
Poland	1	0.8
Prussia	4	3.1
Scotland	1	0.8
Sweden	13	10.0
Switzerland	1	0.8
Unknown	19	14.6
Total	130	100

into clustered communities, whereas other immigrant homesteaders and native-born Americans tended to integrate into mixed-origin neighborhoods. One explanation is relative numbers: being more numerous, central Europeans successfully created communities and networks based on their common region of origin (and perhaps language familiarity), which did not require them to interact as much with communities outside their own. In contrast, immigrants who did not arrive in such large numbers fil-

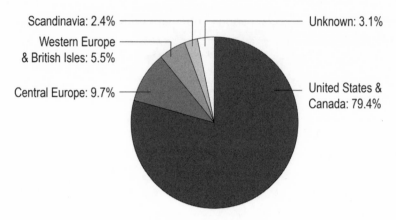

Scandinavia: 2.4%

Western Europe & British Isles: 5.5%

Central Europe: 9.7%

Unknown: 3.1%

United States & Canada: 79.4%

FIG. 7.6. Region of origin for immigrant claimants as a percentage of all homesteaders in study area.

tered into mixed communities, and their locational choices more closely mirrored the behavior of nonimmigrant homesteaders. The clustering of central European immigrants has been well established by Great Plains historians. For example, Betty A. Berglund and Lori Ann Lahlum in *Norwegian American Women* found similar segregation patterns among Norwegian immigrants in Wisconsin, Iowa, Minnesota, and other parts of the West. Karen V. Hansen examined the formation of Scandinavian settlements around Spirit Lake in North Dakota. Our investigation explores how immigrant communities in our study area interacted with local American citizens.[5]

An example of ethnic clustering is T20N, R17W in Custer County, home to the largest central European population in the study area, including eight distinct community groups, of which two are entirely central European. Our network analysis identified Frank Kolousek, an immigrant from Austria, as the most important community leader in the township based on his in-degree connections. His network included fourteen other people, eleven of whom were fellow central European immigrant homesteaders, and the remaining three, while not homesteaders, had central European surnames and spellings. In the same township, Josef Krbel's network similarly extended to eleven people, eight of whom were fellow central European immigrant homesteaders and the remaining three were relatives of homesteaders or had central European surnames. Notably, neither community leader had direct witnessing ties to any nonimmigrant residents, indicating that they were separated socially and for legal business from other residents.

Because they came in such large numbers, central Europeans had less need to integrate with their non-central European neighbors. They constituted the only high-concentration settlement cluster in the study area.[6] Immigrants from Austria, Bohemia, Moravia, and Poland claimed 5,080 acres in Custer County T20N, R17W, or 37.1 percent of all the homesteaded land in the township. Twenty-five claimants listed Austria as their nation of origin, accounting for 89.2 percent of the Austrian homesteaders in the study area. Six other homesteaders listed Bohemia as their nation of origin. With the exception of a few properties claimed by existing American citizens, the Austrians and Bohemians eventually filed homestead claims on the remaining southeast half of the township (fig. 7.7). This settlement of central Europeans in T20N, R17W was swift and purposeful: the first four Austrians filed initial claims by 1887, and within ten years, another nineteen central European homesteaders claimed land nearby. Over the decade 69.7 percent of all central European homesteaders filed claims in the township.

The records do not tell us how later immigrants learned about the earliest homesteaders so they could file claims nearby, but it likely was similar to patterns of ethnic settlement observed elsewhere. Communication probably came as a mixture of word of mouth and other informal communications as well as advertisements and advice from land agents and locators. Since the township's claimants came from all over central Europe and not, for example, from just a few villages, the main attractions to filing here were likely common language and religion. Although Bohemia is currently located in the Czech Republic (now officially a Czech-speaking region), German-speaking people traditionally populated many parts of the country and even non-German speakers probably had some familiarity with German. The Works Progress Administration in the 1930s described the nearby town of Sargent, Nebraska—

not included in our study area—as a "Bohemian and Polish" town, founded just a couple of years before the first homesteaders in the study area filed their claims in the adjacent township.[7] Notably, Alps Road traverses some of the land originally settled by these Austrians in the eastern half of the township (fig. 7.7).

Unlike the central Europeans, other immigrant groups in the study area did not settle in the same volume and thus could not feasibly cluster themselves in distinct communities; these immigrants needed to integrate to succeed. For example, the first Dutch and Belgian settlers began filing claims in August 1890, when Nellie Vosbeek and Godfried Hendricks, Dutch immigrants, applied for their claims in T32N, R50W of Dawes County. They were among the first twenty settlers in the township, and the two chose to claim land on opposite sides of a timber-laden gulch, less than 1,500 feet away from each other. By the following August, Belgian immigrant Cornelius Thissen applied for the land immediately adjacent to Hendricks's. John B. Limpach, also Belgian, soon after applied for a parcel of land that ran along the eastern boundary of both Thissen and Hendricks's claims. Though nearly half of the township's final homesteaded lands were still available at the time, this small group of claimants from neighboring countries in Europe applied for adjacent lands, carving for themselves a square mile of adjoining property in Dawes County (fig. 7.8).

Vosbeek died before she could finalize her claim. Although her neighbor, Jacob Shink, inherited her claim, it was Hendricks who administered her estate. We cannot know for sure why these claimants settled near each other, since the township still had plenty of other land available, but it seems likely that they purposefully chose to settle near each other. They were the only Dutch and Belgian nationals in the study area. Their witnessing patterns were different from central European claimants: while they mutually witnessed for one another, they also witnessed for and called upon their nonimmigrant neighbors. They needed to expand their network beyond their common European compatriots to survive on their new lands.

British or Irish immigrants apparently made little effort to home-

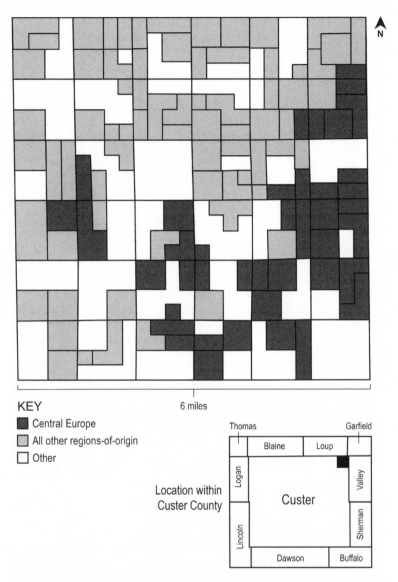

KEY   6 miles

■ Central Europe
▨ All other regions-of-origin
□ Other

Location within
Custer County

Thomas   Garfield

| Blaine | Loup |

Logan

Custer

Valley

Lincoln

Sherman

Dawson   Buffalo

FIG. 7.7. Clustering of homestead claims by central European immigrants in T20N, R17W, Custer County, by the time at which all entries were finalized.

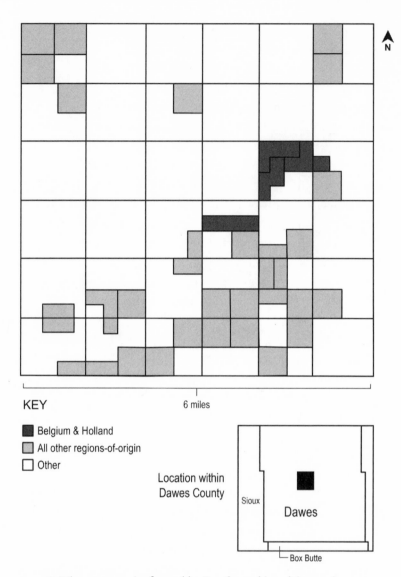

KEY   6 miles

■ Belgium & Holland
▨ All other regions-of-origin
□ Other

Location within
Dawes County

Sioux

Dawes

Box Butte

FIG. 7.8. Microcommunity formed by Dutch-speaking claimants in T32N, R50W, Dawes County, April 1892.

stead near each other (fig. 7.9). Only one cluster developed, in T19N, R21W in Custer County, where eight homesteaders from the British Isles filed nearby claims. For most, the fact that they were native English speakers meant that they did not have the same barriers to integration as the central Europeans or Dutch. And the Irish, having identified themselves as such, were consciously choosing Irish ancestry rather than citizenship under the British monarchy. They rarely drew upon each other as witnesses with the exception of Catharine Jackson and Thomas Loughran, adjacent neighbors. Unlike the central Europeans, these immigrants tended to forge community with whomever their incidental neighbors turned out to be, instead of with their home-country brethren. With the exception of concentrated clusters like the central European population, immigrant homesteaders in our study area generally did not separate themselves from the larger community.

Communities of nonimmigrant homesteaders in our study area emerged incidentally rather than along ethnic or cultural lines. The data reveal an average of eight or nine distinct yet intersecting communities in each township. Only the central Europeans in T20N, R17W formed separate communities of witnesses, but other settlers apparently perceived themselves to be in spatial communities, many claiming residence in "neighborhoods" centered in nearby towns such as New Helena in Custer County or Crawford in Dawes County. The constant among all neighborhoods and settlements, immigrant or not, was the need for homesteaders to find support from their neighbors, whoever those neighbors were.[8]

Neighborhood Leaders

We identified thirty-three keystone individuals based upon their in-degree connections and targeted them for deeper qualitative analysis. With only one exception, the keystone individuals were among the first non-Indian settlers in their respective townships. They began arriving between the 1870s and 1890s, occasionally even ahead of the GLO surveyors. As the longest-residing homesteaders and thus having the most opportunity to get to know their neighbors and the land office requirements, they were natu-

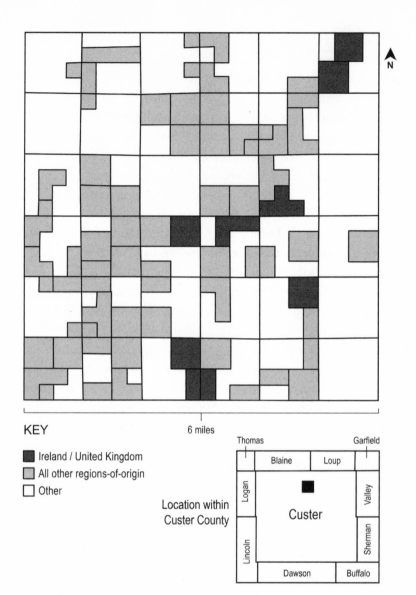

KEY

6 miles

■ Ireland / United Kingdom
▨ All other regions-of-origin
□ Other

Location within
Custer County

Thomas — Garfield

	Blaine	Loup	
Logan	Custer		Valley
Lincoln			Sherman
	Dawson	Buffalo	

FIG. 7.9. Scattered homestead claims by British and Irish immigrants in T19N, R21W, Custer County, by the time at which all entries were finalized.

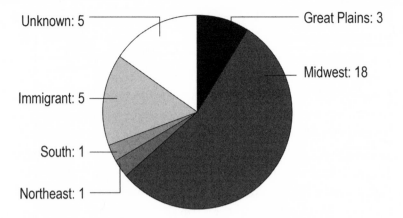

FIG. 7.10. Region of origin for keystone individuals in study area.

ral candidates for recent homesteaders to choose when they drew up their lists of witnesses. Keystone individuals had a median of eight homesteaders who listed them as witnesses, and one-third of them were listed as witnesses for ten or more homesteaders.

The median age of keystone individuals was thirty-three, and 72.7 percent of them were married when they settled their land. Only five of the thirty-three (15.2 percent) were immigrants—from Austria, France, Sweden, and Denmark—and all were located in Custer County. The rest came from various parts of the United States (fig. 7.10). Once settled, they typically remained on their land: 44.8 percent maintained their land ownership for over twenty years, with the median length sixteen years.

Only one keystone individual, John W. Mathews of Custer County, sold his land within one month of finalizing his claim, thus placing him in our "suspicious" category for possible fraud. However, as we discussed in chapter 4, his homesteading circumstances are murky, and sale of his claim could plausibly be classified as due to hardship, although we chose to categorize his claim as fraudulent. His relative, Charles R. Mathews, was another keystone individual who homesteaded in the adjacent township, T19N, R21W; Charles remained on his land for twenty-three years. No other keystone individuals sold their claims within one year. Two sold their land within two years, but these men did not relinquish their land easily—the land transfer records reveal that they mortgaged their property at least once in an attempt to stay in their new homes. They were community leaders, not fraudulent speculators.

No distinct patterns emerge from the spatial distribution of keystone individuals in each township. We hypothesized that community leaders might spread out among the neighborhoods, as evidenced by the number of times they were listed as a witness in distinct neighborhoods. However, this was not the case: community leaders were equally likely to settle in clusters, and their importance was apparently linked to their longevity in the neighborhood. In other words, they sought community when they first arrived in the sparsely populated plains like many future homesteaders did and settled near each other to draw support and improve their chances of success.

Community leaders, as integral parts of the homesteading process in Custer and Dawes Counties, aided their neighbors in the legal act of homesteading, but they also were involved on a civic level. For example, many had a hand in creating the school districts for their townships. Andrew Sommer of Custer County helped organize his school district in 1882 and served as its treasurer during the early years. Willis H. Pullen similarly served as school treasurer in the Crawford neighborhood in Dawes County; though mostly a farmer and rancher, Pullen also helped establish Crawford as a town. Thomas J. Wilson of Dawes County served as school superintendent and preacher for a number of years. Keystone individuals followed other occupations and vocations important to their communities, including carpenter, census taker, constable, judge, justice of the peace, merchant, minister, postmaster, road overseer, and sheriff. These men were not just invested in the land; they were invested in the infrastructure of their neighborhoods, townships, and counties, making the area more appealing to future settlers and their families.[9]

Keystone individuals were typically successful landholders as well, and their civic and social prominence may have derived from and in turn aided their landholding success. Some, however, had to mortgage their land at various times to finance their farming or expand their land holdings. Being a successful home-steader in western Nebraska usually meant finding ways to add to the 160 acres available under the act, as quarter sections simply did not provide enough income. Most successful community leaders bought additional acreage. For instance, local historians remembered Olof Sateren "as a citizen of integrity and worth and a man of industrious and energetic character this gentleman is well known to the people of Dawes County." Indeed, Sateren, a native Minnesotan and clearly of Scandinavian stock, eventually built up his holdings to over 800 acres. Wilson, the Dawes County superintendent and preacher, also purchased an additional 420 acres before selling his land in 1909 and moving into town. Sommer, a French immigrant, served as justice of the peace and helped establish a military post in Merna in 1887. The county history noted, "He has not been remiss in any duty as a citizen and has contributed liberally in time and money to those enterprises which have had to do with the upbuilding of the county." Sommer managed to acquire 1,000 acres by 1920, all within a two-mile radius of his original homestead. "Coming to Custer County without capital," the biographers continued, "success has come to him through his own efforts and it has been justly deserved, placing him among the prominent old settlers of the county."[10]

Purchase of adjacent lands by successful landowners typically came at the expense of a discouraged, injured, widowed, or failed homesteader. While the transaction often meant the end of a home-steader's dream, the purchase sometimes kept the seller afloat, for example, by providing him or her with funds to move to town or start a new life. Such was the case for Ellen R. Abbott, who was widowed and soon thereafter sold her claim worth $890 because, unable to do the upkeep on her farm, she wanted to sell out before her place's improvements fell into disrepair and the property lost value. And while the seller's homestead dream ended, the sale often meant salvation for the purchaser. Buyers benefited because they were able to expand their ranching and farming operations to a more viable scale. In this way, homesteaders created their own economic infrastructure of cooperation and purchase.

Civic responsibility did not always equate to homesteading success, however, and not all keystone individuals were as lucky as Sommer. While some men could afford to expand their holdings, others lost their lands to the county or bank after failing to pay their taxes or mortgage. For example, Charles P. Foote arrived in Custer County before there was even a town and preempted a claim. He turned it into a homestead claim and received patent in 1885. He served as the local sheriff and cofounded the military post in Merna with Sommer.[11] Yet he was forced to mortgage his land six times in the seven years after receiving patent, ultimately losing his land to the county in 1893. Fundamental to the growth and development of his township, Foote's status as an old settler and outstanding community leader did not protect him from the hardships of homesteading.

Though the actual experiences of the keystone individuals varied, the fact that they settled early gave them the opportunity to be founders of their counties. Community leaders in our study area appear to have advanced "the cause of progress," as one biography explained, regardless of their ability or inability to maintain their original homestead claims.[12] They were the core of the local homesteading system as they spent the most time in the local land offices testifying on behalf of their fellow neighbors. Wittingly or not, they formed the heart of community infrastructure on the plains when no other existed. Of course, they also had the most opportunity to commit fraud. Our deeper investigation of each keystone individual, however, suggests that only one, John Mathews—discussed above, whose case is not clear—committed acts suggesting homestead fraud; rather, they spearheaded many of the civic activities in the region.

William Comstock

In a few cases, community leaders were themselves cattle barons, the most important case in our study area being William G. Comstock of T18N, R17W, Custer County. As noted in chapter 4, Comstock was listed as a witness for seventeen homesteaders, the most of anyone in the study area, making him a prime target for further

FIG. 7.11. Capt. and Mrs. William G. Comstock in front of their log house near Westcott in Custer County, Nebraska, ca. 1887. RG2608 PH O 1227. Courtesy Nebraska State Historical Society.

investigation. Comstock was a Civil War veteran who settled on a quarter section, probably in 1874; he was not a homesteader, as he filed no claim. When he settled, he had "very few white neighbors at that time," and Wescott, the closest town, was only established in 1881. Comstock served as the first postmaster in the county, ran a hardware and implement business out of Wescott, served as justice of the peace, and helped organize the school district, like many other community leaders. He also was the local agent for Lincoln Land Company, the company that platted the town of Comstock in 1899. His town effectively put Wescott out of business.[13]

Comstock is mainly known today as the bonanza rancher who partnered with Bartlett Richards to form the enormous Spade Ranch and became infamous for abusing the public domain. Comstock and Richards were prominent figures in the late nineteenth-century struggles over whether public lands would be available for big ranchers or would instead be opened to homesteaders (including Kinkaiders). Initially the big ranchers simply turned their cattle out onto the open range without any authorization, but around the turn of the twentieth century their actions were met with growing protests, and they came under increasing scrutiny. In response, they attempted to obtain federal legislation either authorizing them to use public land or permitting them to lease it; they failed.

Comstock and Richards fenced large tracts of the public domain anyway, and they were indicted for their actions. In 1905 they pleaded guilty to illegally fencing 212,000 acres of public land; they were fined $300 and imprisoned for six hours, a sentence they served—in hardship, we imagine—at the Omaha Club. Interior Secretary Ethan Hitchcock expressed his outrage at the paltry sentence, and President Theodore Roosevelt, frustrated with the tepid prosecution of bonanza ranchers who enclosed public lands, fired both the Nebraska district attorney and the local U.S. marshal. In 1906 the government brought new charges against Comstock and Richards, alleging that they and eight other men conspired to defraud the government out of land by using sixty-three men and women to make fraudulent or otherwise illegal claims under the Kinkaid Act. The success of these prosecutions, including one-year jail sentences, broke the spirits of both Comstock and Richards and resulted in the eventual demise of the Spade Ranch.[14]

Despite Comstock's convictions in 1905 and 1906, however, there is no evidence that he committed fraud under the Homestead Act or in our study area, including specifically with the seventeen homesteaders for whom he was listed as a witness. As noted in chapter 4, none of the seventeen claimants had transferred their homesteads to Comstock (or anyone else) a full year after receiving patents. Comstock had a positive local reputation, albeit a negative national one. As Sandoz described him in *Old Jules,* "Unlike John and Herman Krause [other convicted bonanza ranchers], down near the Burlington, [Comstock was] not found guilty of intimidating settlers," perhaps explaining the glowing record of his service in the local histories.[15] However one views his later actions—and it's hard to see them as anything other than a fraudulent and self-aggrandizing land grab—he did not commit homesteading fraud with the claimants in our study area.

Outliers

As we have discussed, prominent community leaders stand out in the networks through their vast array of connections. What about outliers, or homesteaders who were not connected to the network at all? Outliers are interesting to us because the act, by requiring affidavits from disinterested witnesses testifying that the claimant had met the act's requirements, depended on local relationships as enforcement against fraud. The idea was that fraudulent claimants and bona fide settlers could not coexist. But outliers challenge this assumption, and so they merit further scrutiny. Given that virtually all homesteaders periodically depended on neighbors for assistance as well as for witnesses, being unconnected was atypical behavior. Out of 621 entrymen, only nine claimants appear unrelated to the larger network, having no interconnected witnesses.

Examining the individual homestead and land transfer records of outliers reveals some explanations for why the outliers were not connected. Hardship played a role, but the biggest factor was that our outliers tended to have connections to individuals in abutting townships or counties outside our study area, relationships that would, of course, go undetected by our methodology. In Custer County, for example, three of the four outlier claimants remained on their land post-patent for five years or longer; only David A. Cramer immediately sold his land, thereby flagging his claim as "suspicious" for us. But one of his witnesses, Larkin D. Savage, is actually a keystone individual in the adjacent township. And the individual to whom Cramer sold his land was his neighbor, James Butler, who retained ownership for an additional fourteen years. Cramer's profession after selling his land is unclear, but he remained in the neighborhood and lived in Broken Bow until he died from a hip injury in 1934. Cramer seems disconnected from the local network, but further analysis suggests ties to the community not immediately revealed in the witness network. Similarly Custer County outlier Charles S. Francis was among the earliest in the region. At the time of final proof in 1891, his closest neighbor in the township lived over two miles away. Instead of drawing from witnesses within his own township, he opted for closer witnesses in the adjacent township.[16]

In Dawes County, all five outlier claimants had ties to homesteaders in adjacent townships, although three of these claimants sold their land within one year of receiving patent. However, the individual records reflect a deeper story of hardship. John E. Davidson, for example, sold his claim immediately after receiving patent in 1893, but he did not leave the area. In 1900 he bought land from a previous neighbor near his original homestead and maintained ownership of it until 1904. In 1905 he bought a half-section along another nearby tract, which he mortgaged twice and only kept for five years. Davidson's success in finalizing his homestead claim did not necessarily mean that he succeeded as a rancher or farmer, nor did the sale of land indicate that he tucked tail and left Dawes County. He strove to be a successful landowner, but failed three times. Although it appears outliers had few community ties, in fact they were connected to individuals outside the study area.[17]

By merging geographical and historical methods, we have reconstituted homestead communities in our study area both spatially and socially. In the process we revealed some of the dynamics of homesteader migration—whether from Boston or Bohemia—and ethnic settlements; we also identified community leaders, keystone individuals who helped build neighborhoods and communities. Our analysis has found that the majority were American citizens migrating to the study area, mixing with claimants of diverse backgrounds to settle these spaces and form communities under the watchful eyes of well-connected local leaders. Immigrants from Sweden or England or France likewise staked claims alongside citizens who came from Chicago or New York or Cincinnati, integrating into the social order of their new region. Immigrants from central Europe settled near each other, generated their own community leaders, and created cultural landscapes reminiscent of their homelands.

Community Enforcement

Why does community formation matter for the homesteading story? Community scrutiny and keystone individuals were powerful mechanisms for enforcing the requirements of the Homestead Act. The act embodied a dream, the vision of many "actual settlers" occupying and prospering on the enormous public domain. Homesteaders were to be a property-owning class, a middle class of yeoman farmers who would not only feed the emerging industrial economy but serve as a new foundation for American democracy. This was a different vision from those which had motivated the disposal of so much public land—the public domain had been seen first as an endless reserve to be sold off to finance the central government, then as a plentiful kitty available to fund canals, build agricultural colleges, and reward soldiers' service, then as a lowly regarded disposable asset to be carelessly traded away to stimulate railroad building. All of these uses contained little vision for what should happen *on* the public lands, only the idea that they were a cheap and easy way to pay for *other purposes* deemed worthy, without having to levy taxes. The Homestead Act was different, because it carried a vision of the new society to be built on the public domain. But it contained a huge problem: how to enforce its provisions?

Nominally, the GLO was the federal government's enforcement arm. But the public domain was vast, the number of individuals willing to steal public lands seemingly large, and Congress was unwilling to fund more than a skeleton force of GLO land office registers and receivers. In these circumstances the theft of enormous tracts of public land seemed inevitable. What changed the balance was community enforcement. The act required the claimant to "prove by two credible witnesses that he, she, or they have resided upon or cultivated the same for the term of five years immediately succeeding the time of filing the affidavit aforesaid, and shall make affidavit that no part of said land has been alienated, and that he has borne true allegiance to the Government of the United States." It is unclear whether either Congress or initially the GLO understood the powerful enforcement potential in this requirement; most scholars certainly have not.

Beginning in 1878, however, Congress and the GLO began systematically putting in place a set of laws and regulations to capitalize on the power of community enforcement. That year Congress passed "An Act to provide for the publication of notices of contest" and, as the subsequent GLO 1878 circular made clear, anyone who contested a homestead, preemption, or timber culture claim on the grounds of abandonment was required to publish notice of his or her contest in a local newspaper.

This rule was double-edged: the GLO hoped both to use community vigilance to identify original entries that had been fraudulent and also to mobilize community pressure to minimize fraudulent contestations. Requiring newspaper notices was a first step to making land office transactions transparent. They were already public records, but the public could not easily get access to them or comprehend them, especially before a transaction was completed; thus access came too late to intervene. Requiring publication of a notice allowed members of the public to learn about a proposed transaction before it happened. In 1879 Congress passed a law requiring that entrymen, when making final proofs on their homestead or preemption claims, also publish notice of their intent to finalize their claims, which notice was to appear for five consecutive weeks in a local newspaper. To implement this law, the GLO in its 1879 circular then specified that entrymen must place their notice in the newspaper of the county in which the homesteader resided or, if that area was not yet organized into a county, in the newspaper of the nearest organized county.

In 1880 Congress passed "An Act for the relief of settlers on public land," further regulating relinquishments, as the final piece of legislation needed to develop the system of community enforcement. Unearthing fraud no longer relied only or perhaps even primarily on the personnel and resources of the GLO. The government viewed this shift in policy as so crucial that in 1883 Acting Secretary of the Interior M. L. Joslyn wrote to GLO Commissioner N. C. McFarland "that Congress in various ways invited and encouraged persons to inform against those who are endeavoring to acquire title to the public land fraudulently or illegally, as the only adequate means of protecting the United States." The government protected its interest in giving land to bona fide settlers by placing the responsibility for fraud enforcement on the local community.[18]

We do not wish to romanticize small homesteader communities. They could be riven by jealousies and bitterness as well as marked by solidarity and cooperation. Our point is different: whether they were united in purpose or divided by faction, they provided close scrutiny for how the land laws operated. Self-interest driven by enmity worked as well as public-spiritedness motivated by neighborly solidarity. Local scrutiny would eliminate fraudulent claims by people who were not "actual settlers," either because locals would be unwilling to support illicit claimants with perjured testimony or because they would challenge such claims in contestations. In practice, given the scant investigative manpower available in local land offices, community enforcement became the public's chief protection.

Indeed, the very case that caused Acting Commissioner Joslyn to instruct Commissioner McFarland on the usefulness of community enforcement demonstrates how immediate and helpful it could be. John Brown filed a homestead claim at Larned, Kansas, in Pawnee County, on June 7, 1880. On December 22, 1882, Annie M. Moses initiated contest against it, alleging that Brown failed to cultivate his claim in 1880 and plant in 1881 and 1882. Moses's contest was denied because Brown was not required to cultivate in 1880 and his first year for planting didn't expire until June 7, 1883, which was after Moses had filed her contest. Prior to the decision on Moses's contest, however, Sylvester Brown had also filed a contest to John Brown's claim, which the local land agent had denied because Moses's contest was still in process.

On Sylvester Brown's appeal, Joslyn reversed the denial of Sylvester's contest, on the grounds that Moses's contest "was void on its face" and therefore Sylvester's contest should have been allowed to go forward. But Joslyn then appended this remark-able observation:

> I direct your attention to the fact that it is a Brown who contests Brown's entry, and that the same attorney appears for both Browns. These Browns are perhaps relatives, and it is not an uncommon practice for delinquent entrymen to forestall a bona fide contest by a collusive one, in which it is never intended to produce sufficient evidence to procure the entry's cancellation. I am not satisfied that such is the case here, else I would take summary action [i.e., immediately cancel John's claim] upon it. But in view of its possibility, I think it proper to protect the interests of the Government in this instance. You will, therefore, please notify the local officers that the second affidavit of contest filed by Annie E. Moses [filed after the expiration of John's obligation to plant] shall remain on file . . . until the final determination of the contest between Brown and Brown. If Brown v. Brown is decided in favor of the defendant [John], then Annie E. Moses may have the preference right of contest against him.[19]

John Brown left the area and filed instead on a homestead up in Cheyenne County in the northwest corner of Kansas, proving up in 1894; Sylvester Brown claimed a homestead in Barton County, filing his claim in Larned in 1883; and Annie Moses, also filing her papers in the Larned land office, claimed a homestead in Stafford County in 1890.

Focusing only on official acts of enforcement by government agents misses the community aspect of the act's operation. Newly opened homestead lands filled up fairly quickly, with communities forming and keystone leaders emerging. Community provided a mechanism by which fraudulent claims were kept in check and by which overworked and understaffed land offices could police their region. Sometimes attempted fraud required investigation by the GLO's small staff of professional investigators; sometimes neighbors filed formal contestations; sometimes others—the U.S. attorney general, in the bold defrauding attempt by William Comstock and Richard Bartlett—intervened.

But alongside these formal enforcement systems lay a more

informal system of community enforcement, which provided more pervasive, continuous, and effective scrutiny. It could only operate in a context where functioning local communities with recognized keystone leaders existed. In Custer and Dawes Counties, as we have seen, homesteading encouraged the emergence of just such community infrastructure.

8

Envisioning a New History of Homesteading

We started with the homesteaders Daniel Freeman and Isabel Proctor and the puzzle that, while the public continues to cherish homesteading's place in American history, a generation or more of historians have largely ignored homesteading and, when they do consider it, find it to have been a failure and corrupt. The popular perception perhaps reflects family stories among tens of millions of Americans whose ancestors, like Freeman and Proctor, participated in the homesteading adventure. It may also reflect the ways we form shared memories, from literature like Cather's *My Ántonia* and Sandoz's *Old Jules*, to popular TV shows like the one based on Laura Ingalls Wilder's *Little House on the Prairie*, to films like *Northern Lights* and *Heartland*, to Solomon Butcher's evocative photographs of homesteader families. This homesteading narrative continues to have great power. In 2016 the *New York Times* needed an image to illustrate its story about how today's Americans are less willing to be mobile, so they chose a photograph of homesteaders for their story, "A Dearth of Pioneers."[1]

Scholars by contrast have developed a strikingly different narrative. In the stylized facts that characterize their telling, (a) homesteading was a minor factor in farm formation and most farmers purchased their land; (b) most homesteaders failed to prove up their claims; (c) the homesteading process was rife with corruption; and (d) homesteading caused Indian land dispossession. Taking these points together, they say, means that we can largely forget the whole humbug image about homesteading that the public accepts.

We have tested the stylized facts, primarily relying on analyzing data supplemented with anecdotes and stories. Our studies mainly focus on the period from 1863 to roughly 1900 in the Great Plains, and our findings are mostly limited to that time and place. We found that the first three stylized facts are wrong, and the fourth is true in some states and untrue in others. We believe our work shows that in important ways the scholars' story of homesteading is wrong and that in most respects the popular understanding of homesteading's role is more accurate than the one that scholars have devised.

John Kenneth Galbraith, a mentor for one of us, used to warn that no strong argument is made stronger by exaggeration. We acknowledge that homesteading was not the only way by which white and black settlers gained title to western land and that land purchase was also significant. We also recognize that there was fraud in the operation of the homestead laws. Our argument is not to deny the presence of fraud but rather to ask, how much fraud? We found that homesteading fraud was not copious and pervasive. Finally, while homesteading was largely divorced from the dispossession process in a number of western states, it was, as we noted, deeply implicated in Dakota Territory and Indian Territory. Thus, while our results lean more toward the public's idea of homesteading than the scholarly consensus, neither view is found to be wholly correct.

We hope our work removes the blinders of the stylized facts from scholars' research and teaching. We have seen that Fred Shannon, for one, is a particularly unreliable and misleading guide. This is unfortunate because so many modern writers have uncritically relied on him, often citing as "facts" Shannon's assertions and liberally sprinkling his name among their citations. Like a judge throwing out evidence as the fruit of a poisoned tree, we should thus be skeptical of their writings as well.

Another curious feature of the previous literature is this disturbing pattern: scholars who want to make their case about failure and fraud in homesteading have had a tendency to exaggerate the statistics *of their own cited sources*. James Davenport Whelpley quoted "a prominent Western Senator" who said that 90 percent of the Desert Act final filings were fraudulent. But Whelpley, evidently disregarding any risk that the comment was merely senatorial hyperbole, then upped this figure to report, "It is a conservative estimate to say that fully ninety-*five* per cent. of the final proofs made on desert land were entirely fraudulent" (emphasis added). Shannon, as we have seen, cited Thomas Donaldson's data as covering the period "before 1890" even though the data end in 1880; he then compounded the exaggeration by misusing the data in a way that dramatically biased his results. He concluded (incorrectly) that most initial claimants failed to get patents and that in any event homesteading was a minor contributor to farm formation. Robert Hine and John Mack Faragher write, "After a detailed study, historian Shannon estimated that between 1862 and 1900 half of all homestead entries were fraudulent." However, the Shannon study they cite apparently cannot be found and may not exist. Then Louis Warren, citing Hine and Faragher as his source, extended the span to say, "After 1862, the federal government deeded 285 million acres to homesteaders. Half their claims were fraudulent, backed by false identities, fake improvements, or worse." By omitting Hine's and Faragher's end date, Warren seems to assert that this unsupported fraud statistic applies to the *entire* homesteading period. He immediately reaffirms this interpretation by mentioning the figure of 285 million acres (the amount of land distributed in all homestead patents between 1863 and 1961) rather than, as his source claimed, between 1863 and 1900. As Galbraith warned, evidence mischaracterized as stronger than what the cited source provides does not make one's case stronger—unless it goes undetected.[2]

We suggest a new vision of homesteading, one more true to the digitized data now becoming available. We realize we have made only a small beginning on such a big task. So how is our understanding of the historical process of homesteading changed by our research? We advance the following points as our most significant findings:

1. *Homesteading was a significant, perhaps the most significant, way that western farmers started their farms during the period 1860–1900.*

Virtually all public lands administrators, observers, and scholars in prior generations, from Donaldson and William Sparks in the 1880s and 1890s, to Benjamin Hibbard in the 1920s and Roy Robbins in the 1940s, to Paul Gates in the 1960s, thought the Homestead Act was the driving factor in settlement of the West. Many of them criticized it severely for failing to live up to their high ideals for it, for being administered ineptly and sometimes corruptly, for attracting low types seeking to defraud the government, and for a variety of other sins. But even in their attacks they confirmed its centrality. Shannon, the law's most severe critic, condemned it (strangely) for not being sweeping enough to solve the evils of all the other public land grants and giveaways. In the end, Gates's summing up stands: the act was "one of the most important laws which have been enacted in the history of this country."[3]

Our own reanalysis of the homesteading data confirms Gates's conclusion. In the West, between 1863 and 1900, homesteads accounted for nearly two-thirds of the new farms created. During these years, at least, homesteading was the most common path to making a new farm.

2. *A majority of homesteaders in the West who staked their initial claims before 1900 succeeded in proving up and obtaining their free land.* The best available data must be placed back-to-back: for the period before 1880, we have Donaldson's data on numbers of claimants and those proving up; for 1881 to 1900 we have the *Historical Statistics* data on number of acres initially claimed and proved up. Using these disparate sources, we can say that between 56 percent and 69 percent of homesteaders before 1880 succeeded in obtaining patents, and 55 percent of homesteaders who filed between 1881 and 1900 succeeded in obtaining patents.

3. *The actual frequency of fraud was small: perhaps as little as 3.2 percent and likely not more than 8.5 percent.* Neither the GLO clerks nor most subsequent scholars had access to data or analytic tools which would have allowed them to accurately estimate its extent. As a result, they focused on exceptional cases or reports of exceptional cases. As Gates noted, "A reason for the frequency of these misconceptions of homestead[ing] is the continued reiteration

in the annual reports of the Commissioners of the General Land Office, of the widespread and indeed common violation of the spirit and even the letter of the law by land-hungry settlers, land lookers, petty and large speculators and their agents, and cattle and mining companies.... Historians have reflected this jaundiced view, relying upon these continued reiterations, and not finding much in the reports about the hundreds of thousands of people successfully making farms for themselves." Like TV and newspapers today, which daily report sensational crimes but rarely mention the nation's overall decline in crime and thereby mislead the public, prior observers created a false narrative of rampant fraud.[4]

Stories *about* fraud, like the oft-repeated 12-by-14 dwelling constructed in inches, frequently appear in writings about homesteading and in many American history textbooks, but few actual *cases* of fraud are adduced. One of the most notorious cases, William Comstock's and Bartlett Richards's attempt to grab land under the Kinkaid Act, is sometimes offered as evidence of fraud's persuasiveness. But we would do well to remember that this was a case of *successful* enforcement, the attempted fraud was quashed, and the perpetrators came to ruin—strange evidence to use to support the notion that successful fraud was widespread.

So too, the homesteading fraud we have been able to document constituted what might be classified as petty larceny, as contrasted with the grand theft of the railroads, corporations, and speculators. In most cases the perpetrator was able to gain access to an additional 160-acre claim undeservedly, or a married couple obtained 320 acres when the GLO rules said they were entitled to only 160. Some of these cases occurred in areas which the 1904 Kinkaid Act and 1909 Enlarged Homestead Act later recognized as requiring more than 160 acres to create the viable farms envisioned in the original law. There appears to have been little homesteading fraud, and the fraud that did occur involved small gains. Again, we do not claim there was no fraud, only that scholars have wildly exaggerated its scale.

4. *Community policing of homestead claims was an effective mechanism to deter fraud.* Homesteading scholars focused on what they

assumed must have been paltry enforcement by overworked land office clerks and the miniscule force of GLO field investigators. In these conditions, they concluded, homestead claims *must* have been shot through with fraud; indeed, this conclusion buttressed the larger narrative to which they had already committed.

But it turns out that the Homestead Act also created a local network of watchful eyes. Mapping community relationships in the study area shows the emergence of keystone individuals in homesteading communities who helped create a local-community policing structure when no other existed. Neighbors, extended family members, would-be settlers in nearby towns, and others knew the ground, may have wanted it for themselves or their children, and didn't want it stolen by swindlers and cheats. Just as in farming country today, where neighbors, family members, and others watch closely when ground in their vicinity becomes available due to the owner's death or bankruptcy, so too it was in the homesteading regions. Indeed, Comstock's and Richards's attempted fraud came to disaster precisely because there were too many countervailing watchful eyes. What might have seemed anonymous and beyond scrutiny and hence ripe for fraud when viewed from Washington or New York or New Haven, or even from central Nebraska in the Comstock-Richards case, was in fact far more closely policed than expected.

5. *The relationship between homesteading and Indian land dispossession was more complex than current scholarship assumes.* Our analysis shows that homesteading played a negligible role in dispossession in many states including Nebraska, Colorado, Montana, and Wyoming, while it was a central force in Dakota Territory and Indian Territory.

It could be argued that the Homestead Act inflamed the appetite for land in the rest of the country and in Europe, thereby causing many migrants to move to the region and take up land, whether they obtained the land through homesteading, purchase from the railroads, or by other means, and so in this way the Homestead Act contributed to the general pressure for extinguishing Indian land claims. But in the regions we studied (except Dakota Territory and Indian Territory), Indian land claims had already been extinguished before any large-scale homesteading in those regions began. Here, homesteading's principal role was regulating who in the non-Indian community would benefit from the public domain.

6. *The Homestead Act was not only a "single women's law"; widows also participated at a high rate.* In our study area, nearly as many widows filed initial entry claims as single women. But what greatly increased widows' solitary participation—their *unintended* solitary participation—in homesteading was the deaths of their husbands. Women homesteaders succeeded by forming reciprocal socioeconomic relationships through employment and witness testimony between themselves and males in the wider community; they also created networks with other women that were crucial to their success. Our analysis highlights the need for scholars to further enrich this field.

7. *Homesteading was not a solitary activity; it was a process of Americans from different backgrounds and regions mixing together to settle and form communities.* They depended deeply on each other for survival and success. In our communities, keystone individuals emerged to provide economic, social, and political leadership in their neighborhoods. Immigrants from northwestern Europe tended to stake claims alongside native-born citizens, entering the social order of their new land. Central European immigrants, by contrast, more frequently created their own communities with their own leadership, thereby reproducing cultural landscapes more reminiscent of their homelands.

Settlement patterns and cultural differences thus separated communities of homesteaders. Different languages, religions, civic customs, community expectations, and patterns of family life all served to create distinctions. As Eric Foner noted, "In the late nineteenth century the most multicultural state in the Union was North Dakota," but modern scholars have tended retrospectively to recategorize these varied peoples simply as "white," thereby washing away their diversity.[5] And while the walls between them were never as impermeable as those of race, these groups often required decades to overcome their differences and for diverse communities to become integrated. Even today we are left with certain communities that continue to proudly reflect their ethnic heritage in significant ways.

The Homestead Act ensured that much of the public domain was distributed to "actual settlers." Homesteading's primary impact was ensuring that the government's land distribution among whites and a smaller group of African Americans was more weighted toward the poorer ranks of society than would have been the case—indeed, than *was* the case—had the land been distributed under any other government program, including being sold without restrictions or granted to corporations and speculators.

Even if we eliminate the successful claims that could have been fraudulent using our most conservative (highest) fraud estimate, more than 73 of the 80 million acres granted under the Homestead Act before 1900 were obtained by bona fide homesteaders.

If the same fraud rate persisted in the period from 1900 to 1961—which we cannot know from our data, but is not an unreasonable conjecture—then over the longer span from 1863 to 1961, more than 247 million of the 270 million acres granted under the Homestead Act went to "actual settlers" as the Act intended. Some 1.622 million homesteaders proved up during this period, so (assuming the 8.5 fraud rate) at least 1.484 million were legitimate claimants. These 1.484 million actual settlers gained homestead claims averaging 166.5 acres, including claims under the Kinkaid Act and Enlarged Homestead Act.[6]

So the Homestead Act delivered approximately 160 acres of "free land" in the public domain to nearly 1.5 million "actual settlers," almost exactly what the original Homestead Act intended. Among those actual settlers were Daniel Freeman and Isabel Proctor. Freeman married Agnes Suiter in 1865, and they lived on his claim near Beatrice, Nebraska, for the next several decades, where they raised eight children. In 1899 Daniel again gained national attention when he protested a local teacher's use of the Bible as a textbook. In a landmark case, *Daniel Freeman v. John Scheve, et al.*, decided long before the U.S. Supreme Court took up the issue,

Nebraska's Supreme Court ruled in Freeman's favor, saying that use of the Bible as a textbook violated Nebraska's constitutional separation of church and state. Proctor, after proving up her Montana claim in 1913, retained her ownership but leased her land to nearby farmers. She moved to Stanley, North Dakota, where she led a long and distinguished life of public service to that small plains community; she was especially passionate about enriching Stanley's musical and cultural life. She died in 1982. Freeman and Proctor are emblematic of the continued relevance of homesteading's legacy and the importance of continued homesteading scholarship.[7]

We hope that our findings, preliminary and limited as they are, are at least provocative to this extent: Homesteading requires a whole new look, based on the new evidence that is now becoming available. Reliance on old statistics, old studies, and old anecdotes is no longer sufficient. Repetition of favored old fraud stories is no longer sufficient. So too, the presumed but largely unexamined connection between homesteading and dispossession needs recasting. We believe our work points to a new, deeper, and historically more accurate understanding of the role homesteading played in the history of the American West. We will have succeeded if our work causes other scholars to return to the topic, reexamine old findings and new results, dig deeper into the newly available data, adapt our methodologies, and extend this learning to new and unexpected insights, whether those results ultimately agree with or upend our conclusions.

Appendix 1

An Annotated Review of GLO Circulars, 1862–1904

RHEA WICK

The U.S. General Land Office (GLO) used periodic circulars distributed to its local land agents to announce major changes to homesteading rules and provide clarifications of previous regulations. Tracking these changes helps historians define more concretely how the GLO understood fraud. The circulars helped develop a more robust bureaucracy by ensuring that the local land agents understood the law and that homesteaders met the stipulations of the law, and they provided more comprehensive language intended to reduce uncertainties in administration. The circulars also attempted to clearly identify certain behaviors as fraudulent and establish procedures to deal with these behaviors. The circulars documented the commissioners' responses to unwanted behavior through the creation of additional restrictions and regulations. As such, each change to the GLO circulars denotes an attempt to stop fraudulent behavior, and together they provide scholars with a historically based definition of fraud.

May 20, 1862: An Act to secure Homesteads to actual settlers on the Public Domain

Defined proper residency: The Homestead Act implemented several preventative measures in an attempt to prevent fraud. It stipulated that claimants must reside on the land for five years in order to receive patent.

Proper acreage: The original act also put a limitation on how much land an entryman could acquire through the homestead privilege. It stated that "no individual shall be permitted to acquire title to more than one quarter section under the provisions of this act," although claimants could apply for more land and simply pay the government price for any acreage over 160.[1]

Intent to settle: The law required that applicants swear an affidavit affirming their intent to cultivate and that they intended to use the land strictly for their own benefit. The GLO used these oaths as the main mechanism to identify bona fide settlers. Indeed, "In order to protect the Government from imposition by mere speculators, it was deemed necessary to require clear proof of the intention of the claimant to make the land in good faith his home."[2] The GLO used the affidavit to provide that clear proof. Congress judged an oath, affirmation, or affidavit sworn fallaciously as "deemed and taken to be perjury, and the person or persons guilty thereof shall, upon conviction, be liable to the punishment prescribed for that offense by the laws of the United States."[3]

Abandonment: The act also stated that if a claimant left his or her land for longer than six months, this qualified as abandonment. Since Congress intended the law to benefit bona fide settlers, any claimants who did not establish and maintain residence could not receive patents.

Improper residency in commutations: The law required homesteaders who chose to commute their entries, that is, to pay the established price for the land in order to receive patent before the expiration of the mandatory five years of residency, to prove settlement and residency before they could commute.

1867 Circular

Selling an unproven homestead claim: The 1867 circular made it illegal to sell a claim prior to receiving patent, and the GLO did not recognize any purchaser as having any rights to the title. Moreover, the circular stated that any entryman who sold his or her land would lose the right to the claim. The sale of a homestead "before the completion of title ... would be prima facie evidence of abandonment, and give cause for cancellation of the claim."[4]

Additional homesteads after relinquishment: Further discouraging the sale of unperfected claims, the circular prohibited entrymen from making a second claim if they relinquished or abandoned their original homesteads.

Improper settlement and cultivation: Originally the Homestead Act in cases of commutation only addressed proof of settlement and cultivation. The 1867 circular required settlement and cultivation before receiving patent in the case of both regular and commuted entries.

1870 Circular

Relinquishing a claim to specific people: The circular clarified that if an entryman relinquished his or her claim, ownership of the land reverted to the government. Rights to relinquished land went to the first legal applicant, not a designated person. This was likely a reaction to entrymen attempting to relinquish their homesteads to specific people, possibly for monetary compensation, as a way to circumvent the prohibition on selling unproven homesteads. At this point, before a relinquished claim could be opened to reentry, the local land office clerks had to send the cancellation to Washington for approval.

Improper residency in commutations: Previously the GLO placed no extra restrictions on commutations. The 1870 circular clarified that homesteaders must live on their land and cultivate it continuously for at least six months before they could commute.

Additional homesteads after relinquishment: The 1870 circular amended the restriction that prohibited second homesteads for entrymen who abandoned or relinquished their claims, stating that anyone with an accidentally illegal claim could make a second entry.[5]

June 8, 1872: An Act to amend an act relating to soldiers' and sailors' homesteads

Theft of a soldier's identity: This act amended an earlier act that granted soldiers a number of additional rights under the Homestead Act. This act, however, much like the original Homestead Act of 1862, gave the commissioner the "authority to make all needful rules and regulations to carry into effect the provisions of this act."[6] In order to safeguard the extra benefits given to soldiers, the GLO sent a circular to the land offices stating that applicants claiming military service were required to provide documents proving their eligibility. Soldiers needed a certified copy of their certificate of discharge, an affidavit from two disinterested witnesses proving military service, or an affidavit from the applicant proving the same. In addition to confirming her husband's military service, any widow using her husband's homestead privilege had to provide an affidavit swearing to her widowhood. The GLO also required that guardians assigned to the minor orphan children of deceased soldiers must present proof verifying the father's military service record, establish they possessed power of guardianship, and document the parents' marriage or the mother's death.[7]

1877 Circular

Additional homesteads after relinquishment: This circular altered the 1870 amendment that a homesteader could get a second claim if his or her first was illegal. As of 1877, a claimant could make a second entry—so long as he or she had not abandoned the original entry—if, through no fault of the homesteader, he or she had violated the rules, necessitating relinquishment of the first claim.

June 3, 1878: An Act to provide for the publication of notices of contest . . . and the 1878 Circular

Unfounded contestations: The 1878 circular required that anyone contesting a homestead, preemption, or timber culture claim on the grounds of abandonment must publish his or her notice of contest in a newspaper.[8] By requiring contestants to publish notice of their contestations, the GLO allowed applicants time to assemble an argument against accusations of fraud, which helped diminish frivolous contestations.

March 3, 1879: An Act to provide additional regulations for homestead and pre-emption entries of public lands . . . and the 1879 Circular

Publication of notice and preference right: In 1879 legislators passed an act requiring that anyone making final proof on his or her homestead or preemption entry must publish notice of an intent to finalize for five consecutive weeks in a local newspaper. The GLO required that entrymen publish their intent in the newspaper of the county in which they resided or, if not organized into a county, in the nearest organized county. The circular supplemented this act by giving contestants preference to the land, but only if they submitted an entry on the land along with their contestation. Someone with another claim could still contest a claim, but if the contestation was successful he or she would not receive preference right to the land. These changes enhanced a community's ability to regulate itself.[9]

Additional homesteads on reserved land: This law allowed a homesteader who claimed on a section within a railroad or military road grant to take a second entry or cancel his or her first claim and apply for a new one that made the total holding amount to 160 acres.[10] Making this land available for settlement expanded the homesteading privilege, but the circulars required a claimant to prove the legality of his or her current homestead before making a second claim.

July 1, 1879: An Act for the relief of settlers

Special allowances for environmental disasters: Congress passed a relief act addressing the grasshopper plagues that forced some homesteaders to leave their land for more than six months at a time.[11] The act excused an absence of no more than a year, which previously qualified as abandonment and caused the land to be returned to the government. The law allowed only those with "a loss or failure of crops from unavoidable cause in the year 1879 or 1880" to use this exemption.[12] Furthermore, in order to receive the allowance, homesteaders had to supply an affidavit certifying the extent of their crop losses and apply for leave of absence.

May 14, 1880: An Act for the relief of settlers on public land

Relinquished lands and witnessed relinquishments: This act stated that relinquished land was "open to settlement and entry without further action on the part of the Commissioner of the General

Land Office." In addition, the office could only accept relinquishments that the agents personally witnessed or that included written verification on the back of the duplicate receipt the entryman had received upon applying for the land. After passage of the law, the GLO became concerned that unauthorized people could submit false relinquishments in order to gain control of prime real estate contrary to the Homestead Act's focus on providing public land to bona fide settlers.[13]

Contestants get preference right: The law also formalized the provisions previously implemented in the 1879 circular that gave successful contestants a preference right to the claim they contested; the preference right lasted for thirty days following the cancellation of the contested claim. The law did not require contestants to apply for the land in order to receive this benefit, partially to allow contestants to receive the benefits of the time and money they spent procuring the cancellation of a claim.[14] More important, however, this was the final piece of legislation in a movement to develop a system of unearthing fraud that did not rely on the personnel and resources of the GLO. The government viewed this shift in policy as so crucial that in 1883 Acting Interior Secretary Joslyn wrote to GLO Commissioner McFarland "that Congress in various ways encouraged persons to inform against those who are endeavoring to acquire title to the public land fraudulently or illegally, as the only adequate means of protecting the United States."[15] The government protected its interest in giving land to bona fide settlers by making the local community responsible for rooting out fraud.

June 15, 1880: An Act relating to the public lands of the United States and the 1880 Circular

Retroactively legalizing transfers: In keeping with previous circulars, selling a homestead claim before receiving final patent constituted legal evidence of abandonment.[16] Despite this rule, Congress passed a law in 1880 that retroactively legalized the transfer of homesteads up to the date of the 1880 law's passage. The act permitted homesteaders who previously attempted to transfer their right to homestead to another person to do so; the transferee could purchase the land and receive patent. A circular went out to land office agents imploring them to "exercise all possible care in this matter, as it is not improbable that fraudulent entries will be attempted, and the proper execution of this law will largely depend on your vigilance and discretion."[17] Since the law allowed behavior previously considered fraudulent to become legal, the commissioner required land agents to ensure the lawfulness of attempts to utilize these provisions. The local land offices required that entrymen prove that the original homestead filings were legitimate, that the transfer occurred, and that the transfer occurred within the correct time period. Once the office received satisfactory evidence, the transferee paid the appropriate government price for the land before receiving patent.

March 3, 1881: An Act to amend section 2297 of the Revised Statutes, relating to homestead settlers

Special allowances for environmental disasters: This law allowed certain homesteaders to settle their land twelve months after the date of application (instead of the usual six) if they encountered climatic hindrances.[18] In order to ensure entrymen used this exemption properly, the corresponding circular required that applicants provide an affidavit attesting to the "storms, floods, blockages by snow or ice, or other hindrances dependent on climactic causes which rendered it impossible for him to commence residence within six months."[19]

1884 Circular

Improper residency in commutations: The 1884 circular stated that if applicants never lived on or cultivated the land they applied for and if, after the time allotted, they applied for a commutation, they forfeited "all right to the land and to the purchase money paid." Moreover, making these false assertions to residency rendered entrymen "liable to criminal prosecution."[20] None of the other circulars made this distinction quite so forcefully. This harshly worded proscription suggests the GLO was concerned that some commuters did not actually live on and cultivate the land.

Requiring settlement within six months: The commissioner altered the language of the circular to state that entrymen had six months from the time they entered the land to establish permanent residence and that the period of continuous settlement and cultivation started after the establishment of residence. Previously, the GLO's policy stated that "if a homestead claimant did not establish his residence upon the homestead within six months from date of entry, such entry might be contested and cancelled for abandonment."[21] However, the circulars never before so explicitly stated this policy. Rather, they simply declared that being absent for more than six months at a time or changing residence qualified as abandonment.[22] This additional clarification stated the GLO's intent regarding improper residency more clearly.

Negligence no cause for second homestead: Entrymen did not have a right to a second homestead if they lost their first homestead due to carelessness when choosing it. This change hints at a probable point of frustration for many of the land office clerks. Despite the numerous protections against homesteading failure due to unforeseen circumstances such as grasshopper plagues, draught, or other climactic hindrances, this circular clarified that those provisions were not intended to provide a second chance for use by negligent claimants.[23] "Where a party makes a selection of land for a homestead, he must, as a general rule, abide by his choice. If he has neglected to examine the character of the land prior to entry and it proves to be infertile or otherwise unsatisfactory, he must suffer the consequences of his own neglect."[24]

Soldier's declaratory statement: A previous act gave every soldier the right to make a declaratory statement on a plot of land, meaning he could make claim to the land prior to applying for the right to homestead there. After making his declaratory statement, he could apply for the homestead privilege within six months. If he missed that deadline, he could still apply for a homestead on the same land unless in the meantime someone else had claimed the plot.[25]

The 1884 circular stated that once a soldier made a declaratory statement, he had exhausted his homestead privilege.[26] As such, he could only use his privilege on that same land. The clarification suggests that some soldiers claimed lands without any actual intent to settle on them, instead possibly holding tracts of land for friends or relatives or for sale.

This circular further stated that another person could act as an agent for the soldier only when making a declaratory statement on a tract of land; the agent could not make a regular entry on the soldier's behalf. Previous circulars required an agent to provide proof that he or she had power of attorney for the soldier before the person could serve as agent.[27] In addition to continuing to require certification of the power of attorney, this circular required the agent to prove he or she had no "right or interest, direct or indirect, in the filing of such declaratory statement." Additionally, the agent was required to swear an oath affirming his or her lack of interest "either present or prospective, direct or indirect, in the claim; . . . and that no arrangement has been made whereby said agent has been empowered at any future time to sell or relinquish such claim, either as agent or by filing an original relinquishment of the claimant."[28] The GLO was clearly concerned about the possible theft of soldiers' identities and other abuses of veterans' right to homestead and so chose to require an affidavit and oath as a countermeasure.

Expanded definition of cultivation: The circular broadened the meaning of cultivation to include stock-raising and dairy production in areas more fitted for grazing. Prior to this redefinition, the GLO viewed grazing homesteads as not fulfilling the cultivation requirement.

1889 Circular

More than one homestead through marriage: In the eyes of the law, once married, a husband and a wife became one family unit. If both spouses had been allowed to claim a homestead and proved up, then this family unit would have acquired 360 acres, twice the amount the Homestead Act designated for a family. However, the law itself did not address the complications arising from single female homesteaders who married during the residency period. As such, the 1889 circular stated that a single woman who married before proving up did not automatically forfeit her right to her homestead claim. However, if she abandoned her land (presumably to live on that of her husband) she forfeited her right to the land.

Timber speculation: The circular allowed homesteaders to clear enough timber to make necessary improvements and sell any timber that remained; however, it did not allow them to clear cut all the timber on a claim before it was patented. The GLO considered claimants who left their land after clearing all the timber to be squatters not intending to become actual settlers. This change identified timber exploitation through the homesteading law as a significant problem requiring redress.

Addressing improper residence: Previously, circulars described continuous residence as keeping residence on the claim with no absence from it for more than six months at a time. In 1889 the GLO clarified: "Occasional visits to the land once in six months or oftener does not constitute residence."[29] Homesteaders must actually live there, improve the land, and cultivate it.

Improper residency in commutations: The GLO required that before homesteaders could commute their claim, they needed to have fully complied with the law for the duration of their residency, with no exemptions allowed. "They are not obliged to make proof in the short time in which commutation is allowed, and when such proof is made, full compliance with the law must be satisfactorily shown."[30]

March 2, 1889: An Act to withdraw certain public lands from private entry, and for other purposes.

Special allowances for environmental disasters: This act allowed entrymen to be absent for a year in the event of crop loss.[31] To make his or her absence legitimate, the homesteader needed to apply to the register and receiver for a leave of absence; as part of the application, the homesteader needed to submit a personal affidavit swearing he or she had suffered crop loss as well as the affidavits of two disinterested witnesses.[32] In addition, the entryman could not credit his or her time absent from the claim toward the mandatory five-year residence.

Additional homesteads for claims under 160 acres: The law also allowed homesteaders with unproven homestead claims smaller than 160 acres to apply for a second homestead that would make their combined land holdings total no more than 160 acres. In order for them to make this second claim, entrymen submitted an affidavit swearing that their current claim complied with homestead regulations.[33]

March 3, 1891: An Act to repeal timber-culture laws, and for other purposes.

Improper residency in commutations: This act required entrymen to live on their claims for fourteen consecutive months before commuting their claims.[34] This replaced the previous six-month waiting period.

1895 Circular

More than one homestead through marriage: In 1895 the circular readdressed the issue of married couples acquiring more than one homestead. It clarified that if two applicants married while they each still had unpatented homestead entries, they could prove up both homesteads so long as they resided separately, each on his or her own claim; if, however, they lived together, they could only prove up the claim on which they resided.

Intent to speculate: In this circular, the GLO introduced the most significant changes to the affidavit required to prove an entryman's intent. Earlier versions of the affidavit certified that the applicant met the basic eligibility requirements included in the original Homestead Act. In 1895 the part of the affidavit that included the oath tripled in length, increasing from approximately one hundred words to almost three hundred. The revised affidavit added language making it more explicit that the entryman only intended to use the homestead for his or her exclusive benefit. In addition, the new language clarified that the claimant intended to improve and live upon the land, disavowing any intent of making the claim solely to exploit the resources on the land or transfer ownership of it to a third party. The homesteader was required to assert that he or she applied "in good faith to obtain a home for himself."[35]

Landowners homesteading: The GLO added another stipulation to the affidavit that sought to address the problem of land not going to the landless. In the new affidavit, the homesteader swore that "he has not entered under the land laws of the United States, or filed upon, a quantity of land agricultural in character, and not mineral, which with the tracts of land now applied for, would make more than 320 acres, and that he has not heretofore had the benefit of the homestead laws." Additionally, the entryman was required to swear that he or she had "not heretofore made any entry under the homestead laws." The GLO allowed exceptions because previous laws legalized second homestead entries in certain instances, but applicants had to explicitly state any additional homesteads.

1899 Circular

This circular contained no noteworthy changes.

June 6, 1900: An act to amend the Act of Congress approved May fourteenth eighteen hundred and eighty entitled "an act for the relief of settlers on the public lands" and the 1904 Circular

More than one homestead through marriage: The 1900 law and 1904 circular returned to the issue of married couples' rights to homestead. It stated that marriage did not mean a woman could not perfect her claim, *"Provided,* She does not abandon her residence on said land and is otherwise qualified to make homestead entry: *And provided further,* That the man whom she marries is not, at the time of their marriage, claiming a separate tract of land under the homestead law."[36] This meant that so long as a woman remained eligible and did not abandon her claim, the GLO allowed her to retain rights to her land.

Appendix 2

Sources for Chapter 5 Graphs and Maps

Sources of Data for Graphs

AREA OF INDIAN LAND CESSIONS

The data used in this study were generously provided by J. Clark Archer and David Wishart of the Geography Program of the School of Natural Resources, University of Nebraska–Lincoln. The underlying data were initially extracted in a herculean effort by Wishart from the Indian Claims Commission's proceedings (which cases were mostly decided between 1951 and 1980). He supplemented this source with information from C. C. Royce (*Indian Land Cessions in the United States*), G. J. Kappler (*Indian Affairs: Laws and Treaties*), and other sources; they are extensively described and used in Wishart, "Compensation for Dispossession: Payments to Indians for Their Lands on the Central and Northern Great Plains in the 19th Century." Les Howard vector-digitized the cessions boundaries for the maps that appeared in "Compensation." Steven Lavin (now deceased) and Archer used this boundary file supplemented by additional vector-digitized data on Canada's Prairie Provinces for a map that appears in Archer et al., eds., *Atlas of the Great Plains*. Because most cessions in the Great Plains preceded the formation of states, cession boundaries rarely coincide with state boundaries, and so Archer used GIS to overlay and split cession regions along modern state boundaries. AtlasGIS was then used to calculate the areas of vector-format geocoded polygons of cessions, which then were used to construct the graphs in this study.

The data on homestead final entries and homestead acres claimed are taken from U.S. Department of the Interior, "Homesteads."

Sources of Data for Maps

Most of our maps were drawn by Katie Nieland based on original maps by Michael Cooper, who used several sources: the maps of C. C. Royce, *Indian Land Cessions in the United States*, available at http://www.usgwarchives.org/maps/cessions/; Francis Paul Prucha, *Atlas of American Indian Affairs*, 22–30; National Park Service, "Indian Reservations in the Continental United States," available at http://www.nps.gov/nagpra/documents/reserv.pdf; Edwin C. McReynolds, *Oklahoma: A History of the Sooner State*, 300; James C. Olson and Ronald C. Naugle, *History of Nebraska*, 32, 118; Paul W. Gates, *Fifty Million Acres: Conflicts over Kansas Land Policy, 1854–1890*, 252.

The map of the Great Sioux Reservation (fig. 5.11) was created by Katie Nieland based on data available at the Lakota Sioux Nation website http://www.snowwowl.com/peoplesioux.html and from the North Dakota Studies Project of the State Historical Society of North Dakota, available at http://www.ndstudies.org/resources/IndianStudies/standingrock/historical_gs_reservation.html.

Notes

1. Competing Visions

1. Shanks, "The Homestead Act."

2. *United States v. Wong Kim Ark*, 169 U.S. 649 (1898).

3. Whether Daniel Freeman was actually the first homesteader has been questioned. Dan Jaffe reports that Freeman claims he met the clerk of the Brownville Land Office at a New Year's Eve ball, concocted a story about being a soldier who had been ordered to report elsewhere the next morning and hence had to file right away, and so the clerk opened the land office at midnight. In 1936 Congress passed an act establishing the Homestead National Monument of America and chose Freeman's homestead as its site, designating him as the official "first" homesteader. Jaffe, *Dan Freeman*, 14, 63–64. Isabel Proctor's story is told in Edwards, *Natives of a Dry Place*, chapter 6.

4. Kennedy, "Special Message to Congress on Conservation," in *Public Papers of the Presidents of the United States: John F. Kennedy*, March 1, 1962 [#69], 181; Bush, "Second Inaugural Address," accessed on October 5, 2014, http://georgewbush-whitehouse.archives.gov/news/releases/2005/01/20050120–1.html; and Barack Obama, "Remarks on the Bicentennial of Abraham Lincoln's Birth," February 12, 2009, accessed on June 5, 2016, http://www.presidentialrhetoric.com/speeches/02.12.09.html. On August 3, 1987, Ronald Reagan declared, "Abraham Lincoln signed into law the Homestead Act that ensured that the great western prairies of America would be the realm of independent, property-owning citizens—a mightier guarantee of freedom is difficult to imagine." Accessed on June 22, 2015, http://www.nps.gov/home/learn/historyculture/presquotes.htm. Sandoz; "The Homestead in Perspective," 47; Will, *Washington Post*, January 30, 2005, B7; Center for American Progress, accessed on August 12, 2012, http://www.americanprogress.org/issues/2012/01/middle_class_acts.html.

5. Harris, *Long Vistas*, ix.

6. On women homesteaders see Jameson, "Rachel Bella Calof's Life as Collective History," 135–54; Jameson and Armitage, *The Women's West and Writing the Range*; Harris, *Long Vistas*; Smith, "Single Women Homesteaders"; Garceau, "Sin-

gle Women Homesteaders"; Lindgren, *Land in Her Own Name*; Fink, *Agrarian Women*; Handy-Marchello, *Women of the Northern Plains*; Muhn, "Women and the Homestead Act," 282–307; and Haney and Knowles, *Women and Farming*. Certainly one aspect of Gates's *History of Public Land Law Development* that most urgently needs reformulating is his treatment of women's role in homesteading. On gender dynamics see, e.g., Benton-Cohen, "Common Purposes, Worlds Apart."

7. Gates, "The Homestead Law in an Incongruous Land System," 652–81. On the Homestead Act and immigration, see the recent innovative analysis by Bell, "America's Invitation to the World," accessed July 12, 2014, http://www.nps.gov /home/upload/Immigration-White-Paper.pdf.

8. The figures in this and succeeding paragraphs were calculated from several sources that are inconsistent with each other and in any event should be taken as reflecting only general magnitudes. See Carter, *Historical Statistics*, table Cf78; Department of the Interior, *Public Land Statistics*, tables 1–1, 1–2, and 1–3; Department of the Interior, "Homesteads;" and the websites of the U.S. National Park Service (http://www.nps.gov/aboutus/quickfacts.htm) and the Forest Service (www.fs.fed.us) See also Gates, *History*, 502 and our appendix 1.

9. See Gates, *History of Public Land Law Development*, chapter 10. And for an interesting discussion of this process from outside the usual historical circles, see de Soto, *The Mystery of Capital*, chapter 5. NARA, putting a happy face on this process, says preemption was "an individual's right to settle land first and pay later (essentially an early form of credit)." See "Teaching with Documents: The Homestead Act of 1862," accessed February 27, 2016, https://www.archives.gov /education/lessons/homestead-act/.

10. Quoted in Fite, *Farmer's Frontier*, 18.

11. Quoted in Fite, *Farmer's Frontier*, 18–19; Robbins, *Our Landed Heritage*, 30.

12. Data from Department of the Interior, *Homesteads*. Dakota Territory homesteads were distributed between North Dakota and South Dakota in proportion to total land area; North Dakota has 70,698 square miles (or 47.8 percent) and South Dakota has 77,115 square miles (52.2 percent). This distribution creates the slight uncertainty concerning the homesteading percentages of total land area for North and South Dakota. Counting only homesteads proved up after statehood in 1889, 38.5 percent (17,417,660 / 45,246,924) of North Dakota's land and 31.7 percent (15,660,000 / 49,354,035) of South Dakota's land was homesteaded.

13. Calculated from the data available in the Department of the Interior, *Homesteads*.

14. In our study area, defined in chapter 4 and used in chapters 4, 6, and 7, we limit our analysis to claims under the original 1862 Homestead Act, because the digitized archives at present do not include Kinkaid and Enlarged Homestead claims.

15. Other criticisms have been expressed as well. For example, Fred Shannon voiced an often-repeated complaint: "The trouble with the Homestead Act in operation, as with the Preemption Act, was that Congress merely adopted

the law and then did absolutely nothing in the way of helping the needy persons out to the land or extending them credit and guidance in the first heart-breaking years of occupancy." In Shannon, "The Homestead Act and the Labor Surplus," 644, 646. Geoff Cunfer, a historian, expressed a different criticism in a recent book when he argued, "An important story of Great Plains history is that the rural population in the region rose dramatically for fifty years, from about 1870 to 1920, and has declined steadily since then. . . . One could make a compelling argument that the Homestead Act was a failure if its goal was to spread a strong, prosperous American society across the continent." In Cunfer, *On the Great Plains*, 7. And others have argued that because the government distributed land on the cadastral system rather than on natural or ecological boundaries (such as watersheds), it encouraged farming that was excessively environmentally damaging.

16. Shannon, *Farmer's Last Frontier*, 51; Hine and Faragher, *The American West*, 334.

17. One textbook omitting the Homestead Act completely is Jones et al., *Created Equal*. While the authors did not mention homesteading or the Homestead Act, they apparently decided it was important to discuss the Home Owners Loan Corporation and the Hooker Chemical Corporation, whose index entries bracket the omitted Homestead Act. Other textbooks provide very cursory comment. To give an example:

> The Homestead Act of 1862 gave farmers public land, which they could use and eventually own. In practice, however, the 160-acre unit of the Homestead Act was too small for successful farming; a serious settler had to purchase two or three times that acreage. Nor did the Homestead Act provide the money to go west, file a claim, and acquire the machinery required for profitable farming. . . . Most settlers obtained their land from the railroads or land companies.

Ayers et al., *American Passages*, 2:384. No citation is given for the questionable claim that "most" settlers obtained their land from the railroads or land companies.

18. In 1993 the *Journal of American History* published one article on the emergence of the homestead exemption (from debt collectors, tax liens, etc.) and reviews of books on homesteading by Harris, Lindgren, Brian Cannon, and others; however, not one article on the Homestead Act or homesteading was published in the fifty-year span from 1965 to 2015.

19. Brinkley, *American History*, 2:450. The longer passage is:

> The Homestead Act was intended as a progressive measure. It would give a free farm to any American who needed one. . . . But the Homestead Act rested on a number of misperceptions. The framers of the law had assumed that mere possession of land would be enough to sustain a farm family. They had not recognized the effects of increasing mechanization of agriculture and the rising costs of running a farm. Moreover, they had made many of their calculations on the basis of eastern agricultural experiences. . . . A unit of 160 acres was too small. . . . Although over 400,000 homesteaders stayed on Homestead Act claims long enough to gain

title to their land, a much larger number abandoned the region before the end of the necessary five years.

Indeed, there were "over 400,000" successful homesteaders, a figure reached *by 1891*, but as stated above, without an end date, the correct figure is *1.6 million*. With such neglect, careless presentation of numbers, dated citations, wrong information, and lack of interest displayed in these textbooks, it is little wonder that scholars may know less about homesteading than the general public.

20. Commissioner Sparks wrote, "At the outset of my administration, I was confronted with overwhelming evidence that the public domain was being made the prey of unscrupulous speculation and the worst forms of land monopoly through systematic frauds carried on and consummated under the public land laws." U.S. General Land Office (hereafter USGLO), *Annual Report of the Commissioner of the General Land Office for the Year 1885*, 48.

21. Hibbard, *A History of the Public Land Policies*; Shannon, *Farmer's Last Frontier*; Robbins, *Our Landed Heritage*; Gates, *History of Public Land Law Development*; Hine and Faragher, *American West*, 335–36; and Warren, *Buffalo Bill's America*, 72.

22. Hansen, *Encounter on the Great Plains*, 19; Kaye, *Goodlands*, 166.

23. Hansen illustrates this tendency. She writes, "From the perspective of American Indians, therefore, the Homestead Act amounted to a wholesale scheme for further encroachment. . . . In reaction to the continuing advance by white settlers, Dakota Chief Waanatan, attending a peace commission in July 1868, said, 'I see them swarming all over my country. . . . Take all the whites and your soldiers away and all will be well.'" In *Encounter*, 10. In this construction, Hansen blames the Homestead Act for "them swarming all over my country." But in 1868 there were virtually *no* homesteaders in Dakota country—there were clearly soldiers, gold miners, railroaders, bonanza farmers, land speculators, cattle barons, and other whites, but almost no homesteaders. Their advance was a decade or two into the future and then mostly on the eastern edge of the territory. Despite this lapse, however, Hansen is one of the few who has investigated the link between homesteading and dispossession, although for a later period, as the subtitle of her book makes clear.

24. "In most land-offices a man cannot preëmpt unless he has a house at least twelve feet square. I have known a witness to swear that the house in question was 'twelve by fourteen,' when actually the only building upon the claim was one whittled out with a penknife, twelve *inches* by fourteen." Albert Richardson, *Beyond the Mississippi*, 140-41.

25. Edwards, *Natives of a Dry Place*, chapter 7.

26. Paul Gates provides an interesting case of changing his mind. His 1936 article was quite critical of how homesteading was implemented, but by 1963 he had reversed course, declaring the criticism had gone too far and that scholars were failing to appreciate the significance of the Homestead Act. See Gates, "The Homestead Law in an Incongruous Land System," and "The Homestead Act: Free Land Policy in Operation," 41.

2. Recalculating Homesteading's Reach

1. Shannon, *Farmer's Last Frontier*; Trachtenberg, *Incorporation of America*. Pertinent sections reprinted in Frazier, *Private Side of American History*; Hine and Faragher, *American West*, 335–36; Foner, *Give Me Liberty!* A3.

2. Cochrane, *Development of American Agriculture*, 80–84; Danbom, *Sod Busting*, 24; Hine, *The American West*.

3. Donaldson, *The Public Domain*.

4. See Edwards, "Why the Homesteading Data Are So Poor."

5. Shannon, *Farmer's Last Frontier*, 51; Trachtenberg, *Incorporation of America*.

6. Carter, *Historical Statistics*. Somewhat more accurate figures than Shannon used are given in *Historical Statistics* as 2,044,000 farms in 1860 and 5,739,657 farms in 1900, with the difference being 3,695,657; these figures are based on the *1925 Summary of the Census of Agriculture*; we use the *Historical Statistics* figures, though the difference with Shannon's numbers is insufficient to alter the results much.

7. Shannon, *Farmer's Last Frontier*, 51; Department of the Interior, "Homesteads," 3. Using the figures in note 6, homesteads would represent 16.2 percent of all new farms between 1860 and 1900.

8. This suggests that there are two possible methods of correction (if the data are available): adding the extra in-process homesteads to the numerator or subtracting the not-yet-eligible homesteads from the denominator. The results of these two methods differ only slightly, and the second implicitly shortens the period being analyzed. For consistency, we use the former method throughout.

9. Henretta, Edwards, and Self, *America's History*, 2:499–505; Foner, *Give Me Liberty!* 591. Other textbooks that also place homesteading in the context of the settlement of the West include Goldfield et al., *American Journey*, 539–41, where homesteading is discussed in a chapter called "Transforming the West"; White, *It's Your Misfortune and None My Own*, 143–47; and Berkin et al., *Making America*, 1:366, which incorrectly but revealingly states: "In 1862, Congress passed the Homestead Act ... the law granted 160 acres of the public domain *in the West* to any citizen or would-be citizen" (emphasis added).

10. The included states are Oklahoma, Kansas, Nebraska, South Dakota, North Dakota, Minnesota, Montana, Wyoming, Colorado, New Mexico, Arizona, Utah, Nevada, Idaho, Washington, Oregon, and California. As the BLM noted, "Virtually no land was homesteaded east of the Mississippi, and very little in the first tier of States west of the river." Department of the Interior, *Homesteads*, 1.

11. Hine, *American West*, 161. This argument is retained in the second edition (177) and in the third edition, with John Mack Faragher, where the last statement reads, "Most western settlers, it turns out, were not homesteaders" (334).

12. Cochrane, *Development of American Agriculture*, 83–84.

13. Danbom, *Sod Busters*, 24–25. Danbom seems to be making the same logical error as Hine originally made.

14. Hine and later Hine and Faragher assert without attribution that 700 million acres were *sold* to farmers. How they know this is unclear, and making this

calculation would be very difficult, seemingly requiring access to the files of Union Pacific, etc. There is no evidence they ever conducted such a study. More likely, they are simply and incorrectly reporting as sales all nonhomesteading public-domain land grants to states, railroads, and others, and then assuming that those grant recipients later sold it to farmers. We know this assumption to be false: railroads retained land, states retained land, land was granted to create towns, land was sold to mining companies, some grants were never finalized, and so on. To draw the conclusion that "Most farmers who went west did not homestead" on this basis would seem to require a wild leap of faith.

15. Donaldson, *The Public Domain*, 533. Below we report that homesteading accounted for about one-third of new farmland in the West. Assuming the remainder was purchased, then the ratio of purchased acreage to homesteaded acreage is 2:1. Using this ratio, we can say that only if the average (mean) acreage of a purchased farm was twice the average acreage of a homesteaded farm would the ratio of acreages serve as a proxy for the number of farmers in each group, as Hine assumed. But we would expect the purchased farm mean acreage to be many times that of homestead farms (because homesteads were capped at 160, but purchased farms had no cap, because homesteaders were likely to be poorer than purchasers of farmland, and due to other factors). But without evidence this approach must remain highly speculative, and anyway more direct estimates are possible, as we report below.

16. Foner, *Give Me Liberty!* 604; Maier et al., *Inventing America*, 530 (emphasis in original).

17. Calculated using total farmland acres by state taken from Carter, *Historical Statistics*, tables Da159-224; homesteaded acres by state taken from Department of Interior, "Homesteads."

18. Shannon, *Farmer's Last Frontier*, 54.

19. This is not a logical corollary: homesteading's role in farm creation depends on the number of successful homestead claims as a percentage of total number of farms created, not as a percentage of initial homestead claims. A high failure-to-prove-up rate is consistent with a high total-farm-creation rate if the number of initial claims is sufficiently large compared with the total number of farms created.

20. Unfortunately, while the *Historical Statistics* provides data on the number of initial claims, it does not provide data on the number of claims successfully proved up, so no extension of Donaldson's evidence based on number of claims rather than acres is possible. However, in this case, acres appears to work well as a proxy for numbers; only if the average acres in initial claims was significantly different from the average acres in proved-up claims would there be bias, and we have no reason to believe the averages differed significantly.

21. Calculated from data in tables Cf77 and Cf78 of Carter, *Historical Statistics*. Trina Williams Shanks compiled homesteading data from similar sources. Using her data, the homesteading failure rate for claims filed between 1863 and

1900, taking into account the successful in-process claims between 1901 and 1905, is 54.6 percent, confirming the estimates given in the text. Shanks, "The Homestead Act," 20–41.

22. Shannon, *Farmer's Last Frontier*, 55; Hansen, *Encounter on the Great Plains*, 63.

23. Shannon, *Farmer's Last Frontier*, 55–56.

24. Fite, *Farmer's Frontier*, 22–23.

3. Evolving Views on Homesteading Fraud

1. U.S. Congress, House, *Congressional Globe*, 37th Cong., 2nd sess. (1862): 909–10.

2. "Homestead Act (1862) document info" at Our Documents website (an initiative of National History Day, the National Archives and Records Administration, and USA Freedom Corps), accessed June 16, 2015, http://www.ourdocuments .gov/doc.php?flash=false&doc=31#.

3. Copp, *Public Land Laws* (1890), 58–60. All subsequent publications in this series are referred to as *Public Land Laws*.

4. Gates, *History of Public Land Law Development*.

5. Copp, *Public Land Laws* (1890), 126; Keener, *Public Land Statutes of the United States*, 42.

6. Copp, *Public Land Laws* (1890), preface.

7. Copp, *Public Land Laws* (1875), 243; Homestead Act, Public Law 37–64, May 20, 1862.

8. USGLO, *Circular* (1895), 13. All subsequent publications in this series are referred to as the *Circular*.

9. USGLO, *Circular* (1867), 9; USGLO, *Circular* (1870), 9.

10. USGLO, *Circular* (1880), 16–17.

11. The GLO afforded a contestant a preference right to the land if he or she made entry on the land while submitting the contestation. In addition, Congress passed a law in 1880 giving right to the land to any person who successfully contested a claim without that person needing to file an entry at the same time. USGLO, *Circular* (1878), 15; Copp, *Public Land Laws* (1890), 90–91.

12. Copp, *Public Land Laws 1875 to 1882*, 363–64.

13. USGLO, *Circular* (1889), 13; Copp, *Public Land Laws* (1890), 388.

14. A 1900 law and the 1904 circular mirrored these sentiments: USGLO, *Circular* (1895), 13; Keener, *Public Land Statutes*, 100–101; USGLO, *Circular* (1904), 12.

15. Homestead Act, Public Law 37–64, May 20, 1862.

16. Double minimum refers to one of two classes of land. The first class— minimum land—cost $1.25 per acre, and the law allowed entrymen to take full homesteads of 160 acres. The second—double minimum land—cost twice as much, or $2.50 per acre. Entrymen could claim a full homestead of 80 acres of double minimum land. In practice, the most important application of double minimum land was to the alternate sections retained by the government within the boundaries of railroad grants. The new law allowed servicemen twice the amount of double minimum land. See USGLO, *Circular* (1870), 6–7.

17. Later the circulars expanded this privilege to veterans of the Spanish-American War and the insurrection in the Philippines. Keener, *Public Land Statutes*, 80.

18. Copp, *Public Land Laws* (1875), 107–8. Later Congress made this provision into law during the war with Spain. USGLO, *Circular* (1877), 29–30; Keener, *Public Land Statutes*, 103–4.

19. USGLO, *Report of the Commissioner* (1872), 24–25.

20. Copp, *Public Land Laws* (1875), 264–65; Copp, *Public Land Laws* (1883), 264–65, 465; USGLO, *Circular* (1884), 23.

21. Copp, *Public Land Laws* (1875), 235; Homestead Act, Public Law 37–64, May 20, 1862.

22. USGLO, *Circular* (1867), 8–9; Copp, *Public Land Laws* (1875), 233.

23. USGLO, *Circular* (1880), 68.

24. Copp, *Public Land Laws* (1883), 503.

25. USGLO, *Circular* (1884), 13; USGLO, *Circular* (1889), 15.

26. USGLO, *Circular* (1880), 9–10, 64; USGLO, *Circular* (1884), 14; and USGLO, *Circular* (1895), 20, 170, and 219.

27. USGLO, *Circular* (1867), 9; USGLO, *Circular* (1870), 9; Copp, *Public Land Laws* (1875), 229.

28. USGLO, *Circular* (1877), 7; Copp, *Public Land Laws* (1883), 384–83; and USGLO, *Circular* (1884), 18.

29. Homestead Act, Public Law 37–64; Copp, *Public Land Laws* (1890), 57.

30. USGLO, *Circular* (1867), 5; USGLO, *Circular* (1870), 9; Copp, *Public Land Laws* (1883), 454; USGLO, *Circular* (1895), 203–10.

31. USGLO, *Circular* (1884), 16; and USGLO, *Circular* (1889), 19.

32. U.S. Congress, House, *Report of the Public Lands Commission*, 46th Cong., 2d sess., H. Doc. 46 (1885); Donaldson, *Public Domain*, 350.

33. Donaldson, *Public Domain*, 533.

34. U.S. Congress, House, *Land Office Report, 1885*, 50 (quoted in Gates, *History of Public Land Law Development*, 472); Robbins, *Our Landed Legacy*, 268.

35. Gates, "The Homestead Act", 36; Gates, *History*, 419.

36. Hibbard, *A History of the Public Land Policies*, 408–9, 454–55. Webb provided an equally negative but different evaluation reflecting his southwestern perspective in *The Great Plains*, 428.

37. Donaldson, *Public Domain*, 350; U.S. Congress, Senate, *Report of the Public Lands Commission*, 58th Cong., 3d sess., S. Doc. 189, 123 (1905); Hibbard, *A History of the Public Land Policies*, 386.

38. Danhof, "Farm-Making Costs and the 'Safety Valve': 1850–1860," 327, 354; Atack, "Farm and Farm-Making Costs Revisited," 663–64.

39. USGLO, *Report of the Commissioner* (1885), 50.

40. Shannon, "The Homestead Act and the Labor Surplus," 644 and 646. Internal quotation from U.S. Congress, Senate, *Report of the Public Lands Commission*, 58th Cong., 3d sess., S. Doc., 189, xxiii–xxiv (1905); Shannon, *Farmer's Last Frontier*, 54.

41. Caylor, "The Disposition of the Public Domain in Pierce County, Nebraska"; Okada, "Public Lands and Pioneer Farmers," 73–75; Lang, *Original Land Transfers of Nebraska*.

42. Gates, "The Homestead Law in an Incongruous Land System," 652, 654–56.

43. Gates, "The Homestead Act," 32–33.

44. Gates, "The Homestead Act," 32–33, 43.

45. One eminent outlier is Walter Nugent. He writes about the period from 1860 to the 1890s in the region from Kansas to North Dakota, "The homestead ideal of a land dotted everywhere with industrious and fecund farm families appeared to be the new reality in Kansas and the rest of the plains." In Nugent, *Into the West*, 68–69.

46. Trachtenberg, *Incorporation of America*. Pertinent sections reprinted in Frazier, *Private Side of American History*, 62–63.

4. Estimating the Extent of Fraud

1. Shannon, *Farmer's Last Frontier*, 51. Shannon also discusses abuse and fraudulent dealings under the Timber Culture Act of 1873, the Desert Land Act of 1877, the Timber and Stone Act of 1878, and the various large railroad land grants of the era. We have no quarrel with claims that, under these acts, corrupt and venal operators accepted or stole much valuable land and resources from the federal government. See McIntosh, "Use and Abuse of the Timber Culture Act."

2. Carter, *Historical Statistics*. Using the slightly more accurate *Historical Statistics* figures of 2,044,000 farms in 1860 and 5,739,657 farms in 1900 changes the results only slightly: (1) at the "12.5 percent valid" level, the *Historical Statistics* figures yield an implicit fraud rate of 22.9 percent compared with 22.1 percent using Shannon's figures; and (2) at the "10 percent valid" level, they yield 38.3 percent versus 37.7 percent.

3. For more on the limitations of previous homestead data, see Edwards, "Why the Homesteading Data Are So Poor," 181–90.

4. Lang, *Original Land Transfers of Nebraska*. Lang's map can be found in J. Clark Archer et al., eds., *Atlas of Nebraska*.

5. "Mean Annual Rainfall (in inches) from 1900 to 1979," *Groundwater Atlas of Nebraska*, 24, accessed March 28, 2016, http://nlc1.nlc.state.ne.us/epubs/u2375/x001.0004–1986.pdf.

6. Hayes, Knutson, and Hu, "Multiple-Year Droughts in Nebraska."

7. "The Pre-emption and Homestead Laws. Letter of the Land Commissioner to the Chairman of the Senate Committee on Public Lands—Efforts of Speculators to Defraud the Government," *New York Times*, February 21, 1875; Whelpley, "Homestead Filing Law Is Much in Need of Amendment. Used to Acquire Land Fraudulently. The Law Should Be Made to Apply to Arid Lands and Prevent Perjury," *Los Angeles Times*, September 23, 1901.

8. Reynolds, "Land Frauds," 175; Harris, *Long Vistas*, 37–38.

9. Herbert Edgerly, Homestead Records: Chadron Land Office, Township

3oN, Range 5IW, Section 18, Fold3.com Digital Archive, accessed December 30, 2014, http://www.fold3.com/image/1/291256581/.

10. Thomas Isaacs, Homestead Records: Broken Bow Land Office, Township 18N, Range 21W, Section 3, Fold3.com Digital Archive, accessed December 30, 2014, http://www.fold3.com/image/253/51851470/.

11. Catharine Jackson, Homestead Records: Broken Bow Land Office, Township 19N, Range 21W, Section 1, Fold3.com Digital Archive, accessed June 10, 2016, https://www.fold3.com/image/51661483/; Land Transfer Records, Custer County Historical Society, Broken Bow, Nebraska.

12. John Matthews, Homestead Records: North Platte Land Office, Township 18N, Range 21W, Section 22, Fold3.com Digital Archive accessed June 10, 2016, http://www.fold3.com/image/1/283893430/.

13. John Busch, Homestead Records: Nebraska City/Lincoln Land Office, Township 14N, Range 5W, Section 4, Fold3.com Digital Archive, accessed April 11, 2014, http://www.fold3.com/image/254911329/.

14. U.S. Supreme Court, *U.S. v. Davis*, US 183 (1913).

15. USGLO, "Homestead Affidavit" (form). For an example of such a form, see Jackson, Homestead Records, accessed June 10, 2016, https://www.fold3.com /image/253/51661554.

16. Garceau, "Single Women Homesteaders," 1–2. See also Carter, *Montana Women Homesteaders*, 25.

17. Smith, "Single Women Homesteaders."

18. USGLO, *Circular* (1895), 13.

19. U.S. Census, Dawes County, Nebraska, 1900; Mathias Thein, Homestead Records: Alliance Land Office, Township 30N, Range 5IW, Section 14, Fold3.com Digital Archive, accessed April 11, 2014, http://www.fold3.com/image/287410461/; Bina Thein, Homestead Records: Alliance Land Office, Township 30N, Range 5IW, Section 14, Fold3.com Digital Archive, accessed April 11, 2014, http://www .fold3.com/image/273607544/.

20. The idea that men and women merged at marriage grew from a long tradition of U.S. common law, and women's place as a separate class of citizens only became clearer in 1868 with the passage of the Fourteenth Amendment, which singled out the protection of men's political rights regardless of race. This is not to say that married women could never own property. Arkansas and Mississippi both passed married women's property acts in the 1830s, which exempted a woman's property from being seized for her husband's debts. Similar laws were passed in the North in the 1840s to protect family property from being wasted on a son-in-law's debts. These laws were passed to protect inheritance. However, women advocating for women's rights viewed these property acts as the first step to larger civic recognition. McBride and Parry, *Women's Rights in the USA: Policy Debates and Gender Roles*, 54–56, 165; Sullivan, *Constitutional Context*, 69–70.

21. *Compendium of History, Reminiscence, and Biography of Western Nebraska*, 1097–98; Land Transfer Records, Dawes County Historical Society, Township 33,

Range 47, Section 6; John Kurt, Homestead Records: Alliance Land Office, Township 33N, Range 47W, Section 6, Fold3.com Digital Archive, accessed April 11, 2014, http://www.fold3.com/image/274261715/; Maggie Kurt, Homestead Records: Alliance Land Office, Township 33N, Range 47W, Section 7, Fold3.com Digital Archive, April 11, 2014, http://www.fold3.com/image/287418803/.

22. U.S. Census, Dawes County, Nebraska, 1900; Simon Wright, Homestead Records: Chadron Land Office, Township 30N, Range 51W, Section 7, Fold3.com Digital Archive, accessed April 12, 2014, http://www.fold3.com/image/291397886/; Lillian Wright, Homestead Records: Alliance Land Office, Township 30N, Range 51W, Section 18, Fold3.com digital archive, accessed April 12, 2014, http://www.fold3.com/image/1/273510896/.

23. Lillie R. Bacon filed her claim in August 1888 and married later the same month. Her husband, Lawrence, also homesteaded a tract of land in an adjacent township. He did not establish residence until after Lillie Bacon proved up, technically circumventing the law. Lillie R. Bacon, Homestead Records: Chadron Land Office, Township 30N, Range 51W, Section 6, Fold3.com Digital Archive, accessed June 10, 2016, http://www.fold3.com/image/#1|291441477; Lawrence Bacon, Homestead Records, Alliance Land Office, Township 31N, Range 51W, Section 25, Fold3.com Digital Archive, accessed June 10, 2016, https://www.fold3.com/image/274658915/.

24. Lindgren, *Land in Her Own Name*, 75–81. Lindgren discusses the evolution of laws regarding women homesteading and how contestations could create hard feelings.

25. See chapter 3.

26. White, *Railroaded*, 24, 62.

27. U.S. Government Accounting Office, *Medicare Fraud: Further Actions Needed to Address Fraud, Waste, and Abuse*, GAO-14-712T. The report states: "In 2013, Medicare financed health care services for approximately 51 million individuals at a cost of about $604 billion. The deceptive nature of fraud makes its extent in the Medicare program difficult to measure in a reliable way, but it is clear that fraud contributes to Medicare's fiscal problems. More broadly, in fiscal year 2013, CMS estimated that improper payments—some of which may be fraudulent—were almost $50 billion." Calculation of the fraud rate used these figures, accessed March 5, 2016, http://www.gao.gov/products/GAO-14-712T.

5. Homesteading and Indian Land

1. Many excellent books do explore the process, validity, and fairness or unfairness of Indian land losses; among them are Brown, *Bury My Heart*; Wishart, *An Unspeakable Sadness*; and Banner, *How the Indians Lost Their Land*.

2. Note that all graphs herein show final entries, which means that homesteaders made their initial claims at least five years earlier; see appendix 2 for description of data underlying this and later graphs and maps. Nebraska Indian population estimated from diverse sources at 7,000 in 1870; Nebraska non-Indian

population from Carter, *Historical Statistics*, tables Ag4553 and Ag4555, accessed May 23, 2016, https://hsus.cambridge.org/HSUSWeb/HSUSEntryServlet.

3. Wishart, *An Unspeakable Sadness*, 35; Weltfish, *The Lost Universe*, 3.

4. Wishart, *An Unspeakable Sadness*, 53.

5. Wishart, *An Unspeakable Sadness*, 133, 69.

6. Wishart, *An Unspeakable Sadness*, 53.

7. Boughter, *Pawnee Nation*, xvi–xvii; Wishart, *An Unspeakable Sadness*, 53; Hyde, *Pawnee Indians*, 223–30; Oklahoma Historical Society, "Pawnee," *Encyclopedia of Oklahoma History and Culture*, accessed November 18, 2014, http://digital.library.okstate.edu/encyclopedia/entries/P/pa022.html; and Wishart, "Pawnees," 590.

8. Wishart, *An Unspeakable Sadness*, 180, 182.

9. Starita, *I Am a Man*, chapters 5 and 6.

10. Caylor, "The Disposition of the Public Domain in Pierce County, Nebraska"; Okada, "Public Lands and Pioneer Farmers," 73–75; Socolofsky, *Landlord William Scully*; Lang, *Original Land Transfers of Nebraska*; U.S. Congress, Senate, *Report of the Public Lands Commission*, 58th Cong., 3d sess., S. Doc. 180, 350 (1884); Hibbard, *A History of Public Land Policies*, 386. See the useful discussion in Lang, *Original Land Transfers*, chapter 15 and the studies cited therein.

11. Wishart, *An Unspeakable Sadness*, 202; Edwards, "Changing Perceptions of Homesteading as a Policy of Public Domain Disposal," 194–95.

12. Wishart reports initial settlement in 1886 and a peak in homesteader initial claims in 1888 for the Lamar (CO) Land Office in far eastern Colorado. This influx was approximately a generation after the 1861 settlement with the Arapaho and Cheyenne. Wishart, *The Last Days of the Rainbelt*, graphs 16 and 63; Harris, *Long Vistas*; Ubbelohde, Benson, and Smith, *A Colorado History*, 259; Noel, Mahoney, and Stevens, *Historical Atlas of Colorado*, 46–47.

13. Ubbelohde, *A Colorado History*, chapters 6, 18, and 24.

14. Brown, *Bury My Heart*, 349–67.

15. Decker, *The Utes Must Go*, 121–44; Brown, *Bury My Heart*, 349–67.

16. Carter, *Historical Statistics*, tables Ag381, Aa2606, and Aa2608, accessed May 23, 2016.

17. Malone, Roeder, and Lang, *Montana*, 64, 120–21, 145.

18. As quoted in Hedren, *After Custer*, 33.

19. Hedren, *After Custer*, xiii, 19.

20. Department of the Interior, *Homesteads*, 17.

21. Carter, *Historical Statistics*, tables Ag378, Aa4502, and Aa4504, accessed May 23, 2016.

22. Olson and Naugle, *History of Nebraska*, 118.

23. Hansen, *Encounter on the Great Plains*, 104.

24. Carter, *Historical Statistics*, tables Aa5710, Ag353, and Ag354, accessed May 23, 2016. Dakota Territory's 1880 non-Indian population is reported in the "South Dakota" column; 1880 Indian population is not reported but estimated from 1890 Indian populations for North and South Dakota.

25. White, *Railroaded*, 486.

26. *Congressional Record*, 50th Cong., 1st sess., p. 1838 (March 7, 1888); White, *Railroaded*, 428.

27. University of Minnesota scholar Guy Gibbon reports, "By mid-century, the prevailing attitude among Euro-Americans was that the traditional Sioux lifeway, like that of all Indians, was doomed to extinction before the onrush of settlers. Consequently, Commissioner of Indian Affairs Luke Lea outlined to Congress a new federal program in 1850 for the assimilation of all American Indians." Gibbon, *The Sioux*, 106.

28. *Congressional Record*, 50th Cong., 1st sess., 2923 (April 13, 1888); *Congressional Record*, 48th Cong., 1st sess., 2962 (April 15, 1884).

29. Federal officials' scandalous and criminal mishandling of the trust funds, including depraved management and outright theft continuing over many decades, is one of the low points in a long history with many low points.

30. Harrison, Presidential Proclamation 295, "Sioux Nation of Indians," American Presidency Project, accessed June 10, 2016, http://www.presidency.ucsb.edu/ws/index.php?pid=70952#axzz1mdhak6pe.

31. Edwards, *Natives of a Dry Place*, 16; Carter, *Historical Statistics*, tables Ag353, Aa5146, Aa5148, Ag354, Aa5711, and Aa5713, 331–391, accessed May 23, 2016.

32. *Congressional Record*, 50th Cong., 1st sess., 1842–43 (April 13, 1888).

33. Roosevelt, Presidential Proclamation 771, "Opening of Lower Brulé Indian Reservation Lands," American Presidency Project, accessed June 10, 2016, http://www.presidency.ucsb.edu/ws/index.php?pid=76708#axzz1mdhak6pe.

34. Kohl, *Land of the Burnt Thigh*, 50–51.

35. Kohl, *Land of the Burnt Thigh*, 50–52.

36. Roosevelt, Presidential Proclamation 820, "Rosebud Indian Reservation," American Presidency Project, accessed June 10, 2016, http://www.presidency.ucsb.edu/ws/index.php?pid=76709#axzz1mjzbk0fg; Kohl, *Land of the Burnt Thigh*, 144.

37. Kohl, *Land of the Burnt Thigh*, 158.

38. Johnson and Holtzmann, "When Harry Met Gregory," 37–42; McCullough, *Truman*, 87. McCullough quotes a letter from Truman to Wallace, October 22, 1911.

39. Hansen, *Encounter on the Great Plains*, 95–97.

40. Hansen, *Encounter on the Great Plains*, 79. On degrees of voluntariness and coercion, see Banner, *How the Indians Lost Their Land*.

41. The process of reducing Indian lands continued, notably with the loss of lands associated with the filling of Lake Sakakawea behind Garrison Dam in North Dakota. The cost of this loss is powerfully captured in J. Carlos Peinado's film *Waterbuster*.

42. Strickland, *The Indians in Oklahoma*, 3, 34. After the original dispossession, the land of Indian Territory was formally owned by the federal government but held in (informal) trust for the Five Civilized Tribes and other relocated Indians; thus the second dispossession was not officially a dispossession at all. However, the relocated Indians had gained ownership through

occupation, and therefore it seems proper to treat the second phase as a dispossession as well.

43. Carter, *Historical Statistics*, tables Aa3583 and Aa5874, accessed May 23, 2016; McReynolds, *Oklahoma: A History of the Sooner State*, 285–88; Taylor, "The Origins of the Dawes Act of 1887," 30, 40.

6. Women Proving Up Their Claims

1. Sandoz, "Marlizzie," 59. On the importance of the homesteader's wife's work, see Handy-Marchello, *Women of the Northern Plains*, chapter 3.

2. Carter, *Montana Women Homesteaders*, 21. Anne Effland, Denise Rogers, and Valerie Grim note that as late as the 1950s, women more often held life estates than full title to the land. In a 1940s survey of female landowners in Illinois, for example, one-third held life estates, not full title; see Effland, Rogers, and Grim, "Women as Agricultural Landowners," 238–39.

3. Hallgarth, "Women Settlers on the Frontier," 24.

4. Sheryll Patterson-Black is the first in a line of scholars to use female homesteaders to counter the idea that "most women in the nineteenth century had followed men, and were prostitutes, dance hall girls, or dependent, helpless wives accompanying their husbands." Patterson-Black, "Women Homesteaders on the Great Plains Frontier," 68–70; Dick, "Sunbonnet and Calico".

5. Mari Sandoz's "Pioneer Women" was not published but appeared in revised form as "The New Frontier Woman," *Country Gentleman* 106, no. 9 (September 1936) and reprinted in part as "Marlizzie" in *Hostiles and Friendlies*. For more on drudgery specifically, see Jameson, "Women as Workers, Women as Civilizers," and Handy-Marchello, *Women of the Northern Plains*, 77–79.

6. Hetty A. Hogue, Homestead Records: North Platte Land Office, Township 18N, Range 21W, Section 18, Fold3.com Digital Archive, accessed June 26, 2014, http://www.fold3.com/image/284909334/.

7. Elvira A. Vore, Homestead Records: North Platte Land Office, Township 17N, Range 22W, Section 2, Fold3.com Digital Archive, accessed April 5, 2016, https://www.fold3.com/image/283989347/; Hensley, *Staking Her Claim*, 21.

8. Garceau, "Single Women Homesteaders, 2, 12; Harris, "Homesteading in Northeastern Colorado," 174.

9. Patterson-Black, "Women Homesteaders on the Great Plains Frontier"; Lindgren, *Land in Her Own Name*, 52; Bauman, "Single Women Homesteaders in Wyoming," 39–53.

10. Gates, *History of Public Land Law Development*; Lindgren, *Land in Her Own Name*, 52; and Harris, *Long Vistas*, 61.

11. As quoted in Hensley, *Staking Her Claim*, 36; Hallgarth, "Women Settlers on the Frontier," 24.

12. Lindgren, *Land in Her Own Name*, 19–20; Harris, *Long Vistas*, 67.

13. Hensley, *Staking Her Claim*, 31; Lindgren, *Land in Her Own Name*, 112–13.

14. Lindgren, "Ethnic Women Homesteading," 172.

15. Fink, *Agrarian Women*, 206–207n4; Hogue, Homestead Records; Edwards, *Natives of a Dry Place*, chapter 6.

16. Garceau, "Single Women Homesteaders," 1, 7.

17. Potter, "Postscript: The Chrisman Sisters," 152.

18. Lucy A. Wells, Homestead Records: Chadron Land Office, Township 33N, Range 47W, Section 27, Fold3.com Digital Archive, accessed October 21, 2016, https://www.fold3.com/image/291027317/.

19. Ellen R. Abbott, Homestead Records: Chadron Land Office, Township 32N, Range 52w, Section 26, Fold3.com Digital Archive, accessed June 26, 2014, http://www.fold3.com/image/287524029.

20. Anna Faimon, Homestead Records: Grand Island Land Office, Township 20N, Range 17w, Section 24, Fold3.com Digital Archive, accessed June 26, 2014, http://www.fold3.com/image/301702104/; Lueretia J. McQuiston, Homestead Records: Broken Bow Land Office, Township 18N, Range 21w, Section 15, Fold3.com Digital Archive, accessed June 26, 2014, http://www.fold3.com/image/253/51876831/.

21. Carter, *Montana Women Homesteaders*, 25.

22. Bell, "America's Invitation to the World," National Park Service, accessed May 8, 2014, http://www.nps.gov/home/historyculture/upload/Immigration-White-Paper.pdf.

23. Lindgren, "Ethnic Women Homesteading," 167.

24. Land Transfer Records, Custer County Historical Society, Township 17N, Range 24w, Section 15 and Township 20N, Range 17w, Section 1; Amanda M. Hughes, Homestead Records: Broken Bow, Township 20N, Range 17w, Section 1, Fold3.com Digital Archive, accessed June 26, 2014, http://www.fold3.com/image/68962232/.

25. Lizzie Gilshannon, Homestead Records: Alliance, Township 32N, Range 50w, Section 28, Fold3.com Digital Archive, accessed June 26, 2014, http://www.fold3.com/image/#273499739/; Matilda F. Wescott, Homestead Records: Broken Bow Land Office, Township 18N, Range 17w, Section 22, Fold3.com Digital Archive, accessed June 26, 2014, http://www.fold3.com/image/51863531/.

26. Matilda F. Wescott, Homestead Records: Broken Bow Land Office, Township 18N, Range 17w, Section 22, Fold3.com Digital Archive, accessed June 26, 2014, http://www.fold3.com/image/51863531/; Mary E. Steinman, Homestead Records: North Platte Land Office, Township 17N, Range 24w, Section 31, Fold3.com Digital Archive, accessed June 26, 2014, http://www.fold3.com/image/283873664/; Christian Buchanan, Homestead Records: Chadron Land Office, Township 32N, Range 50w, Section 1, Fold3.com Digital Archive, accessed June 26, 2014, http://www.fold3.com/image/291044525/. For more on the economic benefit of children within the family structure, see Folbre, *Valuing Children: Rethinking the Economics of Family*.

27. Helene K. Rasmussen, Homestead Records: Broken Bow Land Office, Township 17N, Range 24w, Section 12, Fold3.com Digital Archive, accessed June 26, 2014, http://www.fold3.com/image/51870695/; Wells, Homestead Records; and

Josephine Denio, Homestead Records: Grand Island Land Office, Township 18N, Range 17W, Section 4, Fold3.com Digital Archive, accessed June 26, 2014, http://www.fold3.com/image/296631782/.

28. Hallgarth, "Women Settlers on the Frontier," 29; Garceau, "Single Women Homesteaders," 4.

29. Denio, Homestead Records.

30. Elizabeth Cramer, Homestead Records: North Platte Land Office, Township 19N, Range 21W, Section 28, Fold3.com Digital Archive, accessed June 26, 2014, http://www.fold3.com/image/283895307/.

31. Wells, Homestead Records.

32. Wells, Homestead Records.

33. Mary Candee, Homestead Records: Alliance Land Office, Township 30N, Range 51W, Section 35, Fold3.com Digital Archive, accessed June 26, 2014, http://www.fold3.com/image/273498176/.

34. Steinman, Homestead Records.

35. Steinman, Homestead Records.

36. Steinman, Homestead Records and Land Transfer Records, Custer County Historical Society, Township 17N, Range 24W, Section 31.

37. Josephine A. Lane, Homestead Records: Chadron Land Office, Township 32N, Range 52W, Section 25, Fold3.com Digital Archive, accessed June 26, 2014, http://www.fold3.com/image/291372960/.

38. Shumway, *History of Western Nebraska*, 3:334–35.

7. Mapping Community Formation

1. Kooser, *Local Wonders*.

2. All maps and data are available at http://homestead.unl.edu/projects/homesteading-the-plains.

3. Since homesteaders did not uniformly list four witnesses in their Proof of Posting, and also because some of the local community leaders were not necessarily homesteaders and therefore have no out-degree, focusing only on in-degree also eliminates spurious variation in the numbers of out-degrees.

4. Eight of our ten townships do not abut other study area townships (see fig. 4.4), so we would not expect them to share keystone individuals, and none did. But even the two study area townships that do share a border had no keystone individuals in common.

5. Berglund and Lahlum, *Norwegian American Women*, 75; Hansen, *Encounter on the Great Plains*.

6. We used the Index of Dissimilarity to evaluate proportional evenness of immigrant groups relative to U.S. citizens.

7. Nebraska State Historical Society, *Nebraska: A Guide to the Cornhusker State*.

8. For more on the formation of imagined communities on a larger scale, see Anderson, *Imagined Communities*.

9. Gaston and Humphrey, *History of Custer County, Nebraska*, 1058; *Compen-*

dium of History, Reminiscence, and Biography of Western Nebraska, 761; Shumway, *History of Western Nebraska*, 3:676.

10. *Compendium of History, Reminiscence, and Biography of Western Nebraska*, 643; Shumway, *History of Western Nebraska*, 3:676; and Gaston and Humphrey, *History of Custer County, Nebraska*, 324, 1058.

11. Gaston and Humphrey, *History of Custer County, Nebraska*, 172, 324.

12. *Compendium of History, Reminiscence, and Biography of Nebraska*, 1014.

13. *Compendium of History, Reminiscence, and Biography of Nebraska*, 879–80.

14. Reynolds, "Land Frauds," 176–78. For one version of the story of Comstock and his partner, Barton Richards, and their corporation, the Nebraska Land and Feeding Company, as well as the famous (or infamous) Spade Ranch, see Richards and Van Ackeren, *Bartlett Richards*, 78–112.

15. Sandoz, *Old Jules*, 291.

16. David A. Cramer, Homestead Records: Broken Bow Land Office, Township 19N, Range 21W, Section 32 and Township 18N, Range 21W, Section 5, Fold3.com Digital Archive, accessed June 26, 2014, http://www.fold3.com/image/253/53017662/; and Charles S. Francis, Homestead Records: North Platte Land Office, Township 18N, Range 21W, Section 1, Fold3.com Digital Archive, accessed June 26, 2014, http://www.fold3.com/image/1/283996925/.

17. John E. Davidson, Homestead Records: Chadron Land Office, Township 32N, Range 52W, Section 20, Fold3.com Digital Archive, accessed July 6, 2015, http://www.fold3.com/image/291456143.

18. See appendix 1 for review of the relevant legislative acts and GLO circulars; Copp, *Public Land Laws Passed by Congress*, 89; and *Decisions of the Department of the Interior*, 260.

19. *Decisions of the Department of the Interior*, 259–60.

8. Envisioning a New History

1. Patricia Cohen, "A Dearth of Pioneers," *New York Times*, May 25, 2016, B1.

2. James Davenport Whelpley, "The Nation as Land Owner" Part II, *Harper's Weekly*, November 1901, 1238; Shannon, *Farmer's Last Frontier*, 58; Hine and Faragher, *American West*, 335–36; and Warren, *Buffalo Bill's America*, 72.

3. Gates, "The Homestead Law in an Incongruous Land System," 652.

4. Gates, "The Homestead Act: Free Land Policy in Operation, 1862–1935," 32.

5. Foner, *Give Me Liberty!* 604.

6. Calculated using data from Department of the Interior, *Homesteads*, 2.

7. *Daniel Freeman v. John Scheve*, 65 Neb. Sup.Ct. 1902, 853 (Lincoln, 1904), https://www.nps.gov/home/learn/historyculture/upload/W,pdf,Bible%20Case.pdf; and Edwards, *Natives of a Dry Place*, chapter 6.

Appendix 1

1. Homestead Act, Public Law 37-64, May 20, 1862; Lester, *Land Laws: Regulations and Decisions*, 252.

2. Copp, *Public Land Laws 1869 to 1875*, 235.

3. Copp, *Public Land Laws 1882 to 1890*, 62.

4. USGLO, *Circular 1867*, 9.

5. USGLO, *Circular 1870*, 9.

6. USGLO, *Report of the Commissioner of the General Land Office to the Secretary of the Interior for the Year 1872* (Washington: Government Printing Office, 1872), 24–25.

7. Copp, *Public Land Laws 1869 to 1875*, 263–65.

8. Copp, *Public Land Laws 1882 to 1890*, 62–63; USGLO, *Circular 1878*, 7.

9. USGLO, *Circular 1880*, 68; USGLO, *Circular 1879*.

10. USGLO, *Circular 1880*, 67.

11. USGLO, *Circular 1880*, 9.

12. USGLO, *Circular 1880*, 11.

13. Exceptions were limited to sales for churches, cemeteries, schools, or for the right of way of railroads. These transactions had to have bona fide documentation of sale, and the purchaser had to pay at least minimum price. USGLO, *Circular 1884*, 61–62; USGLO, *Circular 1880*.

14. Copp, *Public Land Laws 1875 to 1882*, 497.

15. USGLO, *Circular 1880*, 16; USGLO, *Circular 1884*, 71.

16. Copp, *Public Land Laws 1875 to 1882*, 503.

17. Copp, *Public Land Laws 1882 to 1890*, 89.

18. USGLO, *Circular 1884*, 65.

19. USGLO, *Circular 1884*, 14.

20. USGLO, *Circular 1884*, 16.

21. Copp, *Public Land Laws 1875 to 1882*, 409.

22. USGLO, *Circular 1877*, 29.

23. USGLO, *Circular 1884*, 14.

24. USGLO, *Circular 1884*, 18.

25. USGLO, *Circular 1880*, 21.

26. USGLO, *Circular 1884*, 22.

27. USGLO, *Circular 1880*, 21.

28. USGLO, *Circular 1884*, 23.

29. USGLO, *Circular 1889*, 15.

30. USGLO, *Circular 1889*, 19.

31. USGLO, *Circular 1895*, 170–71.

32. USGLO, *Circular 1895*, 16.

33. USGLO, *Circular 1895*, 28.

34. USGLO, *Circular 1895*, 203–10.

35. USGLO, *Circular 1895*, 13.

36. Keener, *Public Land Statutes*, 100–101; USGLO, *Circular 1904*, 12.

Bibliography

Unpublished Sources

Fold3 Digital Archive. Homestead Records.

Published Sources

Anderson, Benedict. *Imagined Communities: Reflections on the Origin and Spread of Nationalism*. Rev. ed. New York: Verso, 2006.

Archer, J. Clark, et al., eds. *Atlas of Nebraska*. Lincoln: University of Nebraska Press, 2017.

Archer, J. Clark, et al., eds. *Atlas of the Great Plains*. Lincoln: University of Nebraska Press, 2011.

Armitage, Susan, and Elizabeth Jameson, eds. *The Women's West*. Norman: University of Oklahoma Press, 1987.

Arrington, Todd. "Homesteading by the Numbers." *National Park Service: Homestead National Monument*. 2007. Accessed May 4, 2015. http://www.nps.gov /home/historyculture/bynumbers.htm.

Atack, Jeremy. "Farm and Farm-Making Costs Revisited." *Agricultural History* 56, no. 4 (October 1982): 663–76.

Ayers, Edward L, Lewis L. Gould, David M. Oshinsky, and Jean R. Soderlund. *American Passages: A History in the United States*. Vol. 2. 4th ed. Boston: Wadsworth/Cengage Learning, 2010.

Banner, Stuart. *How the Indians Lost Their Land*. Cambridge: Harvard University Press, 2005.

Bauman, Paula Mae. "Single Women Homesteaders in Wyoming, 1880–1930." *Annals of Wyoming* 58, no. 1 (1986): 39–53.

Bell, Blake. "America's Invitation to the World: Was the Homestead Act the First Accommodating Immigration Legislation in the United States?" National Park Service. Accessed May 4, 2015. http://www.nps.gov/home/historyculture /upload/Immigration-White-Paper.pdf.

Benton-Cohen, Katherine. "Common Purposes, Worlds Apart: Mexican-American,

Mormon, and Midwestern Women Homesteaders in Cochise County, Arizona." *Western Historical Quarterly* 36, no. 4 (Winter 2005): 435–39.

Berglund, Betty A., and Lori Ann Lahlum, eds. *Norwegian American Women: Migration Communities and Identities*. St. Paul: Minnesota Historical Society Press, 2011.

Berkin, Carol, et al. *Making America, Volume I: to 1877*. 6th ed. Mason OH: Cengage Learning, 2012.

Boughter, Judith A. *The Pawnee Nation: An Annotated Research Bibliography*. Lanham MD: Scarecrow Press, 2004.

Brinkley, Alan. *American History: Connecting with the Past*. Vol. 2. 14th ed. Boston: McGraw-Hill Higher Education, 2012.

Brown, Dee. *Bury My Heart at Wounded Knee*. New York: Holt, Rinehart & Winston, 1970.

Bush, George W. "Second Inaugural Address." Accessed on October 5, 2014. http://georgewbush-whitehouse.archives.gov/news/releases/2005/01/20050120–1.html.

Carter, Sarah, ed. *Montana Women Homesteaders: A Field of One's Own*. Helena MT: Farcountry Press, 2009.

Carter, Susan, et al., eds. *Historical Statistics of the United States, Millennial Edition*. New York: Cambridge University Press, 2006. https://hsus.cambridge.org/HSUSWeb/HSUSEntryServlet.

Caylor, John Arnett. "The Disposition of the Public Domain in Pierce County, Nebraska." PhD diss., University of Nebraska–Lincoln, 1951.

Center for American Progress, accessed on August 12, 2012. http://www.americanprogress.org/issues/2012/01/middle_class_acts.html.

Cochrane, Willard W. *The Development of American Agriculture: A Historical Analysis*. Minneapolis: University of Minnesota Press, 1979.

Compendium of History, Reminiscence, and Biography of Nebraska: Containing a History of the State of Nebraska Embracing an Account of Early Explorations, Early Settlement, Indian Occupancy, Indian History and Traditions, Territorial and State Organizations; a Review of the Political History; and a Concise History of the Growth and Development of the State. Chicago: Alden, 1912.

Compendium of History, Reminiscence, and Biography of Western Nebraska. Chicago: Alden, 1909.

Copp, Henry N. *Public Land Laws Passed by Congress from March 4, 1869, to March 3, 1875, with the Important Decisions of the Secretary of the Interior and Commissioner of the General Land Office, the Opinions of the Assistant Attorney General, and the Instructions Issued from the General Land Office to the Surveyors General and Registers and Receivers during the Same Period*. Washington DC: The Compiler, 1875.

———. *Public Land Laws Passed by Congress from March 4, 1875, to April 1, 1882, with the Important Decisions of the Secretary of the Interior and Commissioner of the General Land Office, the Land Opinions of the Attorney General, and the Circular Instructions Issued from the General Land Office to the Surveyors Gen-*

eral and Registers and Receivers during the Same Period. Washington DC: The Editor, 1883.

————. *Public Land Laws Passed by Congress from April 1, 1882, to January 1, 1890, with the Important Decisions of the Secretary of the Interior and Commissioner of the General Land Office, the Land Opinions of the Attorney General, and Issued from the General Land Office to the Surveyors General and Registers and Receivers during the Same Period*. Washington DC: The Editor, 1890.

Cunfer, Geoff. *On the Great Plains: Agriculture and Environment*. College Station: Texas A&M University Press, 2005.

Danbom, David B. *Sod Busting: How Families Made Farms on the Nineteenth-Century Plains*. Baltimore: Johns Hopkins University Press, 2014.

Danhof, Clarence H. "Farm-Making Costs and the 'Safety Valve': 1850–1860." *Journal of Political Economy* 49, no. 3 (June 1941): 317–59.

Decker, Peter R. *The Utes Must Go: American Expansion and Removal of a People*. Golden CO: Fulcrum, 2004.

de Soto, Hernando. *The Mystery of Capital: Why Capitalism Triumphs in the West and Fails Everywhere Else*. New York: Basic Books, 2000.

Dick, Everett. "Sunbonnet and Calico: The Homesteader's Consort." *Nebraska History* 47 (1966): 3–13.

Donaldson, Thomas. *The Public Domain: Its History, with Statistics*. Washington DC: Government Printing Office, 1884.

Edwards, Richard. "Changing Perceptions of Homesteading as a Policy of Public Land Disposal." *Great Plains Quarterly* 29 (Summer 2009): 179–202.

————. *Natives of a Dry Place: Stories of Dakota before the Oil Boom*. Pierre: South Dakota State Historical Society Press, 2015.

————. "Why the Homesteading Data Are So Poor (and What Can Be Done about It)." *Great Plains Quarterly* 28 (Summer 2008): 181–90.

Effland, Anne B. W., Denise M. Rogers, and Valerie Grim. "Women as Agricultural Landowners: What Do We Know about Them?" *Agricultural History* 67, no. 2 (Spring 1993): 235–61.

Fink, Deborah. *Agrarian Women: Wives and Mothers in Rural Nebraska, 1880–1940*. Chapel Hill: University of North Carolina Press, 1992.

Fite, Gilbert. *The Farmer's Frontier: 1865–1900*. New York: Holt, Rinehart & Winston, 1966.

Folbre, Nancy. *Valuing Children: Rethinking the Economics of Family*. Cambridge: Harvard University Press, 2008.

Foner, Eric. *Give Me Liberty! An American History*. New York: W. W. Norton, 2004.

Frazier, Thomas. *The Private Side of American History*. 4th ed. Fort Worth: Harcourt College, 1999.

Freedman, David H. "Why Scientific Studies Are So Often Wrong: The Streetlight Effect." *Discover Magazine*, July/August 2010. Accessed July 26, 2014. http://discovermagazine.com/2010/jul-aug/29-why-scientific-studies-often -wrong-streetlight-effect.

Garceau, Dee. "Single Women Homesteaders and the Meanings of Independence: Places on the Map, Places in the Mind." *Frontiers: A Journal of Women Studies* 15, no. 3 (1995): 1–26.

Gaston, William Levi, and A. R. Humphrey. *History of Custer County, Nebraska: A Narrative of the Past, with Special Emphasis upon the Pioneer Period of the County's History, Its Social, Commercial, Educational, Religious, and Civic Development from the Early Days to the Present Time.* Lincoln: Western Publishing and Engraving Company, 1919.

Gates, Paul W. *Fifty Million Acres: Conflicts over Kansas Land Policy, 1854–1890.* Ithaca NY: Cornell University Press, 1954.

———. *History of Public Land Law Development.* Washington DC: Government Printing Office, 1968.

———. "The Homestead Act: Free Land Policy in Operation, 1862–1935." In *Land Use Policy and Problems in the United States*, ed. Howard W. Ottonson. Lincoln: University of Nebraska Press, 1963.

———. "Homesteading in the High Plains." *Agricultural History* 51, no. 1 (1977): 109–33.

———. "The Homestead Law in an Incongruous Land System." *American Historical Review* 41 (July 1936): 652–81.

Gibbon, Guy E. *The Sioux: The Dakota and Lakota Nations.* Malden MA: Blackwell, 2003.

Goldfield, David, et al. *The American Journey: A History of the United States.* 6th ed. New York: Pearson, 2011.

The Groundwater Atlas of Nebraska. Lincoln: Conservation and Survey Division, University of Nebraska, 1986.

Habermas, Jürgen. "Chapter Ten: The Public Sphere." In *Jürgen Habermas on Society and Politics: A Reader*, ed. Steve Seidman, 231–36. Boston: Beacon Press, 1989.

Hallgarth, Susan. "Women Settlers on the Frontier: Unwed, Unreluctant, Unrepentant." *Women's Studies Quarterly* 17, nos. 3/4 (Fall/Winter 1989): 23–34.

Handy-Marchello, Barbara. *Women of the Northern Plains: Gender and Settlement on the Homestead Frontier, 1870–1930.* St. Paul: Minnesota Historical Society Press, 2005.

Haney, Wava G., and Jane B. Knowles, eds. *Women and Farming: Changing Structures, Changing Roles.* Boulder: Westview Press, 1988.

Hansen, Karen V. *Encounter on the Great Plains: Scandinavian Settlers and the Dispossession of Dakota Indians, 1890–1930.* New York: Oxford University Press, 2013.

———. "Land Taking at Spirit Lake: The Competing and Converging Logics of Norwegian and Dakota Women, 1900–1930." In *Norwegian American Women: Migration Communities and Identities*, ed. Betty A. Berglund and Lori Ann Lahlum, 211–45. St. Paul: Minnesota Historical Society Press, 2011.

Harris, Katherine. "Homesteading in Northeastern Colorado, 1873–1920: Sex Roles and Women's Experience." In *The Women's West*, ed. Susan Armitage and Elizabeth Jameson, 165–78. Norman: University of Oklahoma Press, 1987.

———. *Long Vistas: Women and Families in Colorado Homesteads*. Niwot: University of Colorado Press, 1993.

Harrison, Benjamin. Presidential Proclamation 295, February 10, 1890. *The American Presidency Project*. Accessed May 4, 2015. http://www.presidency.ucsb.edu /ws/index.php?pid=70952#axzz1mdhak6pe.

Hayes, Michael, Cody Knutson, and Q. Steven Hu. "Multiple-Year Droughts in Nebraska." Institute of Agriculture and Natural Resources, University of Nebraska–Lincoln Extension. Accessed January 14, 2015. http://ianrpubs.unl .edu/live/g1551/build/g1551.pdf.

Hedren, Paul L. *After Custer: Loss and Transformation in Sioux Country*. Norman: University of Oklahoma Press, 2011.

Henretta, James, Rebecca Edwards, and Robert O. Self. *America's History, Volume 2: Since 1865*. 7th ed. Boston: Bedford's/St. Martin's, 2011.

Hensley, Marcia Meredith. *Staking Her Claim: Women Homesteading in the West*. Glendo WY: High Plains Press, 2008.

Hibbard, Benjamin H. *A History of the Public Land Policies*. New York: Macmillan, 1924; New York: Peter Smith, 1939; and Madison: University of Wisconsin Press, 1965.

Hine, Robert V. *The American West, an Interpretive History*. Boston: Little, Brown, 1973.

———. *The American West, an Interpretive History*. 2nd ed. Boston: Little, Brown, 1984.

Hine, Robert V., and John Mack Faragher. *The American West: A New Interpretive History*. New Haven CT: Yale University Press, 2000.

Hyde, George E. *The Pawnee Indians*. Norman: University of Oklahoma Press, 1951, 1974.

Irish World and American Industrial Liberator, April 30, 1898.

Jaffe, Dan. *Dan Freeman*. Lincoln: University of Nebraska Press, 1967.

Jameson, Elizabeth. "Rachel Bella Calof's Life as Collective History." In *Rachel Calof's Story: Jewish Homesteader on the Northern Plains*, ed. J. Sanford Rikoon. Bloomington: Indiana University Press, 1995.

———. "Women as Workers, Women as Civilizers: True Womanhood in the American West." *Frontiers: A Journal of Women Studies* 7, no. 3 (1984): 1–8.

Jameson, Elizabeth, and Susan Armitage, eds. *The Women's West and Writing the Range: Race, Class, and Culture in the Women's West*. Norman: University of Oklahoma Press, 1997.

Johnson, Jeff, and Roger Holtzman. "When Harry Met Gregory." *South Dakota Magazine*, November/December 2002, 37–42.

Johnston, Sister Mary Antonio. "Federal Relations with the Great Sioux Indians of South Dakota, 1887–1933, with Particular Reference to Land Policy under the Dawes Act." PhD diss., Catholic University, 1948.

Jones, Jacqueline, Peter H. Wood, Thomas Borstelmann, Elaine T. May, and Vicki Ruíz. *Created Equal: A History of the United States*. Vol. 2. 4th ed. Boston: Pearson, 2014.

Kappler, G. J. *Indian Affairs: Laws and Treaties*. 4 vols. Washington DC: Government Printing Office, 1903–38.

Kaye, Frances W. *Goodlands: A Meditation and History on the Great Plains*. Edmonton: Athabasca University Press, 2011.

———. Letter to the editor. *Lincoln Journal Star*, May 23, 2012.

Keener, John W. *Public Land Statutes of the United States: A Compilation of the Principal Statutes of Practical Importance at the Present Time Relating to Public Lands*. Washington DC: Government Printing Office, 1916.

Kennedy, John F. *Public Papers of the Presidents of the United States: John F. Kennedy: Containing the Public Messages, Speeches, and Statements of the President, 1961–1963*. Washington DC: Government Printing Office, 1962.

Kohl, Edith Eudora. *Land of the Burnt Thigh*. 1938. St. Paul: Minnesota Historical Society Press, 1986.

Kooser, Ted. *Local Wonders: Seasons in the Bohemian Alps*. Lincoln: University of Nebraska Press, 2002.

Laegrid, Renee M. "German Russians." In *Encyclopedia of the Great Plains*, ed. David Wishart. Lincoln: University of Nebraska Press, 2004.

Lang, Russell C. *Original Land Transfers of Nebraska: How the West Was Almost Given Away*. Baltimore: Gateway Press, 2001.

Lehmann, Scott. *Privatizing Public Lands*. New York: Oxford University Press, 1995.

Lester, W. W. *Land Laws: Regulations and Decisions. Being a Continuation of Acts of Congress Respecting the Sale and Disposition of Public Lands; and Embracing Land Laws Passed since the Publication of Vol. I. From December, 1859, to January 1, 1870; Together with Selected Decisions of the Interior Department, and Regulations and Ruling of the General Land Office*. Philadelphia: Kay & Brother, 1870.

Lindgren, H. Elaine. "Ethnic Women Homesteading on the Plains of North Dakota." *Great Plains Quarterly* 9 (Summer 1989): 157–73.

———. *Land in Her Own Name: Women as Homesteaders in North Dakota*. Norman: University of Oklahoma Press, 1991.

Maier, Pauline, Merritt Roe Smith, Alexander Keyssar, and Daniel Kevles. *Inventing America: A History of the United States*. 2nd ed. New York: W. W. Norton, 2006.

Malone, Michael P., Richard B. Roeder, and William L. Lang. *Montana: A History of Two Centuries*. Seattle: University of Washington Press, 1991.

McBride, Dorothy E., and Janine A. Parry. *Women's Rights in the USA: Policy Debates and Gender Roles*. 4th ed. New York: Routledge Press, 2001.

McCullough, David. *Truman*. New York: Simon and Schuster, 1992.

McIntosh, C. Barron. "Use and Abuse of the Timber Culture Act." *Annals of the Association of American Geographers* 65, no. 3 (September 1975): 347–62.

McReynolds, Edwin C. *Oklahoma: A History of the Sooner State*. Norman: University of Oklahoma Press, 1954.

Moulton, Candy. "Laying Claim: The Wave of Homesteaders in 19th Century America Included Women Who 'Proved Up' Their Mettle." *American Cowboy*, May/June 1997, 64–65.

Muhn, James. "Women and the Homestead Act: Land Department Administration of a Legal Imbroglio, 1863–1934." *Western Legal History* 7 (Summer/Fall 1994): 282–307.

National Archives and Records Administration. "Homestead Act (1862) Document Info." National History Day, the National Archives and Records Administration, and USA Freedom Corps. Accessed November 21, 2014. http://www.ourdocuments.gov/doc.php?flash=false&doc=31#.

National Archives and Records Administration. "Teaching with Documents: The Homestead Act of 1862." Accessed June 7, 2016. https://www.archives.gov/education/lessons/homestead-act/.

National Park Service. "Indian Reservations in the Continental United States." Available at http://www.nps.gov/nagpra/documents/reserv.pdf.

——. *Land of Dreams: Homesteading America*. Beatrice NE: Homestead National Monument. DVD.

Nebraska State Historical Society. *Nebraska: A Guide to the Cornhusker State*. Compiled by the Workers of the Writers' Program of the Works Progress Administration in the State of Nebraska. New York: Viking Press, 1939.

Noel, Thomas J., Paul F. Mahoney, and Richard E. Stevens. *Historical Atlas of Colorado*. Norman: University of Oklahoma Press, 1994.

Noteware, J. H. "Nebraska. The Garden of the West: 50 Million Acres of Grain & Grazing Land." 1869. In *Emergence of Advertising in America*. Accessed June 15, 2015. http://library.duke.edu/digitalcollections/eaa_B0157/.

Nugent, Walter. *Into the West: The Story of Its People*. New York: Alfred A. Knopf, 1999.

Obama, Barack. "Remarks on the Bicentennial of Abraham's Lincoln's Birth." February 12, 2009. Accessed June 6, 2016. http://www.presidentialrhetoric.com/speeches/02.12.09.html.

Okada, Yasuo. "Public Lands and Pioneer Farmers, Gage County, Nebraska, 1850–1900." *Western Historical Quarterly* 4, no. 1 (January 1973): 73–75.

Oklahoma Historical Society. "Pawnee." *Encyclopedia of Oklahoma History and Culture*. Accessed November 18, 2014. http://digital.library.okstate.edu/encyclopedia/entries/P/pa022.html.

Olson, James C., and Ronald C. Naugle. *History of Nebraska*. 3rd ed. Lincoln: University of Nebraska Press, 1997.

Patterson-Black, Sheryll. "Women Homesteaders on the Great Plains Frontier." *Frontiers* 1 (Spring 1976): 67–88.

Potter, James E. "Postscript: The Chrisman Sisters." *Nebraska History* 89 (2008): 152.

Prucha, Francis Paul. *Atlas of American Indian Affairs*. Lincoln: University of Nebraska Press, 1990.

Reagan, Ronald. "August 3, 1987." Accessed June 6, 2016. http://www.nps.gov/home/learn/historyculture/presquotes.htm.

Reynolds, Arthur. "Land Frauds and Illegal Fencing in Western Nebraska." *Agricultural History* 23, no. 3 (July 1949): 173–79.

Richards, Bartlett, Jr., and Ruth Van Ackeren. *Bartlett Richards: Nebraska Sandhills Cattleman*. Lincoln: Nebraska State Historical Society, 1980.

Richardson, Albert D. *Beyond the Mississippi: From the Great River to the Great Ocean*. Hartford, CT: American, 1867.

Riley, Glenda. *Frontierswomen: The Iowa Experience*. Ames: Iowa State University Press, 1981.

———. "Women on the Great Plains: Recent Developments in Research." *Great Plains Quarterly* 5 (Spring 1985): 81–92.

Robbins, Roy M. *Our Landed Heritage: The Public Domain, 1776–1936*. Princeton: Princeton University Press, 1942.

Roosevelt, Theodore. "Opening of Lower Brule Indian Reservation Lands." Presidential Proclamation 771, August 12, 1907. *The American Presidency Project*. Accessed May 4, 2015. http://www.presidency.ucsb.edu/ws/index.php?pid=76708#axzz1mdhak6pe.

———. "Rosebud Indian Reservation." Presidential Proclamation 820, August 24, 1908. *The American Presidency Project*. Accessed May 4, 2015. http://www.presidency.ucsb.edu/ws/index.php?pid=76709#axzz1mjzbk0fg.

Royce, C. C. *Indian Land Cessions in the United States*. 18th Annual Report, 1896–97. Washington DC: Bureau of American Ethnography, 1899.

Sandoz, Mari. "The Homestead in Perspective." In *Land Use Policy and Problems in the United States*, ed. Howard W. Ottoson. Lincoln: University of Nebraska Press, 1963.

———. "Marlizzie." In *Hostiles and Friendlies: Selected Short Writings of Mari Sandoz*, ed. Virginia Faulkner, 59–66. Lincoln: University of Nebraska Press, 1959.

———. *Old Jules*. Lincoln: Bison Books, 2005.

Shanks, Trina Williams. "The Homestead Act: A Major Asset-Building Policy in American History." In *Inclusion in the American Dream: Assets, Poverty, and Public Policy*, ed. Michael Sherraden. New York: Oxford University Press, 2005.

Shannon, Fred A. *The Farmer's Last Frontier: Agriculture, 1860–1897*. New York: Holt, Rinehart & Winston, 1945, 1989.

———. "The Homestead Act and the Labor Surplus." *American Historical Review* 41, no. 4 (July 1936): 637–51.

Shumway, Grant L. ed. *History of Western Nebraska and Its People: Banner, Box Butte, Cheyenne, Dawes, Deuel, Garden, Kimball, Morrill, Scotts Bluff, Sheridan, and Sioux Counties. A Group Often Called the Panhandle of Nebraska*. Vol. 3. Lincoln: Western Publishing and Engraving Company, 1921.

Smith, Sherry. "Single Women Homesteaders: The Perplexing Case of Elinor Pruitt Stewart." *Western Historical Quarterly* 22 (May 1991): 163–84.

Socolofsky, Homer. *Landlord William Scully*. Lawrence: Regents Press of Kansas, 1979.

Starita, Joe. *I Am a Man: Chief Standing Bear's Journey for Justice*. New York: St. Martin's Press, 2008.

Strickland, Rennard. *The Indians in Oklahoma*. Norman: University of Oklahoma Press, 1980.

"Sudetes." In *Columbia Electronic Encyclopedia*. 6th ed. New York: Columbia University Press, 2013.

Sullivan, Kathleen S. *Constitutional Context: Women and Rights Discourse in Nineteenth-Century America*. Baltimore: Johns Hopkins University Press, 2007.

Taylor, Samuel. "The Origins of the Dawes Act of 1887." MA thesis, Harvard University, 1927.

Trachtenberg, Alan. *The Incorporation of America: Culture and Society in the Gilded Age*. New York: Farrar, Straus & Giroux, 1982.

Ubbelohde, Carl, Maxine Benson, and Duane A. Smith. *A Colorado History*. 9th ed. Boulder, CO: Pruett, 2006.

United States, Public Law 37–64, 05/20/1862, Act of May 20, 1862 (Homestead Act), Record Group 11, General Records of the United States Government, National Archives and Records Administration, Washington DC.

United States v. Wong Kim Ark, 169 U.S. 649 (1898).

U.S. Census Bureau. Dawes County, Nebraska. Washington DC: Government Printing Office, 1900.

U.S. Congress. *Congressional Globe*. 37th Cong., 2nd sess., 1862.

———. *Congressional Record*. 48th Cong., 1st sess., 1884.

———. *Congressional Record*. 50th Cong., 1st sess., 1888.

———. *Journal of the Senate*. Congressional Serial Set. Washington DC: Government Printing Office, 1898.

———. *Report of the Public Land Commission*. 46th Cong., 2nd sess., 1880, House Executive Document 46.

———. *Report of the Public Lands Commission*. 58th Cong., 3rd sess., 1905, Senate Document 189.

U.S. Department of the Interior. *Homesteads*. Pamphlet. Washington DC: Bureau of Land Management, 1962.

———. *Public Land Statistics*. Washington DC: Bureau of Land Management, 2005.

U.S. General Land Office (USGLO). *Annual Report of the Commissioner of the General Land Office for the Year 1885*. Washington DC: Government Printing Office, 1885.

———. *Circular from the General Land Office Showing the Manner of Proceeding to Obtain Title to Public Lands by Purchase, by Location with Warrants or Agricultural Scrip, by Pre-emption and Homestead*. Washington DC: Government Printing Office, 1867, 1870.

———. *Circular from the General Land Office Showing the Manner of Proceeding to Obtain Title to Public Lands under the Pre-Emption, Homestead, Timber Culture, and Other Laws*. Washington DC: Government Printing Office, 1877–1880.

———. *Circular from the General Land Office Showing the Manner of Proceeding to Obtain Title to Public Lands under the Pre-Emption, Homestead, and Other*

Laws. Washington DC: Government Printing Office, 1884, 1889, 1895, 1899, and 1904.

—————. *Circular from the General Land Office Showing the Manner of Proceeding to Obtain Title to Public Lands under the Homestead, Desert Land, and Other Laws*. Washington: Government Printing Office, 1899.

—————. Land Transfer Ledger: Custer County, Nebraska. Custer County Historical Society.

—————. Land Transfer Ledger: Dawes County, Nebraska. Dawes County Historical Society.

—————. *Report of the Commissioner of the General Land Office to the Secretary of the Interior for the Year 1872*. Washington DC: Government Printing Office, 1872.

—————. *Report of the Commissioner of the General Land Office to the Secretary of the Interior for the Year 1885*. Washington DC: Government Printing Office, 1885.

U.S. Government Accounting Office. *Medicare Fraud: Further Actions Needed to Address Fraud, Waste, and Abuse*, GAO-14-712T. 2014. Accessed March 5, 2016. http://www.gao.gov/products/GAO-14-712T.

Warren, Louis S. *Buffalo Bill's America: William Cody and the Wild West Show*. New York: Vintage, 2006.

Webb, Walter P. *The Great Plains*. Boston: Ginn, 1931.

Weltfish, Gene. *The Lost Universe: Pawnee Life and Culture*. Lincoln: University of Nebraska Press, 1965.

White, Richard. *It's Your Misfortune and None My Own: A New History of the American West*. Norman: University of Oklahoma Press, 1991.

—————. *Railroaded: The Transcontinentals and the Making of Modern America*. New York: W. W. Norton, 2001.

Will, George. *Washington Post*, January 30, 2005, B7.

Wishart, David. "Compensation for Dispossession: Payments to Indians for Their Lands on the Central and Northern Great Plains in the 19th Century." *National Geographic Research* 6, no. 1 (1990): 94–109.

—————. *The Last Days of the Rainbelt*. Lincoln: University of Nebraska Press, 2013.

—————. "Pawnees." In *Encyclopedia of the Great Plains*, ed. David Wishart. Lincoln: University of Nebraska Press, 2004. Accessed May 4, 2015. http://plainshumanities.unl.edu/encyclopedia/doc/egp.na.082.

—————. *An Unspeakable Sadness: The Dispossession of the Nebraska Indians*. Lincoln: University of Nebraska Press, 1994.

Index

Hedren, Paul, 109
Hendricks, Godfried, 176
Hensley, Marcia Meredith, 133; *Staking Her Claim*, 137
Hibbard, Benjamin, 14, 198; *A History of the Public Land Policies*, 58
Hickman, Mary A., 149
Hine, Robert, 13, 25, 197, 223n14
Historical Statistics of the United States, 36
History of Public Land Law Development (Gates), 58, 61–63
A History of the Public Land Policies (Hibbard), 58–59
Hitchcock, Ethan, 186
Hogue, Hetty, 140
Holman, William, 114
Homestead Act of 1862: and affidavit of entrymen, 45–46; citizenship requirements of, 172; criticism of, 42, 198, 220–21n15, 222n26; on educational website, 18; impact of, 32–33, 200, 222n23; interpretations of, 14–15, 42–44, 146; opportunities for women in, 133–34; and provision on married couples, 84, 85; purpose of, 10, 202, 221n19; residency requirements of, 2; role of, in farm creation, 32; significance of, for national development, 3, 5; textbook omission of, 221n17; violation of, 59–60; vision of new society offered by, 189; and women's rights, 130–31
homestead communities: citizen homesteaders in, *170*, 171; claims clustering in, 174–76, *177*; cooperation between neighbors in, 169–71; formation of, 201–2; immigrant homesteaders in, 163, *170*, 171, 172, 173, *178*, 188; land locator's role in, 171–72; law enforcement in, 189–93; mapping method for, 163–65; neighborhood formation in, 169–79; neighborhood leaders in, 179–87; outliers among, 165, 187–88; religious affiliations in, 171; roads connecting, 163; and role in homesteading process, 163; scrutiny of land laws by, 191; settlement patterns of, 172–75, 176, *178*, 179, *180*, 201–2; social networks in, 164, 165, 166–67, 169; study of, 164–69. *See also* keystone individuals

homesteading: acreage limit, 32, 40, 54, 164; advertisement, *50*; African American, 2, 5; agricultural disasters and, 150; average land claim for, 12; community leaders, 182; and commutation, 54–55; and corruption and fraud, 15; criticism of, 5, 12–13, 23; definition of, 12; environmental disasters and, 209, 211, 214; evaluation of, 56–57; failure rate of, 14–15, 34–36, 224n21; female vs. male claimants of, 134, *135*, 136; in fiction, 195; filing statistics, 36; historiography, 5–6, 13, 14, 15, 16, 25–26, 60–63; immigration and, 146, 201; Indian land dispossession and, 15–16, 91, 93, 94–96, 127–28, 200–201, 222n23; and local cooperation, 150–56; marital status of claimants of, 130, 136–38, 138, *143*, 148; new vison of, 197–203; and public notices of transactions, 190; percentage of land claimed under, *11*; phases of, 12; in popular culture, 2–3, 18, 19, 195, 196–97; primary sources on, 18–19, 165–66, 196–97, 217–18; proof of claims under, 33–37; public image of, 5, 6, 23; public land transfer to, 6–7; quality of data on, 27; residency requirements of, 2, 51–52; role of, in land distribution, 10; size of claims under, 22, 36, 224n20; and special rights for soldiers, 49, 212–13, 226n17; statistics on, 1, 30, 31, 37–39; stylized facts about, 13–16; in textbooks, 18; and twelve-by-fourteen houses, *17*, 18
homesteading fraud: analysis of occurrences of, 65, 72–73, 196, 198–99; and commutation, 54–56, 59; comparison of, to Medicare program, 90, 229n27; and deployment of antifraud agents, 58; estimated scale of, 15, 89–90, 202, 227n2; and exceeding 160 acres limit, 53–54, 60; historiography, 65–67; and improper residency, 51–53; as intentional strategy, 60; and poverty, 59–60; scholars' consensus about, 41–42; and speculation, 45–47, 74–81; and stolen soldier identity, 49–51, 81–82; through marriage, 47–48, 82–87, 229n23; types of, 44
homesteading's role in farm creation:

evidence of, 19–20, 224n19; scholarly debates about, 13, 27–33, 40, 197–98; statistics on, in selected states, 37–39, 39, 224n15

homesteading states, 11, 29–30, 31, 37–38, 123

homesteading success, 21–22, 40, 198

Homestead National Monument of America, 6, 219n3

homestead records database, 67

Houge, Hetty A., 132

Howard, Les, 217

Hughes, Amanda M., 147–48

immigrant homesteaders: British and Irish, 179, 180; Dutch, 176, 178; and homestead claims clustering, 175, 176, 177; nation of origin of, 173; in Nebraska, 172; Norwegian, 36; region of origin of, 174; settlement patterns among, 172–75

Indian land dispossession: American law on, 91–92; in California and Minnesota, 123, 127; and Colorado pattern, 94–95, 103–7, 127; and Dakota pattern, 95, 111–23; and Garrison Dam, 231n41; homesteading's role in, 15–16, 91, 93, 94–96, 127–28, 200–201, 222n23; in Indian Territory (Oklahoma), 123–24, 125; in Kansas, 124, 126, 127; migration and, 92–93; and Montana pattern, 107–11, 127; and Nebraska pattern, 94–95, 96–103; in New Mexico and Wyoming, 123, 127; phases of, 231–32n42; and "runs" of homesteaders, 126–27

Indian Removal Act, 92

Indian Territory (Oklahoma): acreage of homesteads in, 126; annual homestead entries in, 124; reduction of Indian land in, 123, 124, 125, 126; status of Indian tribes in, 124

Inventing America: A History of the United States (Maier), 33

Isaacs, Thomas, 78, 161

Jackson, Andrew, 92

Jackson, Catharine, 179

Jackson, Joseph, 78

Jaffe, Dan, 219n3

Jefferson, Thomas, 92

Joslyn, M. L., 190, 191, 192, 210

Kansas Farmer, 9

Kansas-Nebraska Act, 98

Kansas population, 124

Kappler, G. J., 217

Karnes, Elizabeth, 149

Kaye, Francis, 16

Kennedy, John F., 3

keystone individuals: age of, 181; civic responsibilities of, 184; fraud committed by, 184; land sales of, 181–82; occupations of, 182; purchase of adjacent lands by, 183; region of origin of, 181, 181; social connections of, 169, 234n3–4; spatial distribution of, 182; as successful landholders, 182–83

Kinkaid Act, 12, 22, 136, 199, 202

Kolousek, Frank, 174

Krbel, Josef, 174

Kurt, John, 85–86, 87

Kurt, Lillian, 86, 87

land: preemption acts, 8; speculators, 8–10; squatting, 7–8. See also public land

Land, William, 107

Land Allotment Act, 111

Land of Dreams: Homesteading America (film), 6

Land of the Burnt Thigh (Ammons), 119–20

Lane, Josephine A., 158, 159

Lane, Julius, 158

Lang, Russell, 69

Lavin, Steven, 217

Limpach, John B., 176

Lincoln, Abraham, 1, 10

Lindgren, H. Elaine, 134, 136–37, 139, 140–41, 146

Little Bighorn, Battle of, 109, 114

Little House on the Prairie (Wilder), 195

Los Angeles Times, 74

Loughran, Thomas, 179

Lynch, Sarah, 78

Malone, Michael, 107

Marshall, John, 124

Mathews, Charles R., 80, 181

Mathews, John W., 80–81, 181

McFarland, N. C., 43, 47, 190, 191, 210

McKay, John J., 55

McQuiston, Lueretia J., 145

66, 227n1; on homestead failure, 33–35; influence of, 25–26; on land speculation, 61, 74, 75; misrepresentation of homestead data, 26–27, 30, 32–33, 36–37; on successful homesteading, 13, 29–30

Shink, Jacob, 176

Shove, Lincoln, 155

Shove, William, 155

Sioux Nation of Indians: alienation of land of, 109–10, 113–15; Euro-American perception of, 231n27; map of Reservations of, *113*, 218; Presidential Proclamation on, 116–17

Sitting Bull, 109

Smith, Oscar, 152

Smith, W. H., 51

Sod Busting (Danbom), 26

Sommer, Andrew, 182

South Dakota: land patented by homesteaders in, 10

Sparks, William, 15, 54–55, 57, 198, 222n20

speculation: possibilities for homestead, 46, 47; of public land, 74

squatting: legalization of, 8, 10

Staking Her Claim (Hensley), 137

Standlea, Catharine, 148

Steinman, Jacob, 155

Steinman, Mary E., 149, 155

Stewart, Clyde, 84

Stewart, Elinore Pruit, 84

Stockslager, Strother M., 48

Strickland, Rennard, 124

Suiter, Agnes, 202

Texas population, 124

Thein, Bina M., 84

Thein, Mathias, 84–85

Thissen, Cornelius, 176

Timber and Stone Act, 227n1

Timber Culture Act, 57, 140, 227n1

Trachtenberg, Alan, 25, 28, 63

Truman, Harry, 121–22

United States treaties with Indian tribes, 105–6

United States v. Davis, 82

An Unspeakable Sadness: The Dispossession of the Nebraska Indians (Wishart), 97

Ute tribe, 106

Vore, Elvira, 133

Vosbeek, Nellie, 176

Waanatan, 222n23

Warren, Louis, 15, 197

Weekly Pioneer, 9

Wells, Delila, 150, 153

Wells, Edward J., 153

Wells, Lucy A., 144

Weltfish, Gene, 98

Wescott, Eliza, 149

Wescott, Matilda F., 149

Wheeler, Theresa E., 156

Whelpley, James Davenport, 196

White, Richard, 90, 114

Wilder, Laura Ingalls: *Little House on the Prairie*, 195

Williams, Hazel, 161

Williamson, James A., 48

Wilson, Amanda S., 160

Wilson, Thomas J., 182

Wishart, David: on bison hunt, 97; on conflicts of white settlers and Indians, 100–101; homesteading data collected by, 19, 230n12; on life conditions of Nebraska Indians, 98, 99; on sale of Pawnee reservation, 102; scholarly works of, 96–97, 217

women: social and legal status of, 228n20, 232n2

women as witnesses: example of network of, *159*; men's use of, 157, 158, 159–60, 161; testimonies of, 157–58; women's use of, 157, 158, 159, 161

women's rights, 131

Wright, Simon, 86

Wyoming: female homesteaders in, 134, 140

Young, Amos W., 171